Harmonic Trading: Volume Two

Advanced Strategies for Profiting from the Natural Order of the Financial Markets

Scott M. Carney

Vice President, Publisher: Tim Moore
Associate Publisher and Director of Marketing: Amy Neidlinger
Executive Editor: Jim Boyd
Editorial Assistant: Pamela Boland
Operations Manager: Gina Kanouse
Senior Marketing Manager: Julie Phifer
Publicity Manager: Laura Czaja
Assistant Marketing Manager: Megan Colvin
Cover Designer: Chuti Prasertsith
Managing Editor: Kristy Hart
Project Editor: Betsy Harris
Copy Editor: Geneil Breeze
Proofreader: Water Crest Publishing, Inc.
Senior Indexer: Cheryl Lenser
Senior Compositor: Gloria Schurick
Manufacturing Buyer: Dan Uhrig

Published by Pearson Education, Inc.
Publishing as FT Press
Upper Saddle River, New Jersey 07458

First Printing May 2010

ISBN-10: 0-13-705151-4
ISBN-13: 978-0-13-705151-9

Pearson Education LTD.
Pearson Education Australia PTY, Limited.
Pearson Education Singapore, Pte. Ltd.
Pearson Education North Asia, Ltd.
Pearson Education Canada, Ltd.
Pearson Educatión de Mexico, S.A. de C.V.
Pearson Education—Japan
Pearson Education Malaysia, Pte. Ltd.

Library of Congress Cataloging-in-Publication Data

Carney, Scott M., 1969-
Harmonic trading / Scott M. Carney.
v. cm.
Contents: v. 2. Profiting from the natural order of the financial —
ISBN-13: 978-0-13-7051519-2 (v. 2 : pbk. : alk. paper)
ISBN-10: 0-13-705151-4 (v. 2 : pbk.)
1. Investment analysis. 2. Investments. 3. Portfolio management. I. Title.
HG4529.C368 2010
332.63'2042—dc22

2009051044

This book is dedicated to Jacob Carney.
This book represents the endless possibility of the future.
Don't ever forget that you are capable of anything in this life.
I love you, buddy, and I will always be there for you.

Contents

	Introduction	1
Chapter 1	Contemporary Market Case Studies from a Harmonic Trading Perspective	11
Chapter 2	Harmonic Impulse Waves	55
Chapter 3	New Harmonic Patterns	73
Chapter 4	Harmonic Patterns Relative to the Trend	111
Chapter 5	BAMM Theory	141
Chapter 6	RSI BAMM	161
	Conclusion	271
	Bibliography	273
	Index	275

Acknowledgments

I want to thank my family. They have been there for me through it all. I am truly grateful for their love, support, and encouragement.

I would like to thank Tracy Knudsen of Lowry Report for her professional insights and friendship. In a competitive industry such as ours, you have always gone out of your way to make me feel accepted. This has meant a great deal to me. Thank you, Tracy.

I would like to thank Peter B. Mauthe of Rhoads Lucca Capital Management. I truly appreciate your interest in new trading ideas and, more importantly, knowing me as a person. Your encouragement has meant a great deal to me. Thanks, Peter.

I would like to thank Veronique Lashinski. It means a great deal that you would show an interest in these new ideas and get to know me personally. Thanks, Veronique.

I would like to thank Jim Kane of KaneTrading.com. More than anything, our friendship is what means the most to me. I miss our dinner meetings at La Indita but know that with one phone call, we can always pick up right where we left off. Thanks, Jimmy.

I would like to thank Guy Cohen of OptionEasy.com for taking the time to show an interest in these new ideas and generously helping to realize the publication of both books.

I would like to thank the special friends that I have in my life—you know who you are without being named, but here you go anyway: Michael and Tania, Wolf, Jav and Missy, John and Carla, Laure, Hans and Dania, Paul and Carmen, Christy, Gus and Maha, Troy and Lauren (Magee Alums), Scott and Christie, Heather, Jon and Jen, Stephen (Quad Connection), Brownie, Rich and Rosaria, Bob, Lisa and Molly, Tom and Danielle, David and Leyla, Bill and Marla, Paul, John, Max and Kim, Larry and Gina, OPCs '87. Although we might not see each other frequently, you are important people in my life, and I think of you often.

A special thanks to Stephanie Kramer. I appreciate your effort with this endeavor and look forward to your continued contribution to Harmonic Trading.

I would like to thank the members of the American Association of Professional Technical Analysis (A.A.P.T.A.) who generously promote the field of Technical Analysis so others may prosper.

Finally, I would like to thank all of those individuals whom I have had the pleasure of getting to know as a result of the Harmonic Trading methodology. I am honored to have this approach be embraced by so many people. Since we are all students of the market, I truly hope that this material facilitates your technical studies. I believe that the Harmonic Trading methodology will dramatically improve your trading results and ultimately benefit your life. It is my purist desire that this material be received as a positive contribution to those in search of answers to the financial markets.

About the Author

Scott M. Carney is President and Founder of HarmonicTrader.com, and the originator of the Harmonic Trading approach. He personally defined this unprecedented methodology that employs a unique system of price pattern recognition and Fibonacci measurement techniques to define opportunities in the financial markets. Among his many discoveries, Scott has defined most of the harmonic patterns, including the Bat, the ideal Gartley, and the Crab. He has been recognized for other contributions to Technical Analysis, including the concept of the Potential Reversal Zone (PRZ), the 0.886 retracement, and the 38.2% trailer. Carney has been a columnist for StockCharts.com, TradingMarkets.com, and eSignal.com, and he has been featured on CNN. He is a full member of the Market Technicians Association (www.mta.org) and the American Association of Professional Technical Analysts (www.aapta.us).

Introduction

After years of research, Harmonic Trading has evolved into a distinct and comprehensive methodology that effectively analyzes the financial markets. The basic tenets of pattern recognition as quantified by harmonic ratios define a system that provides immensely pertinent technical information and identifies trading opportunities unlike any other methodology. It is important to consider the substantial advancement of Harmonic Trading since its inception.

The release of my first book, *The Harmonic Trader*, marked the beginning of the entire methodology. The new measurement techniques presented in this book quantified price action in a unique manner. These new ideas created the framework of an unprecedented Fibonacci measurement and price pattern recognition system that consistently defined profitable trading opportunities. Although it was not my intention to formulate such a system, these strategies were the result of extensive research to discover the most effective relationships that were encompassed by these measurement tools. Through it all, I precisely refined many general concepts and publicly divulged many "secret" strategies that comprised the fundamentals of the Harmonic Trading approach.

The unprecedented combinations of specific ratios that differentiated similar price structures as exact patterns defined an effective trading methodology, yielding relevant technical information in an unprecedented fashion. Although others years before me have utilized Fibonacci ratios within the realm of Technical Analysis, the concept of exact ratio alignments presented a new means to define M-type and W-type price structures. These precise patterns offered greater accuracy in the often vague discipline of pattern recognition for many traders.

Although the rules that define harmonic patterns seem to be common knowledge today, it wasn't too long ago that these strategies were practically considered avant-garde within the field of Technical Analysis. This new application of Fibonacci ratios created a system of rules that defined price patterns in an unprecedented fashion. For example, the common definition for the Gartley pattern—requiring a 0.618 retracement and a 0.786 retracement at the B and D points, respectively—which was originally outlined in *The Harmonic Trader*, has become the standard within the technical community.

These strategies have proven themselves effective through the years, but this success has engendered many Harmonic Trading-related systems that have skewed the basic tenets of the approach. These outfits have espoused the mystical charm of Fibonacci ratios to present more of a "secret code" to the financial markets than a proven system of measurement strategies within the discipline of Technical Analysis. Although I will address the problem of misinformation and unscrupulous "gurus" a little later in this Introduction, there are two critical concepts to be mindful of while studying this material:

- **Harmonic Trading is more than Fibonacci.** Anyone somewhat familiar with this methodology understands that Harmonic Trading is much more than general Fibonacci analysis. The entire Harmonic Trading approach comprises a variety of tools that include more than simple Fibonacci measurement techniques and integrates a complex system of execution and management strategies. Moreover, the new ideas presented in this book incorporate an even wider gamut of unprecedented trading tools.
- **Harmonic Trading is still evolving.** In my first book, I presented a number of technical measurement strategies that quantified price patterns with respect to their alignment of Fibonacci ratios. *The Harmonic Trader* was unprecedented in that it was the first material to emphasize the importance of exact alignments and to employ specific ratio combinations that differentiated a variety of patterns. Although *The Harmonic Trader* outlined the framework of this methodology, *Harmonic Trading: Volume One* represented a substantial advancement to the basic approach. Those two books represent more than 500 pages of some of the most comprehensive pattern strategies within the field of Technical Analysis and dedicate a considerable portion of the material to identification techniques, outlining the strict rules that validate structures as patterns. This book builds upon that foundation and improves upon the entire methodology to outline effective trading strategies from start to finish.

Since its release in 1999, many have tried to lay claim to the ideas that were first espoused in *The Harmonic Trader*. Despite other interpretations, *Harmonic Trading: Volume One* truly distinguished this approach from the often misguided and misappropriated use of basic Fibonacci strategies. Meanwhile, this book advances the basic tenets of Harmonic Trading offering greater "standardization" of pattern structures and improved confirmation strategies that optimize trading decisions.

As these strategies evolve, there will continue to be a need for more thorough statistical validation to improve the application of these methods and to enhance the overall accuracy of the approach. In fact, this is a driving principle behind the entire Harmonic Trading system—always improve upon what works. Although this may challenge the old adage: "If it ain't broke, don't fix it," the effectiveness of this approach (and of any trading methodology) depends upon continual improvement. I offer comprehensive case studies throughout this material. I will continue to compile research to validate the effectiveness of the Harmonic Trading approach. Furthermore, new concepts such as the RSI BAMM and the 5-0 pattern represent substantial improvements upon the initial foundation of this methodology.

New Ideas in Harmonic Trading

The strategies outlined in this book are entirely new concepts that build upon the prior material presented within the Harmonic Trading approach. Many new topics will be presented with particular emphasis on the Harmonic Impulse Waves, patterns within established trends, and

BAMM Theory. In particular, the entire RSI BAMM strategy will be outlined. I will present new patterns such as the 5-0, the Reciprocal AB=CD, and the Alternate Bat. Although *Volume Two* references many of the basic tenets of the Harmonic Trading approach, this material consists of mostly new ideas and trading strategies. The new patterns and expanded measurement techniques significantly advance the primary identification tools established within this approach. For example, the 5-0, the Alternate Bat, and the Reciprocal AB=CD are important new structures within the existing array of harmonic patterns. Furthermore, these new structures also comprise the basic framework of more advanced techniques. Hence, *Volume Two* represents a significant evolutionary step and an essential new direction that enhances the existing methodology immensely.

The most significant concept presented in this book and the most profound advancement of the entire Harmonic Trading methodology is outlined in the RSI BAMM methodology. This new complex system incorporates a standard technical indicator—the Relative Strength Indicator (RSI)—with advanced Harmonic Trading measurement techniques. The RSI BAMM employs precise ratio measurements and exact structural pattern specification to identify critical technical price levels. All of the material in *Volume Two*—especially the RSI BAMM—offers unprecedented strategies that identify the areas where overall trend divergence and harmonic pattern completions define the most critical technical levels. In addition, the new ideas presented in this material advance the basic theory of price pattern recognition by requiring other technical conditions to exist to validate potential opportunities with improved accuracy. Specifically, the advancement of the RSI BAMM separates the minor reactive moves from the more substantial trading opportunities and provides extensive technical information regarding the future potential direction of the price action. Although this material will take some time to digest, I believe these advanced concepts dramatically enhance the entire Harmonic Trading system, furthering its efficacy in pinpointing the best trading opportunities.

Technical Entities Continued...

In *Harmonic Trading: Volume One*, I discussed the importance of specific pattern alignments as defined "technical entities." It is important to note that the prescribed set of harmonic ratios that define these structural entities has been differentiated, analyzed, and refined to develop pattern-specific strategies for each situation. Although I covered it extensively in *Volume One*, it is important to remember that "The Great Gartley Controversy" emphasized the necessity of pattern differentiation and underscored the essential argument that not all patterns (Gartleys) are the same. New "technical entities" in the form of unprecedented harmonic price patterns outlined in this book, such as the 5-0, the Alternate Bat, and the Reciprocal AB=CD, further the basic identification strategies of M-type and W-type price structures. These new patterns adhere to the primary principle of defining specific technical situations based upon their respective ratio alignments. Clearly, the material presented in *Volume Two* furthers the specification of the Harmonic Trading methodology by offering a new level of strategic analysis. The improved measuring techniques enhance the precision and the overall accuracy of this approach in its ability to define the most critical turning points in the financial markets.

Harmonic Trading: Volume One was a major advancement of the principles of the primary pattern identification theory. The addition of unprecedented measurement techniques such as new harmonic ratios, new patterns, and other comprehensive strategies, expanded the existing array of effective trading tools and substantially bolstered the overall Harmonic Trading discipline. *Volume One* presented a step-by-step approach with effective strategies for the entire trading process. From initial identification to trade execution to money management, a comprehensive plan was presented with each aspect thoroughly considered. In this regard, I have been pleased that this material provides a solid decision-making framework of probable answers for all possible questions that might arise during the trading process. From pattern identification to the eventual execution of a trade, all possible actions have been outlined to facilitate decisions, especially when unexpected real-time considerations can affect the outcome.

The material in *The Harmonic Trader* and *Harmonic Trading: Volume* One effectively defined this system. However, through the years, I have continually strived to improve the Harmonic Trading approach and build upon this foundation. Hence, I present *Volume Two.* It is important to note that the material within this book takes Harmonic Trading into new territory. Most of the ideas outlined in *Harmonic Trading: Volume Two* are unprecedented, and they have not been released previously in any other material. *Volume Two* advances the comprehensive methodology of pattern identification presented in *Volume One* to incorporate new technical measures that refine and filter the best trading opportunities. Advanced techniques, such as the RSI BAMM, represent my most sophisticated trading techniques to date. It is my desire to distinguish Harmonic Trading as a serious discipline within the field of Technical Analysis. Such distinction has become increasingly important to me in recent years, as certain individuals have attempted to capitalize on the burgeoning popularity of Fibonacci-related trading strategies, while tarnishing the inherent principles of Harmonic Trading.

Imitators and Agitators

I am compelled to discuss the importance of ethical and accurate reference information regarding these techniques and for that matter, much of the educational material regarding trading the financial markets available today. I have been disappointed with the misinformation and blatant misuse of the concepts first espoused within the Harmonic Trading approach. I'm willing to accept this risk in exchange for the advancement of trading knowledge and for the positive contribution to help others in search of the answers to the financial markets.

When I first began discussing Harmonic Trading on various websites in the 1990s, I was admittedly naive. I openly shared strategies that advanced the basic Fibonacci trading mantra of that era. It was my desire to share with others in the hope that they would provide feedback ultimately furthering this discipline. Although I received a fantastic response from an overwhelming number of traders, I realized that other Fibonacci-related "educators" were picking up on the ideas, as well. I welcomed their response and actively sought to "talk shop" with these traders. Unfortunately, I quickly learned that most of these so-called educators were just teaching basic and somewhat vague Fibonacci strategies. These people promoted their products by making absurd and controversial statements of phenomenal success. In fact, most of these outfits were only in the business of selling products and not really trading. In some instances, certain research of mine was presented as their own. I realized that I needed to exercise greater discretion and to strive to establish Harmonic Trading as a distinct methodology apart from basic Fibonacci analysis.

Harmonic Trading is a distinct approach to the financial markets within the field of Technical Analysis. The main problem relates more to the misinformation or blatant manipulation of the intrigue and mystery that anything related to Fibonacci ratios inherently possesses. With the recent popularity of books such as *The Da Vinci Code*, the subject of mystical conspiracy-type stories that possess a secret order based upon the "golden proportions" of divine numbers has opened a Pandora's box of P. T. Barnums in the investment industry. Their ability to flourish and to attract the general public's attention proves that the inherent curiosity regarding this subject matter can be an easy sell. It seems apparent that harmonic-related trading strategies have become an increasingly popular marketing slogan. Again, I must emphasize that the entire "harmonic concept" of pattern recognition based upon *exact* Fibonacci ratio alignments did not exist until *The Harmonic Trader* was released in the late 1990s. In addition, the entire subject of Fibonacci was a minor niche within the field of Technical Analysis. Harmonic Trading techniques have impacted the technical community and contributed to this recent popularity while others have jumped on the coattails of this approach.

For me, the degree of misinformation spewed to the public with catch phrases such as "market-harmonics, trading in harmony, harmonic secrets" have lumped a great deal of less-than-credible information with the strategies that truly work. It is important for me to take a little time to show some of the troublesome examples that have been offered to the public. I strongly urge people to be cautious regarding outrageous claims of the effectiveness of any system that will make "quick riches" in the financial market, whether it is Fibonacci ratios or fundamentals.

The problem with such claims, especially when the subject of Fibonacci is involved, is that it is simply exploited for its marketing value. In this business, marketing is the key to selling your financial products, as I have unfortunately realized. Unlike many of the financial product vendors, I am not dependent on book sales to make my living. I do this because I am passionate about trading the financial markets and the strategies that unlock its secrets.

I strongly recommend that you perform thorough due diligence before signing up for seminars, purchasing software, or spending substantial money for educational products and services that make outlandish claims. Believe me, Harmonic Trading possesses some of the most effective trading strategies available, but success still depends upon diligent and dedicated work to turn patterns into profits.

Market Gurus Again

These concerns lead into another discussion regarding my disdain for so-called market gurus. Anyone who purports to be a market guru must be cautiously regarded. Simply stated, there are *no market gurus*. Let me repeat: There are *no market gurus!* In fact, many of these gurus are just people who have failed to be successful traders and have resorted to selling products to make their living. It's such a shame. It is so easy to believe these people and their hype. My question is if they were really making money trading the markets with their methodology, why would they spend the majority of their time selling products? In addition, it's amazing to me that these guys have so much time to dedicate to the marketing of their financial products when the market consumes so much time as a full-time trader. It can be difficult to know the real deal from the jokers selling their products just to make money. In my experience, after thoroughly investigating many of these professionals—either going to their seminars or reading their books and talking with them personally—you quickly realize who's really trading and who is not. It's unbelievable that many of these individuals get so much exposure in the media yet they rarely trade and derive most of their income from selling products. If you want to find the most pertinent material on successfully trading the markets, you must seek out the people who have been or are in the business of trading.

Even more incredulous is the number of people who have come to me after spending thousands—if not tens of thousands of dollars—trying to learn how to trade from self-proclaimed gurus like these. Many of these people have been swindled out of their money while not learning any meaningful trading strategies. I believe that this is one of the greatest pitfalls as a beginner. Engulfed in a sea of (mis)information, it is easy to bounce from one system to the next looking for the answers to the financial markets. I have been there—searching for the answers to the market. Years ago, I struggled to find the best systems, spent thousands of dollars on books and software, and lost even more money attempting to trade these fantastic systems that held no real trading value. Sitting in front of my computer screen, I spent countless hours researching the best techniques. I was willing to look at any approach that proclaimed to have the answers to the market. Unfortunately, most of this research yielded strategies that failed to be reliable techniques in real trading situations.

From a general perspective, I must emphasize that searching for the Holy Grail to the financial markets is just not a realistic approach to achieve consistent success. What is realistic is discovering the order within the chaos in the financial markets, defining that order and being willing to take some risk in return for financial reward. I've dedicated a substantial portion of my life to the intensive study of the financial markets in an attempt to discover the best techniques that are consistently profitable. Through my years of research, I have put together a series of books and a software program that is sufficient to help anyone learn the dynamics of harmonic price action and provide a comprehensive method for effectively trading the financial markets. Whether you are a hedge fund manager with a billion in assets, a retiree trying to maximize your IRA, or a novice trader just beginning, I'm confident that these tools will help you decipher price action better than any other system. In my opinion, the Harmonic Trading methodology offers some of the most reliable and pertinent technical information to identify profitable opportunities and interpret price action.

Then Why Give It Away?

Why give it away? I could simply retain these techniques for my own research and trading. However, I firmly believe that knowledge not shared is worthless. It does not matter that I have taken the necessary legal precautions to protect my intellectual property. Although I am bothered by blatant plagiarism, it is my greatest desire to encourage an open and frank discussion of this material, while freely sharing this information with the public. The most important reason why I'm releasing this book is that I truly want to set Harmonic Trading apart from all of the other Fibonacci-related strategies that have sprouted up in recent years. I believe that the advanced concepts within *Volume Two* demonstrate that Harmonic Trading is one of the most effective and reliable methods to understand the complex dynamics of the financial markets. The material in this book advances the entire system to a new level of accuracy and provides even more effective trading strategies to achieve consistent success.

It's Still Up to You...

I can share these strategies, but the overall success is still dependent upon your dedication and determination to work diligently to follow the markets, analyze price action, and adhere to this methodology. You must be willing to do the work. Although it can be easier to relinquish control to an advisor or professional money management outfit, the ultimate responsibility for success in the financial markets is still up to each individual. The pursuit of market knowledge can be daunting. But it is essential to refuse to allow anyone to deter you from the success that you seek.

The ability to succeed in trading is 100% self-directed. You must find the opportunities, determine which trades to execute, and remain focused on your goals, as no outside element can distract you from your objective. Although this can seem overwhelming at first, Harmonic Trading does possess a comprehensive, start-to-finish methodology to successfully guide you throughout the decision-making process. Despite sharing my most advanced research, it is still entirely up to you to dedicate yourself to this endeavor to realize success.

Although trading can be a solitary pursuit, it is important to remember that you know what's best for yourself—regardless of your level of experience. Many experts and their "immensely successful systems" can be intimidating at first. It can be easy during the early stages of learning any trading system to relinquish control of your own decision-making process to others because they seemingly have better answers or appear to know more than you. Again, the truth is that only you know what's best for yourself, and you must make your own assessments regarding any trading methodology. I encourage questions and welcome any comments and/or criticism to extend an open debate regarding this material. Despite my own beliefs and personal success, I truly encourage you to evaluate this material for yourself.

The Benefits of Advanced Harmonic Trading Techniques

I have always said that Harmonic Trading and the pattern identification techniques in particular within this approach are merely a starting point. These techniques serve as a comprehensive framework that accurately measures and analyzes price action. The ultimate objective of this book attempts to outline specific technical situations within the course of trading that will yield a high degree of reward while minimizing risk. Advanced Harmonic Trading techniques can offer information regarding the potential state of price action unlike any other methodology. When combined with other technical studies and analyzed within the predominant trend, Harmonic Trading strategies can pinpoint the potential "hot spots" where reversals may complete or important continuations of the prevailing direction may develop.

The combination of pattern identification techniques and the utilization of Fibonacci ratios to quantify price action is the greatest asset within the Harmonic Trading approach. As this methodology has become more refined, I've realized that there are many other technical indicators that form repetitive patterns in the same manner as price action. In the past, I tended to be exclusive in the application of other technical measurement tools with harmonic price patterns. However, I began to notice over time how frequently many of these indicators were acting as valid confirmation signals in conjunction with the basic pattern recognition techniques. Although many of these integrative strategies are simple applications of standard indicators, the combination of these existing measures with the Harmonic Trading approach yielded more accurate technical information.

The advanced Harmonic Trading strategies offer immense confirmation signals, and they have led to more precise executions within a pattern's Potential Reversal Zone (PRZ). Essentially, the integration of other measures has resulted in even more accurate projected reversal points for trade executions and hence, more reliable technical information regarding the state of potential price action. At first, the simple integration of many of these indicator readings was generally beneficial. However, as I expanded the use of other technical indicators, I noticed many similar harmonic traits that formed in the indicator readings as did in the actual price action itself. Once I began to see these relationships, I thoroughly explored a variety of indicators to find those that correlated best with the Harmonic Trading techniques and provided the most accurate confirmation signals to validate patterns.

The Best of the Best

This book like the others has been years in the making, and it represents a collection of my best ideas. I'm proud of this book because the techniques that I present in this material are truly original within the field of Technical Analysis. While combining the basic approach of several established technical methodologies, I believe the new ideas in this material integrate the existing unprecedented strategies of Harmonic Trading to create one of the most comprehensive and effective trading systems available today.

It is important to note that I only release strategies that I have tested thoroughly in real trading situations that have produced consistently successful results for me. In my opinion, successful strategies must stand up in real market conditions that reflect the realities of trading and not just shine in well-chosen examples at a weekend trading seminar. I understand that many products and services, especially Fibonacci-related ones, make absurd claims of fortune and success if you spend "only 15 minutes a day." NO! I make no false promises of quick riches. I offer effective trading tools that help those people who are looking for the answers to the financial markets, as long as they are willing to study and apply themselves through diligent work to achieve consistent success.

My goal in this book is to present a significant advancement of the Harmonic Trading approach that integrates new applications of existing technical measures beyond their standard interpretation. In fact, the extent of new ideas and concepts practically doubles the existing amount of material on the subject. The advanced techniques outlined in this book incorporate only the most pertinent technical measures that substantially increase the accuracy of harmonic patterns to identify the critical turning points in the financial markets. In particular, the RSI BAMM exemplifies the effectiveness of these advanced techniques to identify unique technical situations where the completion of harmonic patterns has even greater importance and serves to filter the more meaningful setups from those that possess less significance.

In closing, I want to thank you for taking time to read my material. I want you to know that I'm using these techniques every day to make financial decisions for my clients and myself. I have a responsibility to serve their best interests to the best of my ability. I extend this level of dedication and commitment to all career endeavors. This book reflects such dedication and commitment. I just want you to know that you are getting the real deal here and that I'm grateful to share this information with you. Let's get started!

Chapter 1

Contemporary Market Case Studies from a Harmonic Trading Perspective

Since the inception of my website, HarmonicTrader.com, I have released a variety of reports that have assessed critical long-term turning points in the markets. Specifically, the Dow Jones Industrial Average, the Standard & Poor's 500 Index (S&P 500), and the NASDAQ Composite Index have experienced a wide variety of market extremes in the past two decades. Despite such extreme volatile long-term price action, Harmonic Trading effectively and accurately provided reliable analysis of the most critical turning points and outlined precise possibilities of probable future action that these markets were facing. In fact, the challenging environment of the past two decades has proven to be a comprehensive test for Harmonic Trading techniques. For example, the Dow Jones Industrials and the S&P 500 have both experienced multi-year bull and bear markets since 2000. This era compares on par with some of the most volatile market environments in history. Notwithstanding, these markets pale in comparison to the incredulous tech bubble in NASDAQ Composite Index at the turn of the century. This index rallied several hundred percent at the end of the 1990s only to lose 80% of those gains in less than three years. These long-term situations challenged the measurement strategies of this approach to decipher the most critical levels of support and resistance and to determine the overall future direction of the markets. The ability of the Harmonic Trading methodology to define the critical long-term market turning points has tremendously validated this approach. For example, the bear market of 2008-2009 possessed a substantial weekly 5-0 pattern that defined the clear make-or-break support zone for the index. Although I no longer operated an advisory service, I posted an initial report of the long-term possibilities outlining the situation earlier in 2008 before the dramatic decline. Since the market environment has changed drastically from the 1990s, it is important to review some historical developments that were a crucial element in the evolution of this approach.

Harmonic Trading was conceived during a particularly bullish era for the markets. Stocks were traded mostly, as currencies and commodities experienced far less public participation than today. Despite the entrenched bullish trend of the 1990s, the market manifested evidence of trouble soon after the decade ended. Although the "pre-9/11" market climate seems as if it is ancient history, these events hold tremendous significance for today and the future. The technical significance of the price action in these markets impacts long-term structural considerations and serves as the established price limits for Harmonic Trading measurements going forward.

The following analysis of these major U.S. indices has two purposes. First, the review of such historic action underscores the importance of these techniques to be analyzed in long-term cases with the same considerations as intra-day situations. The primary difference is that instead of minutes to react as is the case for intra-day opportunities, these markets involved days and weeks of analysis to accurately assess their validity. Second, these markets distinguished the Harmonic Trading approach more than any other situation. At each turn, the reports posted on the website and in related Internet articles accurately outlined the reason for the change in trend based upon distinct harmonic pattern completions and other technical considerations.

The bear market of 2000 and subsequent low in 2003 impacted this approach immensely. The importance of pattern failures during this time was one of the discoveries that expanded the scope of Harmonic Trading. The price action of 2008 reinforced this principle further and engendered an even more vigilant monitoring of the markets in general. Unlike the decisive bullish trend of prior decades, the long-term structure of these indices has vast implications for the future direction and influence on other markets, such as commodities and currencies. The following case studies review these historic patterns and illustrate the clear signals outlined by the Harmonic Trading approach that defined each situation. Starting with actual market reports from my original advisory service from the early 2000s, this review represents a live assessment of the action as it happened. Furthermore, my ability to predict the bear decline of 2008 was directly influenced by the lessons learned from those early days.

The Bear Market of 2000—Same Patterns, Different Day

The true challenge of these changing market environments required a thorough assessment of weekly and monthly harmonic price levels to offer relevant information—let alone pinpoint exact lows and highs of multiyear trends. It is important to remember that Harmonic Trading concepts were relatively new in 2000. The strategies were yielding tremendous success in short-term situations, but the question that loomed in my mind as I refined the approach was whether weekly, monthly, and even yearly Harmonic Trading measurements would be as reliable.

The other dilemma that preceded the turn of the century was the predominant bullish bias of the 1980s and 1990s. The incredible advancement of the Internet in particular opened financial markets to a generation of new online traders. This bullish fervor was the backdrop for unrealistic aspirations and distorted long-term realities. As the bull market of the late 1990s waned, many were locked into a one-sided bias and were unable to adapt to the impending changes. Although bullish harmonic patterns were accurately defining significant opportunities in those early years, the powerful bear market of 2000 overwhelmed many substantial setups. The failure of daily and weekly bullish patterns forced me to step back and take a hard look at the flexibility of this methodology. It became apparent that I had to adjust the approach, employ a more balanced system of pattern analysis, and interpret price action from a more neutral perspective. Although bearish patterns were yielding success, there was a period of time—at least for me—where the major bear market scenario was still not clear and required time to be entirely confirmed. After 13 years, was a major correction at hand? But, an entire meltdown of the preceding bull market still required a violation of many harmonic support levels before I would consider an official bear position. I found myself locked into a bullish mode until enough patterns failed that the information—like a brick being slammed over my head—was indicating significantly more downside than a minor correction. The predominance of the strong uptrend of the prior decades created an inherent bullish bias that favored trading these setups more than bearish patterns. Although the bearish patterns were still effective in determining excellent selling opportunities, the lasting bias of the prior bull market needed to be overcome. As more bullish patterns failed, the technical evidence mounted to respect the severity of the price action. Not to mention, the information provided by this analysis was accurately pinpointing that the overall market direction had changed to a bearish bias. The trend was clearly reversing and heading lower.

The Importance of Pattern Violations

The bear markets of 2000 and 2008 possessed critical long-term harmonic setups that clearly defined the most relevant technical levels within their overall respective trends. Critical long-term support levels and distinct harmonic patterns consistently marked important turning points and clearly signified the extent of the trouble at hand in each case. The recognition of such price action led to a greater understanding of the importance of these formations as significant technical signals. Within the context of the primary bearish trend, especially in 2000, the repeated pattern failures provided the evidence needed to effectively validate the state of the market. Also, this helped me to focus mostly on bearish patterns for my trading and favor the short side until the major market indices stabilized in both cases.

I must emphasize the importance of this adjustment as a critical advancement in my thinking regarding the entire Harmonic Trading methodology. Instead of staying locked into a bullish mentality, I was able to reassess the current environment of the financial markets at this time and make the adjustments necessary to adapt to the changing environment. Regardless of whether a particular setup was valid, the price action at the completion of many harmonic patterns in the major U.S. indices provided accurate information regarding their future direction. If a pattern was a valid opportunity, the price action typically reversed at the completion point. However, price action that exceeded the completion point for a critical pattern normally resulted in a further extension of the primary trend. In the case of both markets in 2000 and 2008, the failure of long-term bullish patterns led to a substantial downside continuation.

"A Signpost for Future Price Action"

Another result of these bear markets was a reinforcement of the fact that a pattern is more a signpost of potential future action and not an "end all, be all" signal for trading. I have discussed this principle in each of my three books. In fact, in *The Harmonic Trader*, I discussed this concept as a critical first step to enable an unbiased perspective and not get locked into one side of the market or the other. Throughout early 2000, a problem quickly emerged when many of the people who initially embraced the Harmonic Trading concepts became disparaged as the bear market progressed. In fact, I received e-mails from people who claimed that harmonic price patterns no longer worked. The problem was not the failure of harmonic patterns, rather their interpretation and analysis of the technical information provided by such failures was flawed. Instead of getting locked in to this mentality, I realized that the overwhelming pattern failures of the time were indicating a further substantial decline in the financial markets. Furthermore, the bullish pattern violations were in fact frequently providing clear trading opportunities, as each breakdown in price action below the projected harmonic support area typically accelerated after failing the setup. In this manner, particular patterns did serve to pinpoint the continuation areas of the major reversal at hand, time and time again.

At a minimum, the price levels determined by Harmonic Trading measurement techniques were consistently identifying the key areas within the primary trend to examine for clues of potential future price action. Distinct long-term Potential Reversal Zones (PRZ) were defining the make-or-break support and resistance levels. Furthermore, the effectiveness of long-term harmonic ratios to gauge price action was particularly impressive. Regardless of the type of setup, the effectiveness of this methodology was consistently accurate in pinpointing the most critical technical levels throughout these volatile times.

The Proving Grounds—A Comprehensive Test

From a longer-term perspective, the experience of these reports of the prior decade resulted in a definitive substantiation of the Harmonic Trading techniques as an effective technical approach to analyze price action. As I mentioned previously, the rules within the Harmonic Trading methodology were relatively new at this time. My ability to navigate through the difficult trading environment during that period was put to the test. In the end, I believe that my overall advisory record and detailed reports prove that Harmonic Trading techniques passed the test and substantiated the validity of this approach. I say this because these reports represent one of the most accurate long-term case studies that have been compiled for this approach.

In each of these markets, I correctly determined the major market trend changes of the time and identified the critical long-term price levels in each instance. The ability to accurately quantify critical price levels was a direct result of applying the Harmonic Trading measurement techniques. The various reports consistently identified the most important levels of support and resistance, utilizing Fibonacci ratios exclusively to project long-term technical areas as critical price targets. Furthermore, the price action at these projected harmonic levels frequently provided early warning signs, as the primary trend remained strong—especially in both bear markets—and indicated that the larger historic price targets were to be tested before a major trend change could occur.

When analyzed within this context and in accordance to the basic rules of harmonic pattern recognition, these reports were capable of anticipating the overall changes in the financial markets and successfully pinpointing the precise levels where these changes would occur. Although this analysis required immense consideration and attention to the daily market action, the ability of these techniques to interpret the overall direction proved increasingly reliable throughout those early years. In the time since, the advancement of the Harmonic Trading methodology, in particular the new strategies outlined in this book, has improved the overall effectiveness and serves to provide a more comprehensive perspective on the basic pattern recognition approach.

Frankly, I was challenged by the market environment during those first few months of reports. Beginning with the extreme multiyear rally of the 1990s and followed by a near-liquidation of the entire market, the remarkable volatility created one of the most difficult market environments of the past 100 years. From a harmonic pattern perspective, the bull market of the late '90s possessed many bearish patterns that were continually violated. The strong price action overwhelmed many of these setups. Conversely, the bear market from 2000-2003 annihilated what seemed to be once-in-a-lifetime buying opportunities. I learned a great deal during this time. In the long run, this was an important evolutionary process for the entire Harmonic Trading methodology. The lessons learned during this time made me focus on price action in the completion area of harmonic patterns more than the patterns themselves, which led to a more accurate and unbiased analysis of the overall direction of the markets. This opened my eyes and spawned a more flexible interpretation of harmonic price action. In addition, the change in thinking led to a greater integration of applying these patterns within the constraints of the overall trend, especially when related to other standard technical measures. Although this advancement required many years to develop, the time and research invested has yielded significantly improved the strategies and substantially enhanced the already potent capabilities of the Harmonic Trading approach.

Market Positions

As a part of my advisory service for HarmonicTrader.com, I wrote market reports for the three primary U.S. indices—the Dow Jones Industrial Average, the Standard & Poor's 500, and the NASDAQ Composite. The following synopsis of these reports represents an accurate research study on the effectiveness of these techniques in real-time situations. Throughout this time period, my reasons for particular market positions and specific price targets were clearly stated and presented well in advance. From a general perspective, my advisory service official positions for each of the three major U.S. indices were as follows:

- **1998–September 2000: Bullish**
- **September 2000–April 2003: Bearish**
- **April 2003–November 2003: Neutral**
- **November 2003: Bullish**

I will explain the various pattern developments of the times and my reasons for the analysis presented. The recommendations of the advisory service were exclusively based on Harmonic Trading measurement techniques. It is important to be mindful of the progression of pattern analysis and the associated price action, as various harmonic scenarios unfolded. The most important point is that distinct harmonic measurement techniques provided consistently reliable technical information throughout this entire time period. The end result was an extremely accurate collection of monthly reports that defined critical technical price levels and the major changes in the overall market direction during a rather volatile long-term market environment.

Standard & Poor's 500 Review

Of the three major U.S. indices, the Standard & Poor's 500 was a leading index that frequently formed distinct harmonic patterns and responded well to critical long-term Fibonacci levels of support and resistance. In fact, the S&P 500 was my baseline index for the entire market. In essence, the price action on the S&P 500 and the validity of the various harmonic setups effectively indicated the probable future price action for the markets in general. For example, it was common for the markets to form different harmonic patterns within each index simultaneously. The S&P 500 was typically forming the most distinct patterns with price action that provided clues of the impending direction before the other two indices. Therefore, a failure in a pattern in the S&P 500 would typically translate into a failure of another pattern in one of the other two indices.

Bearish Gartley Marks the Beginning of the Bear

In my S&P 500 analysis, I identified some significant harmonic developments that pointed to a major reversal at hand. After the bull market of the 1990s ended with the decade, the index quickly violated some critical technical levels that suggested a greater correction was in the works. In fact, the index formed a Bearish Gartley on the weekly chart in August 2000 that marked a significant failure of the prior all-time high. This pattern turned out to be the structure that initiated the multiyear bear market.

The reversal from the Bearish Gartley was the first significant failure of a prior high within the established bullish trend in nearly five years. The price action from 1995–2000 was among the strongest bull markets in history. Although I maintained a bullish position from 1998 until September 2000, this pattern was clearly signaling trouble for the S&P 500 on a long-term basis. The reversal from its completion was one of the primary reasons for my bearish position.

Standard & Poor's 500 (^SPX): Weekly Bearish Gartley

It all started with this weekly Bearish Gartley just above the 1500 area (see Figure 1.1). Although the CD leg was a bit extended, the structure possessed a precise alignment of harmonic ratios to validate the pattern. The interesting aspect of the price action was the decisive downside continuation following the completion of the pattern. I outlined this setup as early as June 2000, stating in the monthly report:

"The S&P 500 has held the lows set in the past two months.... Despite this strength, there is a nice shorting opportunity at the 78.6% retracement from the high that would complete a Bearish Gartley pattern. There are three harmonic numbers just above 1500 that define the potential reversal zone:

- ***AB=CD at 1505***
- ***1.27BC at 1515***
- ***.786XA at 1510***

I would focus closely on the 1510 area where the .786XA completes. Although the index may exceed this area slightly, if the bearish pattern is valid, the index should not rally too far above this zone."

(HarmonicTrader.com http://www.harmonictrader.com/members/harmonic/markets/spx0600.htm)

Figure 1.1

The decisive downside continuation following the completion of this pattern clearly indicated the change in trend that was occurring. In fact, in my September 2000 market report three months later, I outlined this breakdown:

> ***"As we enter the historically ominous September-October period, it is essential to consider such bearish possibilities.... The most critical levels to examine in the next few weeks are the short-term .618 and .786 retracements from the July low to the August high.. I would become extremely bearish if the index sold off sharply through these support levels. In that event, I would look for the index to sell off well below the 1400 level. For now, stay on the sides and watch these levels closely."***
>
> (HarmonicTrader.com http://www.harmonictrader.com/members/harmonic/markets/spx0900.htm)

The index declined steadily in the months that followed and triggered the next set of harmonic levels at the 1300 level.

Two More Failed Harmonic Scenarios—1300 and 1150

Despite the bearish downtrend, the index still possessed critical support levels that continued to maintain the long-term bullish trend. The next set of long-term harmonic support was well-below the prior Bearish Gartley at 1500. Although the index possessed a Bullish AB=CD on the weekly chart at the 1300 level, the price action failed this area decidedly. Within a few months later, the price action was clearly headed for the 1150 area, where the next set of long-term harmonic retracements converged. I outlined this scenario in my December 2000 market report, stating:

> ***"The test of 1150 will be one of the most critical market events of the New Year. The 1150 area represents a convergence of significant Fibonacci projections or retracements for each of the past six years. From each of the previous years' low to this year's high, these retracements converge in the mid-1100 area:***
>
> - ***1999 1.27 @ 1145***
> - ***1998 .618 @ 1165***
> - ***1997 .5 @ 1145***
> - ***1996 .382 @ 1190***
> - ***1994/95 .382 @ 1135 (general area)***
>
> ***A convergence of numbers like this will most likely act as a magnet and pull the index down to test all of the numbers in this area. A capitulation sell-off could happen quickly and signal the end of the bear trend. But, the index must hold this price level. Therefore, the picture for the S&P is clear: A violation of the 1300 lows will cause a decisive move to 1150."***
>
> (HarmonicTrader.com http://www.harmonictrader.com/members/dow/harmonic/markets/spx1200.htm)

The Road to 800

It didn't take long for the index to fail the 1300 level and test 1100. In fact, three months after the December 2000 report, the index reached this area. Although the price action bounced on the initial test, there was little upside continuation, and the index quickly stalled in the following months. As the daily price action stalled, I became increasingly concerned and issued this warning in November 2001:

> ***"The S&P is stuck in this sharp bear trend. <u>Although there are a few Bullish AB=CD patterns beginning to form, these patterns complete at much lower levels—around 800</u>. In the next few weeks, the index will most likely encounter resistance as it tests the upper range of the channel. A violation of the 1075 level would trigger a retest of the September lows. Therefore, I remain bearish on the index."***
>
> (Harmonic Trader.com http://www.harmonictrader.com/members/dow/harmonic/markets/spx1101.htm)

Although the 800 area was starting to shape up, it is important to note that this was nearly a blasphemous statement at the time. Despite already losing one-third of its value, it was apparent that the index clearly was heading toward the completion of the multiple AB=CD patterns at the 800 level.

Standard & Poor's 500 (^SPX): Weekly Bullish AB=CD Patterns

A decline to 800 was going to represent a 50% "hair cut" in the index, which would eventually result in one of the most significant bear market declines in history (see Figure 1.2). Despite such a bold prediction, I did not waver, as these patterns converged with a few long-term retracements to clearly define the 800 level as critical harmonic and historic support. This scenario was clearly coming together, signaling its fruition nearly 18 months prior to its eventual completion. Although this scenario required some time before being realized, the harmonic factors of the long-term downtrend were clearly dictating the direction of the price action. Furthermore, it became apparent that the market direction was still down because the overwhelming harmonic setup that completed at the 800 level represented such a fantastic buying opportunity.

Figure 1.2

After the first test of this projected support zone, I reiterated the 800 target a year later in my November 2002 Standard & Poor's market report, stating:

> ***"It is important to note that the S&P 500 possesses the most harmonic scenario of all of the indices. The historic retracements and the distinct bullish AB=CD patterns defined the 800 area as a major potential bottom. The critical element to validate this long-term Potential Reversal Zone (PRZ) is time. If the index can hold these levels and move higher, the stronger the support at 800 will become... the index still needs more time to resolve the larger bearish trend. The index is close to challenging the three-year downtrend and decisively changing its course. But, it must provide more constructive bullish action before ending the downtrend. For these reasons, the official position remains bearish."***
>
> (HarmonicTrader.com http://www.harmonictrader.com/members/dow/harmonic/markets/spx1102.htm)

The Historic Low at 800

After the S&P 500 bounced sharply on the initial test of the long-term Bullish AB=CD pattern convergence, the index formed a distinct Bullish Bat in this significant Potential Reversal Zone (PRZ). The completion of this smaller pattern within the larger PRZ was the defining harmonic signal that confirmed the entire 800 area as historic support. In my March 2003 Standard & Poor's 500 market report, I outlined my argument for the completion of the bear market:

> ***"Without question, the next two weeks will be a historically defining time period for the markets. The Standard & Poor's 500 has been the Harmonic bellwether for all of the indices. The index has consolidated for the past nine months in a considerable Harmonic support zone at the 800 level.... It is amazing to consider the significance of the 800 area and the price action of the S&P 500 for the past 9 months. <u>The clear Bullish AB=CD patterns and the longer-term trend line support are defining this area as a historic point for the index</u>."***
>
> (HarmonicTrader.com http://www.harmonictrader.com/members/dow/harmonic/markets/spx0303.htm)

Standard & Poor's 500 (^SPX): Weekly Bullish Bat Completing Within the Bullish AB=CD(ab=cd) Potential Reversal Zone (PRZ) @ 800

Although the ultimate bear market low reversed at 770—slightly beyond the weekly PRZ, the Bullish Bat pinpointed the precise area within this long-term support zone that marked the beginning of the new bull market. In fact, in my April 2003 S&P 500 market report, I wrote:

> ***"The 'tea leaves' of the entire Harmonic convergence at 800 says that the bottom has completed for the index. The impending breakout of the bear market channel will be significant, and it will confirm this 800 as a historic low. For these reasons, the official position is now NEUTRAL with a bias to the upside. Although the index still needs to take out some resistance levels—namely a strong move above the 950 area—the index has resolved this long-awaited Potential Reversal Zone (PRZ)."***
>
> (HarmonicTrader.com http://www.harmonictrader.com/members/dow/harmonic/markets/spx0403.htm)

Figure 1.3 shows the distinct Bullish Bat that developed within the larger PRZ in the 800 area.

Figure 1.3

Standard & Poor's 500 Conclusion

My experience in writing these market reports for the Standard & Poor's 500 Index in the early days was one of the most educational endeavors of my life. The harmonic measurement strategies proved incredibly reliable, as distinct patterns and Fibonacci ratios effectively defined the critical turning points in the index for a period of many years. It is important to emphasize that these techniques were new during the time that I offered my advisory service (1998–2004). However, I knew that this new approach effectively analyzed price action on all time frames. Therefore, I knew that if I properly applied these measurement strategies to the daily and the weekly time frames as I did for intra-day trading, I would be able to accurately decipher the long-term price action. The history of these reports clearly shows how the harmonic measurement techniques consistently predicted the overall market direction and defined those critical areas where the trend would potentially change.

NASDAQ Composite Review

In much the same manner as the S&P 500, the NASDAQ Composite Index possessed many harmonic patterns and responded well to long-term Fibonacci ratios. Although the price action was much more volatile in the NASDAQ, the predominant trend throughout this time was dictated by several distinct "harmonic events" that accurately defined the future price action in each case.

One notable aspect of the bear market in the NASDAQ Composite was the overwhelming failure of many significant long-term patterns. The violation of many of these setups seriously questioned the integrity of the entire Harmonic Trading approach. Although the overwhelming failure of most bullish patterns during this time might have presented a frustrating environment for the bulls, the technical phenomenon of these pattern violations was signaling a severe decline at hand. I address these situations a bit later in this section, but there was as much to learn about failed harmonic price action on the upside as well as the downside.

The Parabolic Rally to 5000

It was amazing. Incredible. Simply stated, the rally from August 1999 to the top in March 2000 was the greatest bullish price action that I have ever witnessed. This was an era of insanely priced tech stocks that frequently traded 10–20 point price swings every day. Stocks such as Dell, Microsoft, Qualcomm, Yahoo!, and others were among the greatest bull markets of all time—right up there with the Tulip Bulb and 1929 manias!

NASDAQ Composite ($COMPQ): Daily The Rally to 5000

Despite the unprecedented rally, the price action continued higher. Figure 1.4 shows the incredibly bullish price action from early 1999 to the top in March 2000. I discussed the significance of the violated 3.14 extension in my January 2000 NASDAQ Composite market report.

Figure 1.4

"This latest NASDAQ rally has been incredible. The volatile action in some of the biggest NASDAQ stocks, such as Qualcomm and Yahoo, has left many wondering if this is truly a "blow-off" top. And that is the big question! In the past few weeks, the index has rallied above the extreme 3.14 projection from the August correction. Although the NASDAQ did sell off after exceeding this level, it has found support in this area. One note of caution: With such sharp action, the index could rally to the 1.618 of the XA leg, which would put it at 4500! Believe it or not, I think this is possible. Stay cautiously long but watch the first area potential resistance area at 4300."

(HarmonicTrader.com http://www.harmonictrader.com/members/dow/harmonic/markets/nasdaqjan00.htm)

The Inevitable Decline

It was coming. You could feel it. Tired and drunk on 30% year-over-year gains, the NASDAQ Composite was sitting like Humpty Dumpty on the wall, and he was ready to fall! The index tested the 5000 area briefly and started to stall. The one question on everyone's mind was: "Is this sustainable?" Clearly, it was not. Although making an arbitrary decision that the 5000 level is critical psychological resistance does not represent the most cogent argument for a top, the inability of the index to rally significantly above this area was the first sign of trouble. The index started to roll over shortly after testing 5000, as it completed the all-time peak of the bull market. Although the 5000 level had the ominous feeling of a historic top, the price action still needed to exhibit technical behavior of the breakdown at hand. In my opinion, the top could not be confirmed until the price action actually started to break down and begin to exhibit bearish behavior. As a side note, I have spoken to many market technicians in past conversations regarding the top in the NASDAQ at 5000. Many of these analysts made accurate predictions, calling for a peak in the 5000 area. Intuitively, this seemed the right call. However, the price action still needed to begin to manifest such behavior. From a Harmonic Trading perspective, the NASDAQ Composite offered several distinct signals that confirmed the top at 5000. The first was a distinct Bearish Bat that was forming on the retest of the initial peak above 5000. In my NASDAQ Composite March 2000 market report, I outlined this setup:

"The NASDAQ formed another clear pattern, as the bearish Gartley that completed recently has yielded a nice reversal. The pattern was projected to complete around 5000—just past the .786 off the high."

(Author's Note: I had not released the Bat yet, and I was calling this a Gartley.)

(HarmonicTrader.com http://www.harmonictrader.com/members/dow/harmonic/markets/nasd0300.htm)

NASDAQ Composite ($COMPQ): Daily Bearish Bat—March 2000

Much like the Bearish Gartley in the S&P 500, the Bearish Bat shown in Figure 1.5 was the harmonic pattern that marked the beginning of the bear market for the NASDAQ.

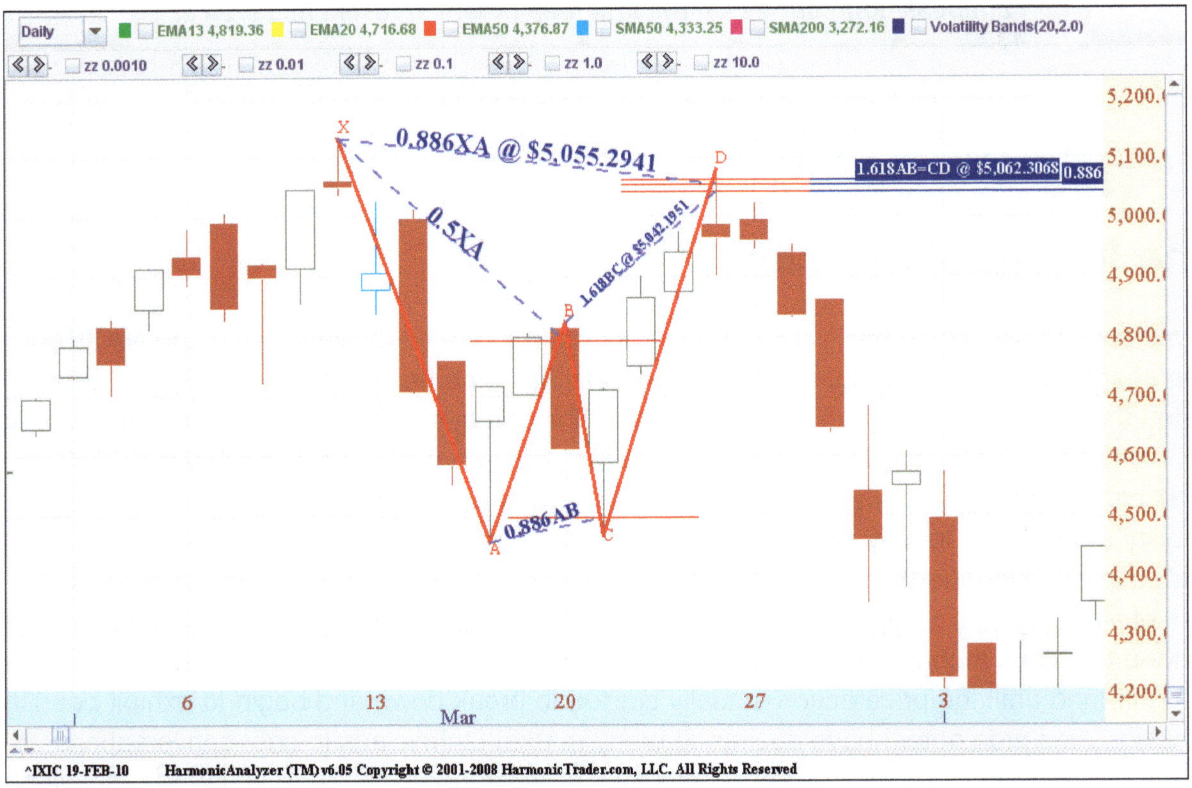

Figure 1.5

This was the first significant failure of a prior high within the established bullish trend in nearly five years. For the NASDAQ Composite, the prior two years represented one of the strongest bull markets in history. Although I maintained a bullish position from 1998 until September 2000, this pattern was clearly signaling trouble for the NASDAQ Composite on a long-term basis, and its completion was one of the primary reasons for my bearish position.

NASDAQ Composite ($COMPQ): Daily Bearish Bat—August 2000

After the initial decline from the peak at 5000 was complete, the NASDAQ Composite consolidated to form another Bearish Bat pattern at the 4200 level in August 2000 (see Figure 1.6).

Figure 1.6

The price action following the completion of the pattern signaled another devastating continuation of the severe bear market at hand. In fact, this Bearish Bat resulted in an acceleration of the entire bear market, as the index quickly declined from just above 4000 to well below the 3000 level.

NASDAQ Composite ($COMPQ): Daily Bearish Bat—January 2001

As if 2000 was not devastating enough, the index formed its third Bearish Bat for the year. Although the NASDAQ Composite reversed shy of the 0.886 retracement, the index reversed sharply, as another distinct PRZ marked the continuation of the devastating bear market (see Figure 1.7).

Figure 1.7

After losing nearly half its value, this pattern marked another corrective peak within the downtrend. Although it might have seemed that the pattern would not result in a significant decline due to the devastation of the past year, this Bearish Bat led to largest percentage decline of the entire bear market.

The Monster Bullish Gartley That Failed

After a few nasty continuations from distinct Bearish Bat patterns, the index was clearly in the midst of a historic decline. The decisive bearish continuation throughout this decline was indicating the severity of the downtrend. In fact, as early as October 2000 in my NASDAQ Composite Market Report, I discussed this technical possibility long before it was actually realized.

> ***"If the index breaks below these lows at 3000, the NASDAQ will most likely fall quickly in crashing fashion... there is 'nothing but air' below this area... the overwhelming convergence of harmonic numbers is in the 2200 area. This would be an extreme target on the downside and represent a significant buying opportunity."***
>
> (HarmonicTrader.com http://www.harmonictrader.com/members/dow/harmonic/markets/nasd1000.htm)

NASDAQ Composite ($COMPQ): Weekly Failed Bullish Gartley—April 2001

After realizing the next convergence of weekly projections indicated that the index was headed for the 2200 area, as illustrated in Figure 1.8, I truly believed that this would be a substantial low for the NASDAQ Composite Index. However, this was merely a brief stop in a further slide that would take the index much lower. Although it did not seem possible at the time, I knew that a severe violation of this long-term harmonic support would trigger another steep continuation of the bear market. Although a minor bounce was experienced on the initial test of the upper range of the PRZ, the price action severely lagged in this area. Furthermore, the eventual continuation of the decline underscored the severe bearish condition that would require much more time to stabilize and to reverse the downtrend.

Figure 1.8

NASDAQ Composite ($COMPQ): Weekly Failed Bullish Gartley Potential Reversal Zone (PRZ)

The chart in Figure 1.9 shows the overwhelming convergence of harmonic numbers that defined the PRZ range between 2165–2275. The weekly PRZ clearly shows the decisive price action that violated this harmonic support. In fact, the index bounced briefly after exceeding this area on the initial test, only to continue lower after reversing from the prior failed PRZ. I remember thinking at this point: "Can it get any worse?"

Figure 1.9

No More Harmonic Scenarios—Now What?

At this point, the persistent downtrend that violated the monster weekly Bullish Gartley was signaling more trouble ahead. One of the dilemmas with the monster Bullish Gartley was that its structure could have possibly been interpreted as a Bat pattern. Specifically, the B point of the pattern was not an exact 0.618 retracement. Hence, the possibility that the entire four-year price structure could actually result in a completion of a Bullish Bat in the 1700 area quickly became reality, as the index sank under the 2200 level. Below the multiyear 0.786, the only other harmonic number to consider was the multiyear 0.886 retracement at 1750. This scenario was difficult to imagine at the time, but the overwhelming bearish trend eventually drove the index to test under this area, as well.

Although the alignment of the structure was somewhat in question, the pattern was distinct enough to have been interpreted as a Bat and not a Gartley. Regardless, the index continued well beyond this level too. Eventually, the NASDAQ Composite even violated the original low point (X) of the pattern that was established in 1998—essentially erasing all of the gains made from the past four years.

NASDAQ Conclusion

Despite bottoming above the all-important psychological 1000 level, the total destruction of this multiyear bear market was on par with the greatest declines of all time. Quite frankly, the multiyear NASDAQ Composite chart is similar in structure and magnitude to the Dow Jones Industrial Average Crash of 1929. Although the Crash of 1929 was more severe, the NASDAQ Composite lost an astounding 80% of its total value and the devastation remains to this day. Despite the upside progress since the bear market low, the index has languished in comparison to the other major indices, as it has barely retraced to the all-time 38.2% minimum bear market level, as of this writing date.

The parabolic rise and ultimate decline of the NASDAQ Composite during this time was one of the most challenging trading environments that I have ever faced. Although I realized the extent of the impending bear market early on and stayed exclusively on the short side for most of this period, the initial failures of substantial bullish patterns, especially in those first nine months, taught me a great deal about their importance as continuation signals. Furthermore, the action in the NASDAQ Composite led me to respect the importance of the predominant trend in all trading situations more than ever before. Whether I am trading on a 5, 15, 60-minute, or daily time frame, I now analyze all setups with respect to the predominant trend. For the NASDAQ Composite, the price action eventually broke out of the multiyear established downtrend channel after reversing from the bear market low. But, this required quite a bit of time before the trend reversal was confirmed.

The most important consideration from the NASDAQ Composite advisory experience was the respect that I now possess for the ability of distinct patterns to define critical turning points in the price action. Whether a harmonic pattern reverses successfully or fails the PRZ, the technical information provided by this phenomenon to act as "action spots" of the overall direction of the price action that can define excellent trading opportunities.

The lessons learned from the NASDAQ's performance during this time reinforced some important concepts within the Harmonic Trading approach. Despite the devastating decline, the various harmonic patterns and long-term Fibonacci ratios proved to be extremely effective measurement tools that provided consistently accurate information in the NASDAQ Composite analysis during an era of market extremes that comes along once every century!

Dow Jones Industrial Average 2000-2010 Review

Although the 2000 bear market in the Dow Jones Industrial Average was severe, the index endured an even more devastating decline in its second bear market of the decade. The drop in 2008 was sudden in comparison to the price action earlier in the decade, which required most of three years to reach its ultimate low.

The volatility of the Industrials during the last two decades is remarkable. Starting with a substantial drop in 2000, the index rallied to new highs by mid-decade only to retrace the entire move and more. As the index enters another decade, the action of these two bear markets holds tremendous long-term significance. The action of the 2000 bear market established the parameters for the rest of the decade. After the decline of 2008, the long-term price history has established several critical technical and structural considerations. First, let's review the conditions of the 2000 bear market that preceded 2008's demise.

The 2000 Bear Market—The Top, the Distribution, and the Eventual Decline

Throughout 2000 as the other indices were breaking down substantially, the Dow Jones Industrials were still consolidating after violating their multiyear uptrend. Although many have argued that the bull market of the 1990s began from the 1987 (some suggest the 1982 low was the real bottom) the bull market mania began in earnest with the breakout in 1995. For the next several years, the Dow Jones Industrial Average rallied sharply, as the index continued to attain year-over-year new highs. The interesting aspect of the longer-term price action during this five-year accelerated period between 1995 and 2000 was the fact that the index was able to hold at a critical Fibonacci retracement of each of the prior year's rally. In essence, the weekly price action possessed a strong technical upside, as the index was able to make higher highs and higher lows for five years in a row. After the peak in early 2000, the index stalled and started to roll over on the weekly chart. The long-term trend line starting from the 1995 low was violated in mid-2000, and the index languished from that point forward. The five-year series of weekly bullish retracements was violated at this time, as well. Therefore, the price action was clearly beginning to signal a change at hand.

As I mentioned previously, the Dow Jones Industrial Average did not suffer the extent of the decline as did the NASDAQ Composite in the early stages of the bear market. In fact, the action in this index appeared weak, but it managed to hold in the 10,000 area for quite some time before declining sharply. On its own, the price action in the Industrials was not terribly negative until the latter half of the bear market. However, the steady distribution as evidenced by the weak sideways action in combination with the severe declines of the other two indices were the most critical factors that signaled lower prices.

Dow Jones Industrial Average (^DJI): Weekly Bullish Retracements 1994–2001

The weekly chart in Figure 1.10 shows the sequence of annual harmonic retracements. The structural pattern each year rallied to a new all-time high, retraced to a distinct Fibonacci retracement of the prior year, and continued higher.

Figure 1.10

As long as the index was able to maintain this uptrend, holding the prior year's critical retracement, the long-term trend remained up. However, the series of retracements came to an end in 2000, as the index violated its critical 50% retracement.

Dow Jones Industrial Average (^DJI): Daily Bearish Retracements

After an initial sharp decline from the early 2000 peak where the index sank to the low 9000 level, the Industrials consolidated in an ever-tightening series of bearish retracements for the rest of that year (see Figure 1.11).

Figure 1.11

In my June 2000 Dow Jones Industrial Market Report, I wrote:

> ***"The action in the Dow Industrials continues to trade in a tighter range. Sooner rather than later it is going to break in a direction that will define the trend for the next few months. As the chart illustrates, the index has traded in a downward trending channel, where it has continually rallied to the 78.6% retracement of each prior sell-off."***
>
> (HarmonicTrader.com http://www.harmonictrader.com/members/harmonic/markets/dow0600.htm)

The 9/11 Crash, Rebound, and Another Sell Signal

As terrible as the events of September 11, 2001, were, the crash in the Dow Jones Industrial Average as a result of that fateful day had been building for quite some time. The clear distribution from the year prior and the more severe action in the other indices were dominant factors that contributed to the severe bearish trend developing in the Industrials. Furthermore, the index lacked any clear patterns or distinct harmonic bullish setups on either the daily or the weekly chart to suggest that a low had been completed. Although the 9/11 crash was severe, the net result after the crash and corresponding bounce was actually a further reinforcement of the existing bearish channel. The 9/11 crash was a challenging technical situation due to the fact that it did appear to be the capitulation event, which most market pundits believed would mark the bear market low. Despite the bullish consensus, I did not share this view. In my Dow Jones Industrial Average March 2002 report, I wrote:

> ***"For now, the index is trading above its current downtrend channel.... The whole scenario appears to be another monster bear trap. Also, the impulsive action off the September lows does not represent a "stable" and "maintainable" trend. In fact, the 1974 and 1987 collapses required years to recover their losses—which is a more favorable technical scenario than the current recovery. In addition, the existence of many bearish patterns that have yet to completely resolve their action suggests that the index needs time, if it is going to assert itself to new highs. For these reasons, I remain bearish on the index."***
>
> (HarmonicTrader.com http://www.harmonictrader.com/members/dow/harmonic/markets/dow0302.htm)

As I stated in the March report, I believed that the index needed to retest the 9/11 crash low or at least retest a portion of this initial rally. The impulsive nature of the rally following the crash was not sustainable, as the index started to stall at the top range of the bear market channel. Although the technical action was clear, many "gurus" were calling for a new bull market. In my April 2002 market report, I reiterated my case for a continuation of the bear market:

> ***"The Dow Industrials have chopped around quite a bit in the past month without much net result. The index has sold off recently, closely testing the 10,000 mark. The action has been lackluster, as most of the rallies are a one-day phenomenon, while the declines have slowly dragged. ... There are many market analysts making claims of the beginning stages of the first bull market of the 21st century. I've heard overly bullish targets anywhere from 15,000 to a recent call by a well-known money manager for 30,000 in six years. I think these claims warrant caution. Technically, these price targets cannot be even considered until certain resistance levels are breached.... The 'Line in the Sand' for such a breakout is above the 11,300 area—the all-time 0.886 retracement from the January 2000 high to the September 2001 low. It is a number that I have in the back of my mind and I have mentioned it in a few past reports. But, I continue to stick with my bearish overall position for several reasons."***

- ***First of all, the trend is still down. It is amazing that some analysts are calling for a new bull market when there are no technical signs that would support such an argument. As noted by the red channel, the Dow Industrials have failed to break out of the two-year downtrend.***

- ***Lower highs and lower lows. Each successive critical high and low since the January 2000 peak has continued to trade at lower levels.***

- ***Lack of clear pattern. Throughout the Dow's history, the index has signaled new market uptrends with distinct bullish patterns, including distinct secondary tests of prior critical lows. The rally since September has been more impulsive than constructive. This impulsive action can be observed in the Dow Jones Transports, as well. Essentially, the index must provide a significant retest of the September low to establish a constructive and stable base.***

...I will outline my longer-term downside targets over the next few Dow Industrial reports. Although it is a long way down from current levels, my first target for the Dow Jones Industrial Average is 6800. There, I said it. In May's report, I will explain my reasons. In the short term, the Industrials have declined after testing an important 0.618 retracement at 10,400, serving as the critical resistance. I favor a continuation of the recent selling, and I'm looking for the index to begin to break under 10,000 to as low as the 9500 level. Remember, the longer-term trend remains bearish and unless convincing upside action materializes, the Industrials will continue to slide."

(HarmonicTrader.com http://www.harmonictrader.com/members/harmonic/markets/dow0402.htm)

Finally, A Low in Sight...One Problem, It's 3000 Points Lower

Quite simply, the index was clearly stalling at a critical 0.618 retracement at the top range of the bear market trend channel. As the index continued to slide further, I knew that the next breakdown and continuation of the primary bearish trend could lead to a much further decline. As the index started to roll over, it became apparent that this next leg down would possibly trigger a massive Bullish AB=CD.

Dow Jones Industrial Average (^DJI): Weekly

Figure 1.12 shows the actual chart from the April market report. Clearly, the breakdown was beginning to accelerate. The impending breakdown of the sharp up trend line and the reversal at the weekly 0.618 retracement were distinct signs of the continuation of the bear market.

Figure 1.12

Dow Jones Industrial Average (^DJI): Weekly Monster Bullish AB=CD

The chart in Figure 1.13 is the original post from the initial prediction of an eventual low in the 6800 area. The breakdown following the test of the 0.618 weekly retracement turned out to be a critical continuation point within the predominant bearish trend. In fact, it was probably the best shorting opportunity of the entire bear market, as the index accelerated to the downside after reversing at the C point of the massive AB=CD.

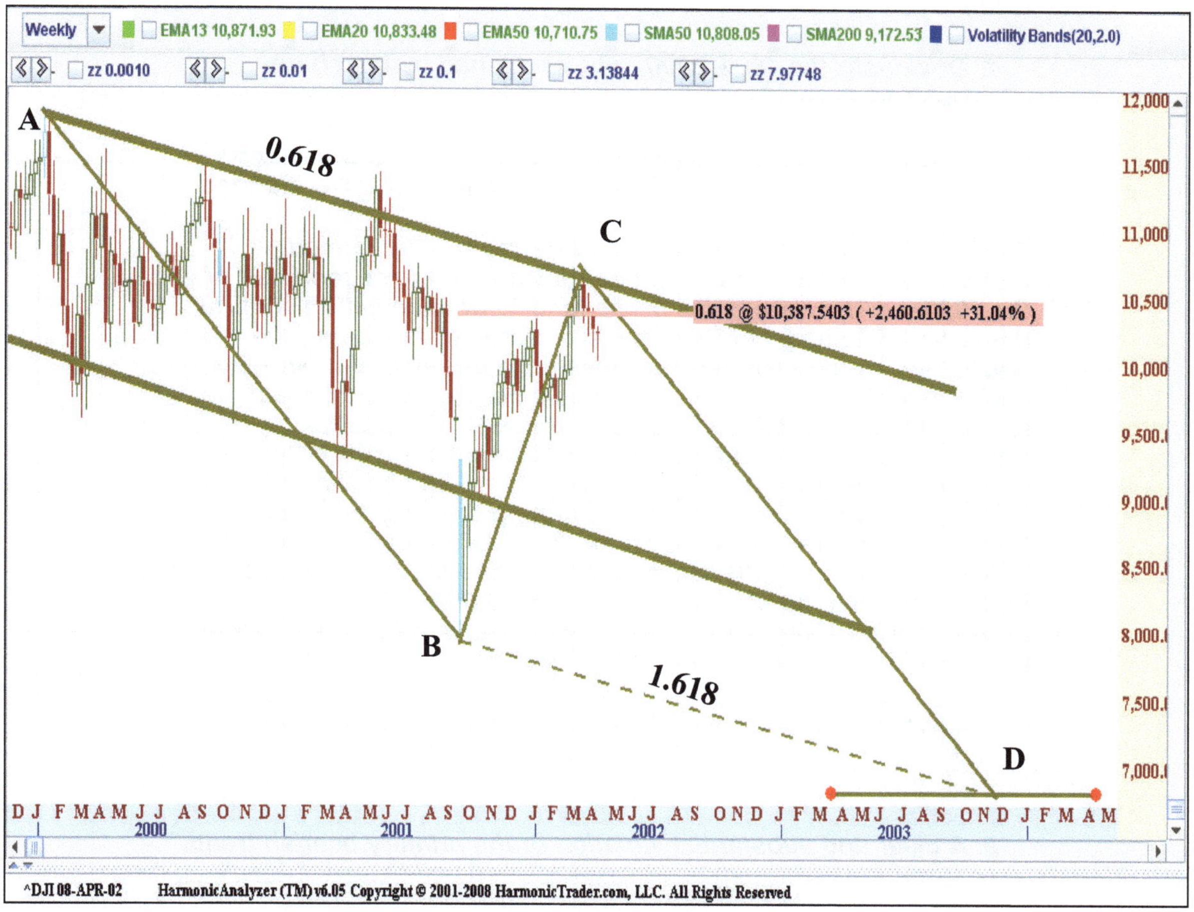

Figure 1.13

The steady downside continuation in the months following confirmed the continuation of the bear market. I reiterated this position in my May 2002 Dow Jones Industrial Average market report and explained the longer-term reasons for the bear market low to occur at the completion of the Bearish AB=CD:

> ***"As I mentioned in last month's report, the longer-term picture remains bearish. This 15-year chart—starting from the crash low of 1987—reveals several interesting aspects of the future action. Clearly, the sharp uptrend from the 1994 low to the 2000 high has been violated. Furthermore, the chart shows that the 15-year bull trend from the 1987 low is quite a distance from the current level. It is important to be mindful of these two trend realities:***
>
> 1. ***Obviously, the 1994–2000 rally, as defined by the sharp uptrend, is over.***
>
> 2. ***The 15-year trend line represents substantial support and defines the lower limit of any significant potential correction.***
>
> ***The Dow Industrials are consolidating—more aptly termed distributing—below the bull market uptrend of the second half of the 1990s.... The Harmonics of the long-term price action confirm the potential support of the long-term uptrend. Assuming the current year's high will remain untested, a potential Bullish AB=CD completes at 6,700. This area is complemented by two critical retracements from the 1987 low and the 1994 low, a 50% retracement at 6,760 and a 61.8% retracement at 6,700, respectively. These levels converge with the 15-year trend line and would represent a correction worthy of resuming the long-term bullish trend.... The overall market position for the Dow Jones Industrials remains bearish.... I felt compelled to outline the larger scenario that I have been monitoring for quite some time. I have been officially bearish on this index for two years, and I will not change this position until one of two things happens:***
>
> 1. ***A significant correction to the aforementioned long-term levels.***
>
> ***or***
>
> 2. ***A clear and substantial violation of the primary bearish trend."***
>
> (HarmonicTrader.com http://www.harmonictrader.com/members/harmonic/markets/dow0502.htm)

Price Action Just Above the Potential Reversal Zone (PRZ): The Bullish Bat at the Bear Market Low

The Industrials continued to slide for another year after making the initial call for the bear market low in the 6700–6800 range in April 2002. In combination with the psychological 7000 level, I firmly believed the index would test this immensely critical long-term harmonic support. As the price action sank under the 7500 level, I knew the index was close. But, I firmly believed in the "magnet effect" of so many technical factors to "attract" the ultimate low to occur in this area. Furthermore, the S&P 500 possessed a similar long-term setup, and both indices were in the midst of completing their respective harmonic patterns. In October 2002, the index nearly tested the 7000 level, as the Dow declined sharply during this ominous seasonal time period. The Industrials sank under the 7200 level before bouncing sharply. Despite another near-completion of the long-awaited PRZ, I remained bearish. In my opinion, the harmonic support in the 6700–6800 area was so substantial that the index would eventually test it. Furthermore, the Industrials lacked any other substantial technical possibility.

After a sharp but brief rally, the index rolled over again, sinking to retest the October lows. This retest presented a dilemma, as the Dow Jones Industrial Average formed a distinct Bullish Bat. In addition, the S&P 500 formed the same pattern; however, it had already tested its long-term harmonic support zone. In my April 2003 Dow Jones Industrial Average market report, I discussed this dilemma:

> ***"After completing this Dow Bullish Bat, the index has continued to move higher and hold weekly lows. This is crucial for the stability of the index. But what about 6800? The patterns indicated at a minimum that this was a primary target for this bear market.... Recent weeks have confirmed these lows as critical support, indicating inherent strength.... Since last summer, the index has tested the low 7000s three times and has been able to hold this area for eight months. With this type of action, the index is poised to make another attempt to retest the upper bear channel—at a minimum. For the Dow Jones Industrials, its defining resistance is the 9000 area. As I stated in last month's report, 'The next few weeks, if not days, will likely resolve the entire Dow Jones 6800 scenario.' The following few days were the beginning of this resolution, as the index was able to hold the third test of the 7000 area.... The biggest question of all is: 'Are we looking at a historic low for the index?' Possibly. However, the index must provide confirmation and take out the aforementioned resistance levels before committing to such a stance...."***
>
> (HarmonicTrader.com http://www.harmonictrader.com/members/dow/harmonic/markets/dow0403.htm)

Dow Jones Industrial Average (^DJI): Weekly Bullish Bat

The weekly chart in Figure 1.14 shows the Bullish Bat in the Dow Jones Industrial Average that formed over the course of six months just above the 7000 level. The precise reversal and decisive bullish continuation in the weeks and months that followed confirmed this pattern as the definitive technical signal marking this area as the bear market low.

Figure 1.14

The Bullish Bat was considerably large, as the entire pattern comprised approximately 2000 points from high to low. Therefore, this was a substantial harmonic factor in my overall analysis. It is important to note that I did not immediately switch from bearish to a bullish position. Officially, I switched to a neutral stance in my April 2003 Dow Jones Industrial Average market report after the Bullish Bat completed, and I clearly stated that the primary bearish trend was coming to an end:

> ***"The biggest question of all is: 'Are we looking at a historic low for the index?' Possibly. However, the index must provide confirmation and take out the aforementioned resistance levels before committing to such a stance. There are several basic long-term factors, such as historic trend, decennial cycles, and significant retracements that must be considered. And these factors indicate that the index is close to resolving this multiyear downtrend. For these reasons, the official position is now NEUTRAL. Essentially, this position is respecting the signs of the market and anticipating an eventual new uptrend. Before committing to a bullish stance, the index has some work to finish. But the upside is becoming the prevalent bias."***
>
> (HarmonicTrader.com http://www.harmonictrader.com/members/dow/harmonic/markets/dow0403.htm)

At a minimum, the price action and the completion of the Bullish Bat were key signs that the primary downtrend of the past three years was coming to an end. Furthermore, the decisive upside in the months following its completion signaled inherent long-term strength at hand, as the Industrials eventually climbed to new all-time highs within three years after its completion.

The 2008 Bear Market

The ability of the Industrials to rally to new all-time highs was remarkable. The multiyear uptrend of the 1990s was clearly over. It seemed as if a new multidecade trend was beginning. Surely, the 2000 bear market represented a significant historic correction—enough to possibly justify a new bull market. Despite such rationalizations, the 2008 bear market did provide early signals of a significant decline at hand. Specifically, the price action reversed sharply from the prior year's peak. In fact, the index lost nearly 15–20% of its value before anyone really knew what was unfolding.

From a Harmonic Trading perspective, the index established a distinct Bullish 5-0 structure on the weekly chart that possessed a smaller Bullish AB=CD. The initial points of the pattern were well defined. As the price action declined in the final leg of the setup, it became apparent that this structure was the make-or-break support of the prior multiyear rally (see Figure 1.15). Although I was not actively operating my advisory service, I was compelled to outline these developments in a report on my website.

Figure 1.15

In a report in July 2008, I wrote:

> ***"The Dow Jones Industrial Average has sustained remarkable damage the past 12 months. Although the index recently declined sharply—nearly 10 percent in 30 days, the trend is still clearly down. Remarkably though, the index has formed an exact 5-0 pattern on the weekly chart. The distinct structure clearly points to a critical technical test in the coming months at slightly lower levels.... With the prevalence of the weekly Bullish 5-0 pattern and the AB=CD pattern, there are several substantial technical events about to unfold. Following this short-term bounce, I expect a complete test of the entire Potential Reversal Zone (PRZ) at the 10,400 range.... Back in March, I outlined the entire scenario for the Dow Jones Industrial Average at a group presentation in Atlanta. In particular, I was addressing the numerous Harmonic levels at the 11,600 are.... As I stated in my presentation in March, I was very concerned and still am about the long-term state of the Dow Jones Industrial Average. More importantly, a failure beyond the mid-10,000 area would essentially trigger a massive continuation and an eventual retest of the entire 2003 low. For now, it is important to focus on the current action and impending roll over of the recent rally. The eventual test of the mid-10,000 area will dictate the long-term action. It is critical to prepare for this impending technical action and upcoming test of this substantial harmonic support zone. Until then, it is important to stay with predominant trend, which is still down."***
>
> (HarmonicTrader.com http://www.harmonictrader.com/hownowdow708.htm)

Figure 1.16

Figure 1.17 shows how the price action failed this projected support in dramatic fashion and actually exceeded the 2003 low. Although the 5-0 pattern failed, the decisive breakdown was a clear continuation of the predominant trend. Not to mention, the extreme warning sign of the sharp sell off at the pattern's completion contributed to the bearish trend.

Figure 1.17

The index has rallied from these lows, but it is still bound by the respective multidecade limits of support and resistance. For the Industrials, the lows of the 2000 and 2008 bear markets—approximately in the 7000 area—possess incredible significance for the next decade and beyond. Regardless of the end result, more than anything the volatile action of the past decade has mandated a greater attention to the market's behavior and a greater readiness to capitalize on *both sides* of the market.

Dow Jones Industrial Average Conclusion

More than any other index, the Dow Jones Industrials required a bit of discretion and confirmation to decipher the long-term trend. For example, in the 2000 bear market, the price action failed to completely test the 6700–6800 area. Despite falling shy, it is important to note that this prediction was accurate within the context of the time period. At a minimum, the harmonic measurement techniques provided a reliable ballpark area that effectively identified the long-term potential support for this multiyear bear market. Also, the actual low was approximately 400 points above—or less than 10% of the entire move—from the projected target. Most important, this target was identified nearly 18 months prior to its realization.

From a harmonic perspective, this was not an ideal conclusion to the multiyear bear market. It would have been a perfect situation if the index would have reversed from the completion point of the long-term Bullish AB=CD. But it did not. Similar to this discretion, the failure of the 5-0 pattern in 2008 was not an ideal situation. However, these events still pinpointed the critical areas to examine for market turning points.

Did Harmonic Trading techniques fail to provide the correct conclusion in these situations? I don't think so. In real trading situations, there has to be some degree of flexibility in the overall market analysis to allow for the variations that may arise from the model situation. Although the market failed to react ideally, the performance of Harmonic Trading measurement techniques throughout this period was extremely accurate. At both the all-time peak and the bear market lows for the index, the approach warned of the impending changes about to unfold in the predominant trend.

The Lessons from the Bear Markets of 2000 and 2010

The experiences of the past two decades have facilitated an evolution of the entire Harmonic Trading approach. I realized that the patterns were not ultimate buy or sell signals in their own right. Although I always stressed the principle that harmonic patterns are first and foremost "signposts of potential future price action," the overwhelming failure of the bullish patterns during the multiyear bear markets in particular required a broader perspective to interpret what the market was really indicating at this time. Specifically, the failure of harmonic patterns was to be regarded more than I had in the past. This was a difficult admission for me because in a way it devalued the significance and potential for the patterns themselves to comprise a stand-alone trading methodology. Regardless, a more comprehensive interpretation of harmonic price action was required to recognize the market's signals and to determine the overall direction of the primary trend.

Without a doubt, I learned a great deal during this time. In the long run, this was an important evolutionary process that was essential to the advancement of the Harmonic Trading approach. These lessons refocused my attention on price action in the completion area of harmonic patterns, especially with respect to the predominant trend. Furthermore, this strategic adjustment led to new strategies that expanded the technical tools employed within the Harmonic Trading arsenal.

It's Not the Pattern's Fault...

The structural significance of harmonic patterns has been debated in recent years. I encountered some criticism in those early years regarding the effectiveness of patterns. For example, some maintained that since the monster bullish setups failed from 2000–2002—especially the NASDAQ Composite—Harmonic Trading failed to work. No! In fact, the numerous bullish pattern failures were screaming that the predominant trend in many of these equity markets would remain bearish for quite some time. Again in 2008, the index violated a significant weekly setup—the critical Bullish 5-0 pattern—which underscored the extent of the damage at hand. Therefore, I would have to argue that the system did not fail. Throughout these bear declines, the demonstrative price action signaled their overwhelming continuation, as most of the significant bullish patterns on daily and even weekly time frames yielded little to no support at these harmonic zones. In short, my point is that the bear markets of 2000 and 2008 represented a unique test of the Harmonic Trading strategies as an effective methodology. But, these difficulties inspired a more integrative approach that has expanded the application of the basic interpretations immensely.

A Feel for the Markets

In *The Harmonic Trader*, I discussed the importance of developing a feel for the markets, especially as it relates to harmonic price behavior. Developing this "intuitive feel" for the markets is where the lines of the art and the science of trading merge. Again, despite the fact that incredibly harmonic price action helped to determine the overall market positions, these conclusions still fall under the "artistic side" of trading. I prefer to call these types of decisions "educated assessments." Regardless, this situation truly manifests the "feel for price action" that is required to successfully navigate the financial markets.

One of my favorite classic books on the markets—*How to Make the Stock Market Make Money for You* by Ted Warren—aptly describes this feel as a technical "know how" to be successful:

> ***"Learn to recognize the variety of bases, consolidations, trends, false ceilings, false support levels, false starts, and shakeouts. There are internal changes which take place, all of which have an important bearing on the future action of a stock. If you can detect these formations, you will acquire the 'know-how' in forecasting stock price movements."***
>
> (*How to Make the Stock Market Make Money for You* [Grants Pass, OR: The Ted Warren Company, 1966] 66).

I believe that the "feel for the markets" must always be based upon the established principles and technical rules that define the Harmonic Trading approach. Throughout my experience operating an advisory service based exclusively on this approach, my decisions were always based upon the application of the standard harmonic measurement techniques. This adherence to a "strict constructionist" view of the Harmonic Trading rules is the primary reason I was able to anticipate the critical changes and stay with the predominant trend throughout this era for all three major U.S. indices. Furthermore, this experience permanently validated the effectiveness and importance of these techniques to determine probable future price action in the financial markets.

Now What—Long-Term Harmonic Projections

Elliott Wave Principle by Alfred Frost and Robert Prechter was a revolutionary technical book for its time. In addition to integrating price structures with Fibonacci ratios and outlining precise wave counts, the book presented some remarkable future projections for the markets. The book was written during a period of time when the markets were still languishing in an extended long-term sideways range. After crashing in 1974, the markets experienced a volatile few years, as equities failed to recover. Despite the unfavorable conditions of their time, Frost and Prechter presented some bold predictions for the next decade. At the very end of the book (in their third edition), they called for an all-time target of 4000 on the Dow Jones Industrial Average by 1990. In fact, on page 188, they outlined their case:

> ***"...based on Elliott's channeling methods, to the upper channel line, wage in this case cuts through the price action in the 3500-4000 range in the latter half of the 1980s...therefore, one point to be watching for a possible market peak is five years from 1982, or 1987. Coincidentally, as we pointed out in the text, 1987 happens to be a Fibonacci 13 years from the corrections low point in 1974, 21 years from the peak of wave 3 in 1966, and 55 years from the start of wave want in 1932. To complete the picture, 1987 is a perfect date for the Dow to hit its 3686 target sense to reach at the Dow would have to burst briefly through its upper channel line in a 'throw-over,' which is typical of exhaustion moves (such as the 1929 peak). Based upon a 1.618 time multiple to Wave I and upon equality to the 1920s fifth cycle wave, and a year wave V would point to 1990 as the next most likely year for a peak."***
>
> (*Elliott Wave Principle* [Gainseville, GA: New Classics Library, 1978]).

The interesting aspect regarding this study was that Frost and Prechter were utilizing prior measurement techniques to project future targets. Although Harmonic Trading does not discuss wave counts, similar comparative measurement techniques from the past can be employed to determine critical future price levels. Surprisingly, their predictions were accurate as the Dow Jones Industrial Average crashed in 1987 and managed to test the 3000 level by 1990—a mere 15% shy of their long-term target.

It must have been alarming to hear someone predict that the Dow Jones Industrial Average would more than triple from the current level in 1983—the date of the market report from their third edition. In fact, the 3500–4000 area represented a critical technical level where the index consolidated briefly before accelerating sharply in a historic breakout. Similar to Harmonic Trading, their prediction was based upon the analysis of specific price waves that established their technical measurement methods. This type of analysis was unprecedented for the time, yet the methodology held its own throughout the following years, and remains to be a reliable framework to analyze price action. Although the price levels from this Elliott Wave study have been vastly exceeded in the years since, the effectiveness of such techniques to gauge critical long-term technical areas in advance is impressive.

In much the same manner, I believe Harmonic Trading techniques will continue to hold their own as an effective methodology to analyze price action. Regardless of the time frame—either long-term multiyear price projections or intra-day short-term analysis—harmonic measurement techniques offer an effective means to decipher market movements in a similar fashion as Elliott Wave.

Harmonic Projections—The Year 2025

It's the year 2025 and the Dow Jones Industrial Average is trading at 36,000! Am I kidding? Partially. However, the analogous prediction of Frost and Prechter's decade forecast related to current levels would equate to over a 300% gain or a Dow Jones Industrial Average reading of approximately 25,000 points from current levels of 10,000. Although the relative market position is different than that of the early 1980s when Frost and Prechter made their historic prediction, such long-term forecasts must be based upon cogent measurement tools and thorough technical reasoning. I am not making a prediction that this will occur. Rather, I am merely speculating along the same lines as the Prechter forecast.

In that vein, I present a similar analysis within the context of the Harmonic Trading approach. Historically, the markets have responded to long-term technical levels as defined by respective substantial harmonic retracement and projection ratios of prior price history. The incredibly harmonic long-term price action in both the bear market of 2000 and 2008 exemplified the ability of these measurements to provide an effective framework of critical technical levels to consider.

Standard & Poor's 500 (^SPX): Weekly Historic Harmonic Projections

Although this may seem oversimplified, the progression of harmonic ratios serves as a general framework to analyze future long-term price action (see Figure 1.18). For the S&P 500, the price action recovered following both the bear market of 2000 and 2008. Although the index has retraced 50% of the prior decline since the 2009 low as of this writing date, the all-time historic 0.886 bearish retracement will serve as the true historic test. Eventually, the index will test new highs. But, the price action at the long-term 0.886 retracements in cases like these has frequently provided a great deal of indication of whether it will happen sooner or later. Aside from the all-time 0.886 retracement as resistance, the index has established historic support since the bear market low of 2003 and 2009 that completes in the 700 area. This type of long-term price action could be manifesting a stable recovery like many prior historic cases—namely the 1929–1934 and the 1987–1992 markets.

Figure 1.18

As long as this multiyear uptrend is maintained, I truly believe that the index will retest historic resistance at the long-term 0.886 retracement level above 1500. This is attainable within the context of the 2025 scenario. Again, this framework depends upon steadily maintaining the uptrend support from the recent bear market low.

NASDAQ Composite ($COMPQ): Weekly Historic Harmonic Projections

This long-term chart of the NASDAQ Composite, shown in Figure 1.19, is strikingly similar to the price action in the Dow Jones Industrial Average following the Crash of 1929. If these are similar situations, it will likely take the same 25 years for the NASDAQ to recover all of its losses as the Industrials did following the Crash of 1929. One indication of this is the fact that the NASDAQ has failed to exceed the minimum 38.2% bear market retracement in the past decade.

Figure 1.19

The most interesting long-term harmonic level for the NASDAQ is the 0.886 retracement at 4675. This essentially represents a 100% gain from current levels, but it just might be the year 2025 or later before it is realized!

Dow Jones Industrial Average (^DJI): Weekly Historic Harmonic Projections

The Dow Jones Industrial Average possesses the best chance of testing the long-term harmonic resistance levels. Having already recovered half of the 2008 losses, the index has established substantial multiyear support in the 7000 area (see Figure 1.20).

Figure 1.20

The most significant harmonic level within the next few years for the index is the 0.886 retest above of the prior all-time high. Given the volatility of the last decade, 14,000–15,000 is possible. If the next ten years are anything like the last, an even higher target is not as far-fetched as it might seem. Given the year 2025, the Dow Jones Industrial Average would need to triple from current levels. Although such speculation can be interesting, this does not excuse complacency, as the 80% washout in the NASDAQ demonstrated. However, it is important to be mindful that such long-term levels have provided reliable technical projections in the past. Furthermore, future harmonic areas will help to decipher the progress of the predominant trend.

Markets Review Conclusion

Before we continue with the new concepts within the Harmonic Trading approach, I believe that this review was an essential foundation to lead into the new material. I'm proud of the advisory service that I provided for so many years. The ability to accurately assess such volatile price action over the course of that time proved that these techniques are truly effective in deciphering price action in the financial markets. In addition, I believe that these market reports represent accurate case studies, further substantiating the Harmonic Trading approach.

Over the course of the past two decades, there have been many advancements in the basic approach of Harmonic Trading. New patterns, new ratios, and unprecedented measurement techniques have evolved directly from the lessons learned from the experience of providing this advisory service. I believe that the new techniques presented in this book substantially increase the arsenal of technical tools within the Harmonic Trading approach, and enhance the ability of existing strategies to effectively decipher price action and define profitable opportunities.

In conclusion, it's important to understand the state of the major indices relative to any other market that you might be trading. It is essential to have a solid understanding regarding the state of the predominant trend and to be able to determine the potential critical turning points in the markets. In essence, the ability to understand and to interpret "the big picture" of the overall technical condition of any market is an essential aspect of successful trading. With the tools within the Harmonic Trading approach, it is possible to decipher the relative state of price action within any market. But it is essential to consistently analyze all markets within the framework of the Harmonic Trading methodology, as this will provide the clearest of signals regarding the state of future potential price action.

Chapter 2

Harmonic Impulse Waves

Harmonic Ratio Progression

Regardless of the methodology that is employed to analyze trading opportunities, it is critical to have some type of framework to assess price action and to establish limits. Most technical tools utilize some type of numeric limits to establish discerning levels that categorize price action. One of the earliest of technical approaches, Dow Theory employs basic ⅓ percentages in its approximation of price movements. Although such approximation does not represent exact measures for real trading purposes, they serve as an effective means of gauging various technical levels of price action. In the same manner, the gamut of harmonic ratios serves as a framework of potential areas of support and resistance. It can be argued that standard fractional percentages could be utilized in the place of harmonic ratios and be as effective to analyze price action. However, the application of the primary harmonic ratios—the 0.618 and the 1.618—along with their respective derivations are the primary means of defining harmonic price action.

As I discussed in *Harmonic Trading: Volume One*, the ability of these measurements to be effective technical tools is founded in the notion of the *Principle of Harmonicity*. J. M. Hurst defined this technical phenomenon as:

> ***"The periods of neighboring waves in price action tend to be related by a small whole number."***
>
> *(J .M. Hurst Cycles Course* [Greenville, SC: Traders Press, 1973]*).*

However, in *Volume One*, I adapted this notion to replace "a small whole number" with "harmonic ratios." Again, the 0.618 and the 1.618 ratios serve as the primary basis for all measurements, since they are directly related to the Fibonacci sequence. Although I explained the technical phenomenon of harmonic ratios in *Volume One*, the relative measurement ability of these ratios is the primary strength of this approach. It is true that the essence of Harmonic Trading is founded in the combination of these ratios as the most effective means to analyze price action. But, simple retracements and extensions can serve as an effective general approach to measure price action.

This framework of harmonic ratios represents the basic model to analyze harmonic behavior for all measurable price moves. Of course, the entire series of retracements and extensions cannot be applied to every situation. However, this illustration is typically best applied to the largest price leg within the time frame analyzed. Regardless of the time interval, this spread of ratios represents the fundamental framework that most effectively categorizes price action relative to the prior dominant price leg.

Bullish Harmonic Ratio Progression

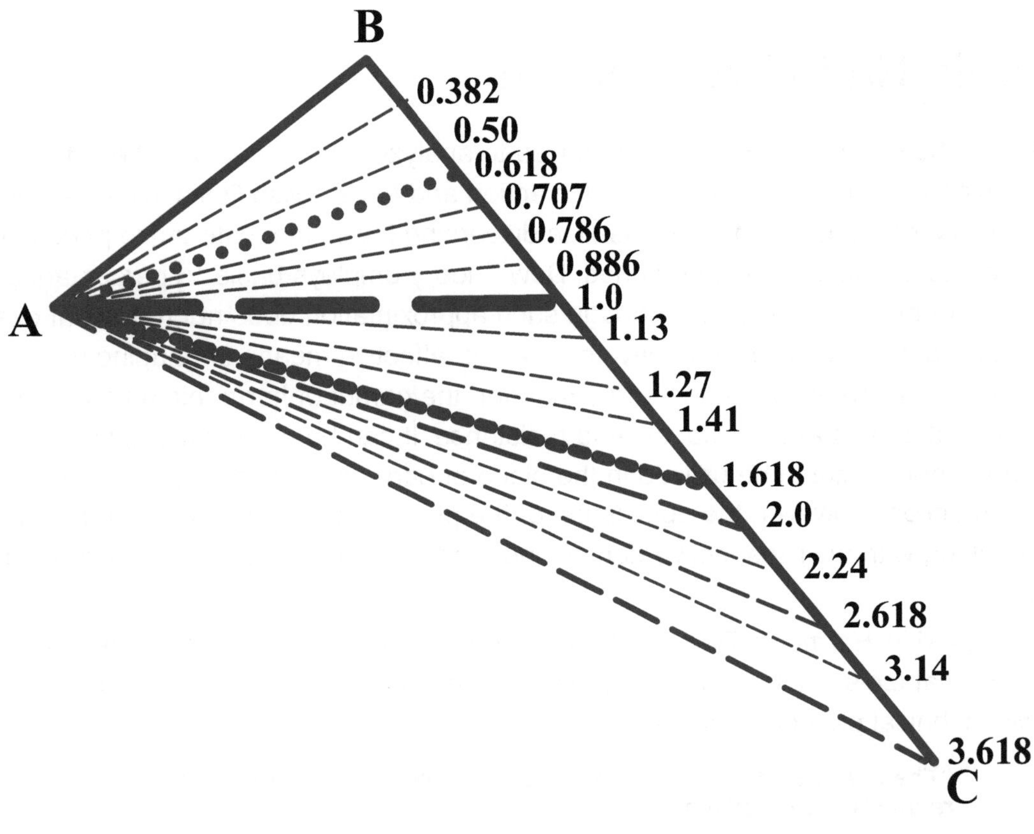

Figure 2.1

Bearish Harmonic Ratio Progression

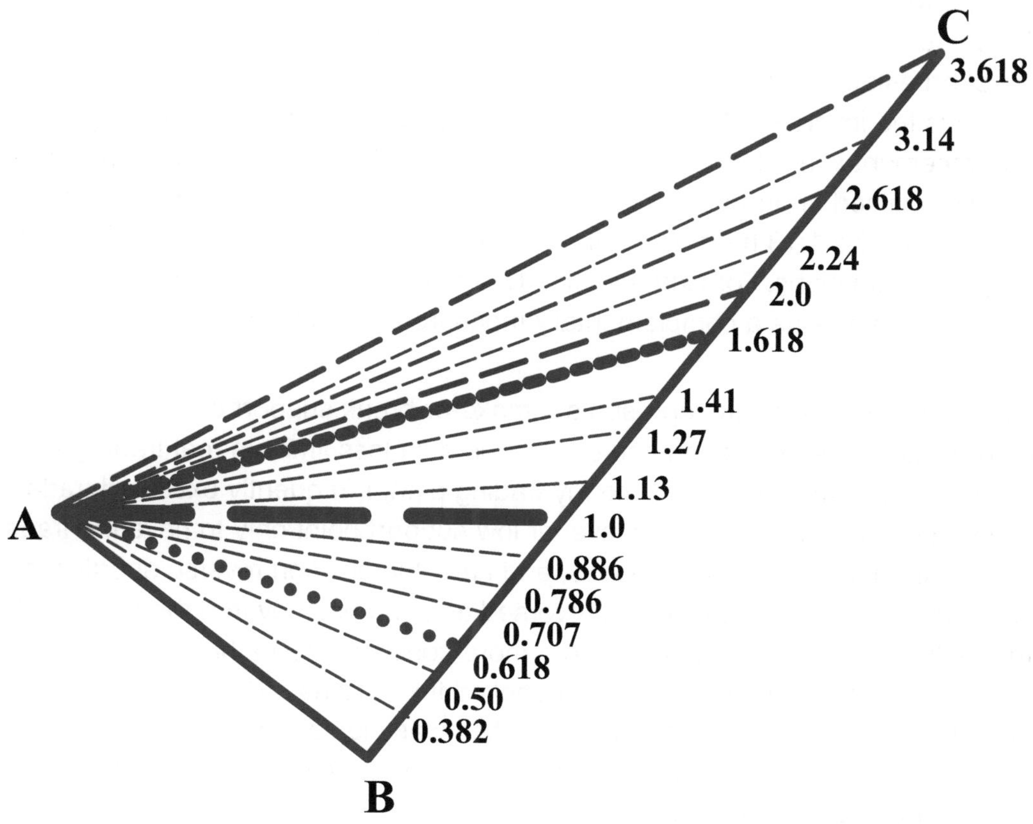

Figure 2.2

Harmonic Impulse Waves

Harmonic impulse waves are unique price movements that exhibit specific ratios that can be extreme and temporary in nature. Harmonic impulse waves respond to specific ratios and establish the initial price legs of complex patterns. Although these formations typically possess only three simple harmonic ratio points, they offer reliable and consistent indications of future price action. In much the same manner that complex patterns define areas of potential support and resistance, harmonic impulse waves can provide a great deal of technical information and can signal trade opportunities. Furthermore, these structures should possess distinct symmetry and adhere to specific harmonic ratios as complex patterns do. Although there are many harmonic impulse structures that can be defined, the following represent the most reliable combinations of distinct price waves with specific ratios that yield the most relevant technical information.

1.13 Extension—The Failed Wave

Although I refer to the 1.13 extension as "The Failed Wave," the name aptly refers to the true nature of the price structure. The 1.13 extension usually represents a failed breakout or breakdown of an established prior resistance or support point, respectively. The 1.13 harmonic ratio is the inverse of the 0.886. As I discussed in the *Harmonic Trading: Volume One*, the 0.886 retracement is a relatively new discovery within the technical community. The 0.886 retracement has gained enormous acceptance and is now widely cited. The inverse of the 0.886 retracement—the 1.13 harmonic ratio—is not as well known, but it is as effective when applied to specific situations. For example, the 1.13 ratio represents a critical aspect of the RSI BAMM, and it serves as a complementary measurement within other specific harmonic structures.

The 1.13 extension frequently represents a make-or-break support or resistance level in many technical situations, and it can serve to define stop loss limits in real trading scenarios. Before I integrated this measurement into my trading plan, I frequently executed trades that were retesting a critical high resistance level or low support point only to have the trade violate the target area, trigger a stop limit for a loss, and have the position reverse shortly thereafter. It seemed that these whipsawed shakeouts reversed as soon as I covered the position. I realized that the true validity of these trades required a more consistent level that defined a pattern's violation from a harmonic perspective. After I applied the 1.13 as a defining stop loss limit, the price area that marked a pattern's ultimate validation was clearly defined. In particular, this integration resulted in an advancement of the 1.13 extension within the Bat pattern, leading to the discovery of the Alternate Bat structure.

The simple 1.13 extension represents a critical level in confirming breakouts and breakdowns, as well. It has been my experience that price action that exceeds a critical 1.13 extension level frequently will continue farther to the 1.27 or 1.618 areas. Although this is a broad generalization, the rule of thumb serves to guide trading decisions within the framework of the progression of harmonic ratios. In the case of the 1.13, the failed aspect of the price structure in valid reversals reflects a seemingly false move in the primary trend's direction before dramatically changing course. Typically, such price action is associated with the final wave of either a corrective structure or a complex formation that reverses at the 1.13 projected extension of the prior move. In fact, I believe that this can be one of the most frustrating trading situations possible. However, the 1.13 serves as an effective defining limit in many of these cases.

In a real trading situation, this type of action can make you feel as if trading is not fair. Despite such injustice, these situations can be defined and handled properly when placed in the proper context. It is important to understand that such shakeouts manifest similar technical conditions as harmonic patterns to help identify these situations. Let's examine a few situations and the conditions that signal such potential price action.

Bullish 1.13 Extension—The Failed Wave

A simple bullish 1.13 extension is usually preceded by an extended down leg that experiences a quick bounce, only to roll over yet again slightly under the prior low. Although this may be a difficult structure to identify at first, price action in these circumstances is typically void of any distinct harmonic pattern and possesses more of a line segment character. In particular, as the AB price leg completes and begins to decline to the C point, the price action typically will adhere to the general structure (shown in Figure 2.3) and move decisively to the final completion point at the 1.13 extension. As Figure 2.3 demonstrates, the price action quickly violates the initial low point (A) and reverses decidedly thereafter in valid situations.

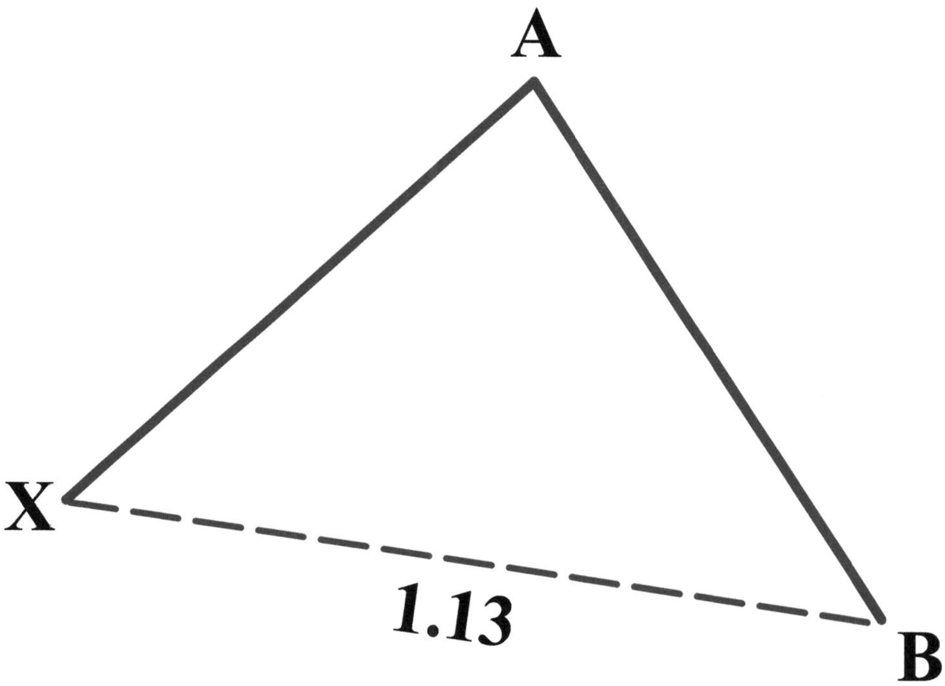

Figure 2.3

Google (GOOG): 5-Minute Bullish 1.13 Extension

In the example illustrated in Figure 2.4, Google possessed a sharp decline after the open of trading. The stock completed a final intra-day sell off at a distinct 5-minute 1.13 extension at 492. This type of price action is common for reversals in many short-term trading situations. Although it might have been difficult to buy the stock simply from the 1.13 extension area, in conjunction with larger harmonic setups or other important technical levels, this type of price action can help identify significant opportunities that are in the final phases of their decline.

GOOG 09-FEB-10_13:55 HarmonicAnalyzer (TM) v6.05 Copyright © 2001-2008 HarmonicTrader.com, LLC. All Rights Reserved

Figure 2.4

Bearish 1.13 Extension—The Failed Wave

A simple bearish 1.13 extension is usually preceded by an extended rally that experiences a quick reaction near the peak and reverses sharply after nominally exceeding the prior high (see Figure 2.5). In many cases, this type of price action is typically void of any distinct harmonic pattern structure and possesses more the character of a simple line segment.

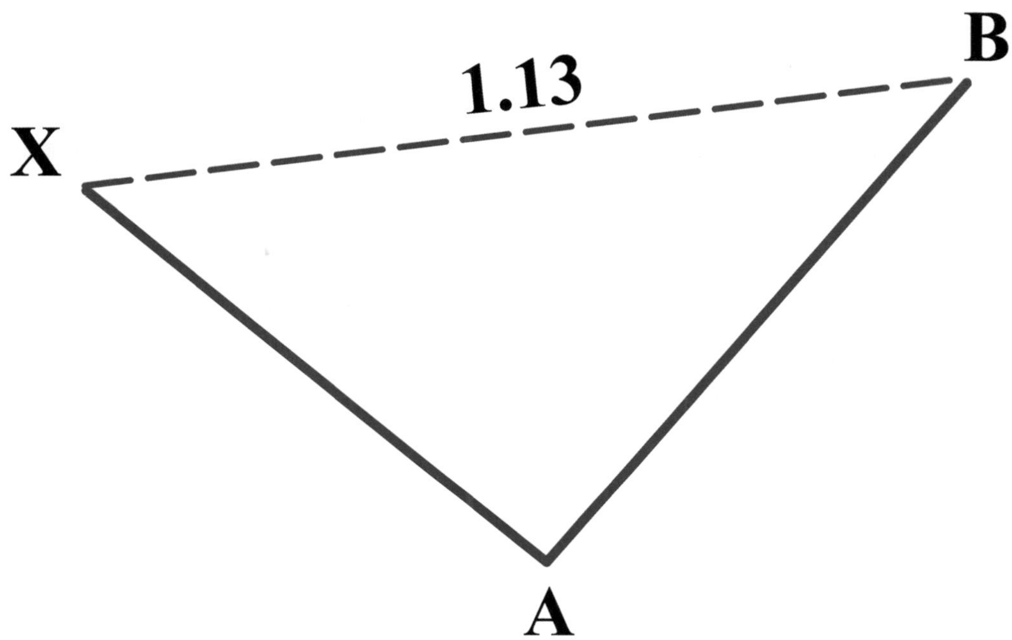

Figure 2.5

In particular, after the AB price leg completes and begins to rally to the C point, the price action typically will adhere to the linear structure and move decisively to the final completion point at the 1.13 extension. As Figure 2.5 demonstrates, the price action usually violates the initial high point (A) and reverses shortly thereafter.

Eurodollar (EUR_A0-FX): Daily Bearish 1.13 Extension

The daily chart of the Euro in Figure 2.6 shows a distinct bearish 1.13 extension that failed to continue higher. In fact, it marked a temporary top for the market in late 2009.

Figure 2.6

This is an excellent example because it clearly represents the nature of the 1.13 extension as a failed breakout. In this case, the index reversed a few points above the completion of the extension. Furthermore, the price action rolled over quickly and declined shortly after testing this critical resistance. The lack of continuation just above the prior peak at the 1.13 extension was indicative of a trend that is not going to continue. Situations like these underscore the importance of the 1.13 extension in defining critical potential resistance.

Extreme Bullish Harmonic Impulse Wave

The Bullish Harmonic Impulse Wave is a distinct structure that possesses several harmonic ratios. The structure typically can be the precursor to the 5-0 pattern, and it commonly forms as the down leg following a failed rally. In particular, the AB segment takes the shape of a failed harmonic impulse wave that can possess a range of ratios from a 1.13 extension to a 1.618 extension (see Figure 2.7).

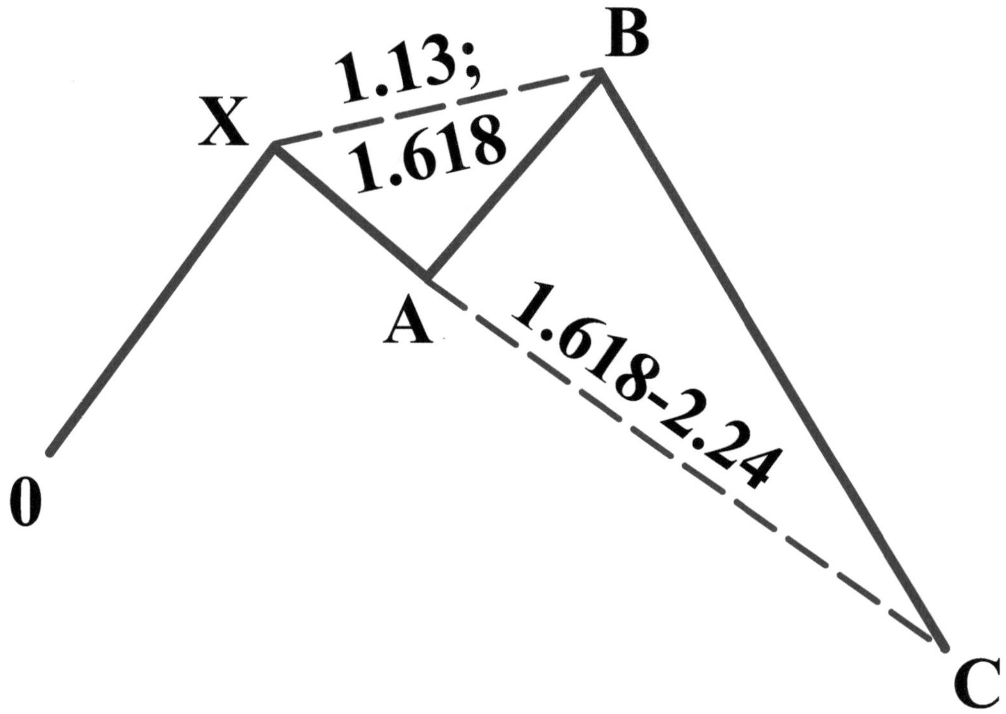

Figure 2.7

The first half of the structure is typically distinct, and it possesses price action that reverses precisely at each harmonic ratio. The final decline to the C point is typically a sharp move that is a 1.618–2.24 extension of the AB leg. One of the reasons for this type of price action is due to the preceding AB price leg that is usually a failed continuation of the prior extended 0X leg. Although the conditions for a valid harmonic impulse structure are general, the best situations are typically distinct and possess ideal price action.

Standard and Poor's 500 December 2009 Mini-Contract (ES_Z9): 60-Minute Extreme Bullish Harmonic Impulse Wave

This example of the S&P 500 December 2009 mini-contract on the 60-minute chart shows an ideal situation of an Extreme Harmonic Impulse Wave that possesses a perfect structure (see Figure 2.8).

Figure 2.8

The prior Bearish 1.13 extension established the structure, as a sharp reversal following the failed breakout resulted in an extended decline. In this case, the ES mini-contract sold off to the short-term 1.618 extension of that failed 1.13 breakout attempt and reversed exactly at this level.

Extreme Bearish Harmonic Impulse Wave

The Extreme Bearish Harmonic Impulse Wave is a distinct structure that requires a few essential elements to validate the structure. After an extended decline (0-X), the price action typically experiences a brief consolidation that results in a nominal new low. This consolidation area (X, A, B) is followed by an extended rally to at least the 1.618 AB extension area, as illustrated in Figure 2.9.

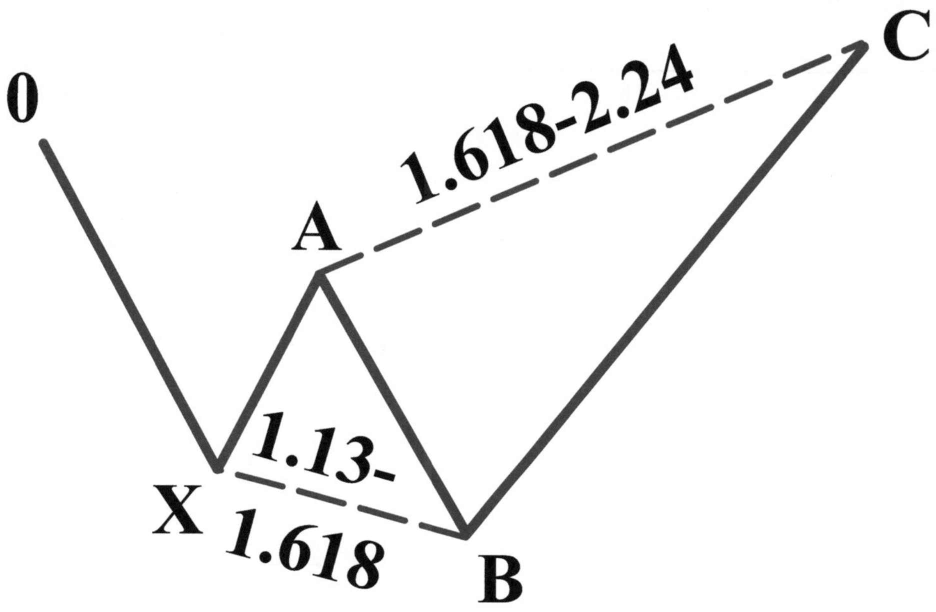

Figure 2.9

This BC segment rally is the most important aspect of the structure, as it manifests the extreme and impulsive nature of the setup. In fact, these structures frequently form within many defined bearish channels, and they can offer excellent opportunities to sell overextended rallies that are counter to the primary trend.

Light Sweet Crude March 2006 Contract (CL_H0): 15-Minute Extreme Bearish Harmonic Impulse Wave

The nature of the Extreme Bearish Harmonic Impulse Wave is exemplified in the chart in Figure 2.10. The 2010 March Crude Oil contract was declining steadily on the 15-minute chart until it rallied sharply to form the Extreme Bearish Harmonic Impulse Wave. The price action bounced quickly to test the intra-day 1.618 impulse extension.

Figure 2.10

The price action reversed quickly after testing the impulsive extension and continued lower, as the predominant downtrend squashed the brief rally. Situations like these develop frequently on intra-day charts, and they can identify excellent opportunities to take advantage of overextended short-term rallies within established downtrends.

Extreme Bullish Harmonic Impulse Wave @ 0.886 Retracement

The Extreme Bullish Harmonic Impulse Wave at an 0.886 retracement, illustrated in Figure 2.11, is a special situation that combines two critical harmonic measurements to define the trade opportunity. The combination of the 0.886 support with the extreme impulse extension frequently provides a brief reversal in most cases. This initial reaction provides many short-term trades at a minimum.

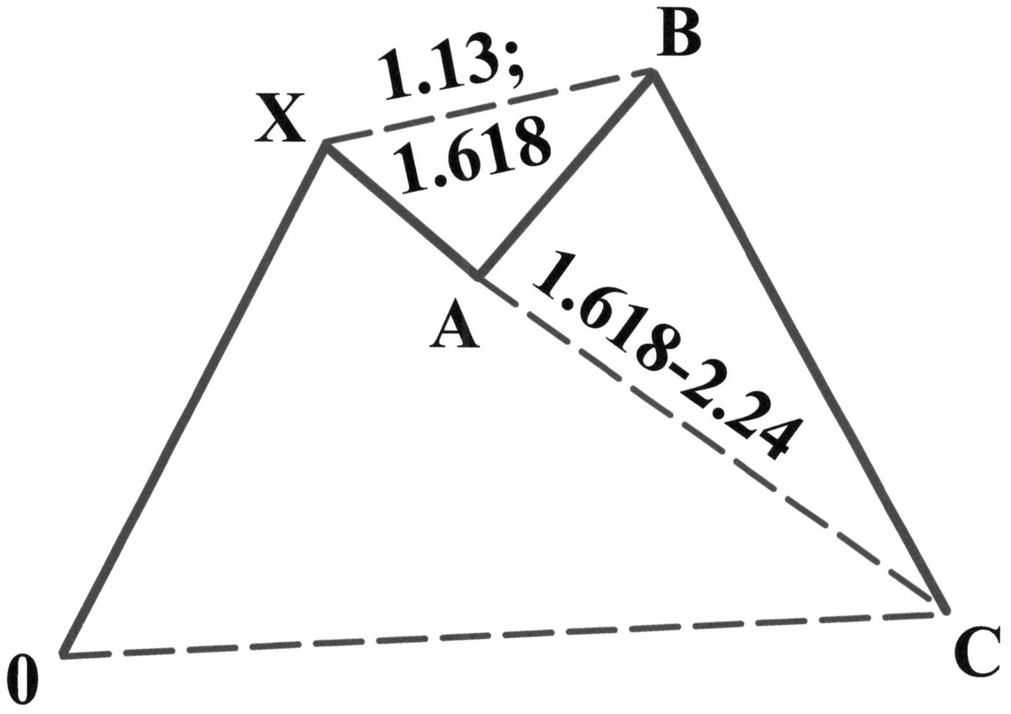

Figure 2.11

The structure represents a unique test of a critical prior support point. Although the bullish 0.886 retracement is a powerful potential support point on its own, an Extreme Bullish Harmonic Impulse Wave that possesses at least a 1.618 extension provides a short-term technical phenomenon that produces many reliable setups. It is important to note that many of these situations result in only brief reversals and require decisive continuation following the completion of the setup to signal a larger move at hand. But this unique structure can offer many profitable opportunities, as long as the trade is executed on the initial test of these harmonic numbers and the management of the position is handled tightly. Furthermore, reversals in these situations require an aggressive profit-taking approach, since many of these reactions are sharp but brief rallies.

AMEX Gas and Oil Exchange ($XOI): Daily Extreme Bullish Harmonic Impulse Wave @ 0.886 Retracement

This example of the XOI possessed all the ideal elements to validate the Extreme Bullish Harmonic Impulse Wave at an 0.886 retracement (see Figure 2.12). The failed rally of the AB leg preceded the sharp decline that resulted in a convergence of the 2.0 Bullish Harmonic Impulse Wave extension and the 0.886 retracement.

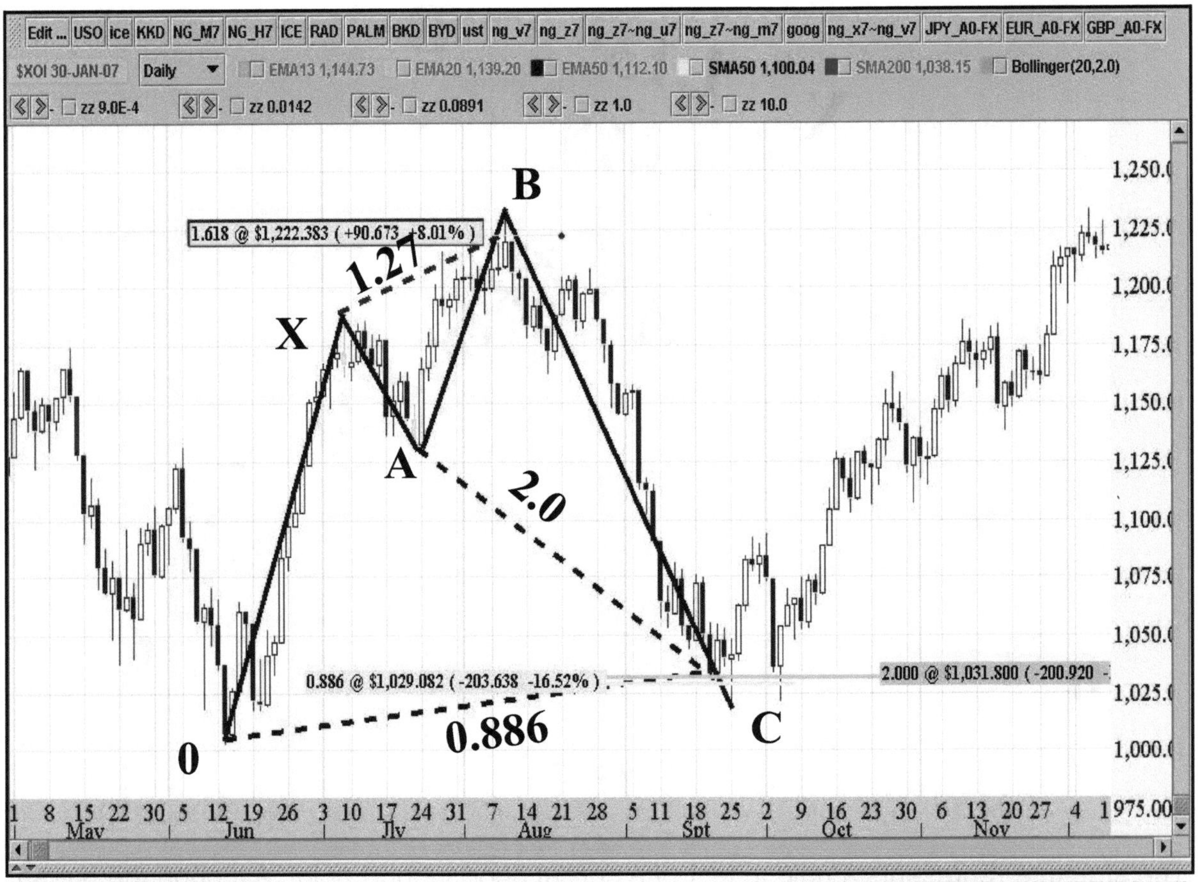

The Harmonic Analyzer (TM) : $XOI

Figure 2.12

The structure defined a precise area at 1030 for a short-term bounce at a minimum. In fact, both of these critical harmonic measurements completed within two points of each other. Although the price action required a secondary test of the PRZ, the decisive continuation following the completion of the structure clearly indicated a strong rally at hand.

Bearish Harmonic Impulse Wave @ 0.886 Retracement

The Extreme Bearish Harmonic Impulse Wave at an 0.886 retracement, illustrated in Figure 2.13, is a special situation that combines two critical harmonic measurements to define the trade opportunity. The combination of the 0.886 resistance with the extreme impulse extension frequently provides a tradeable, short-term opportunity at a minimum.

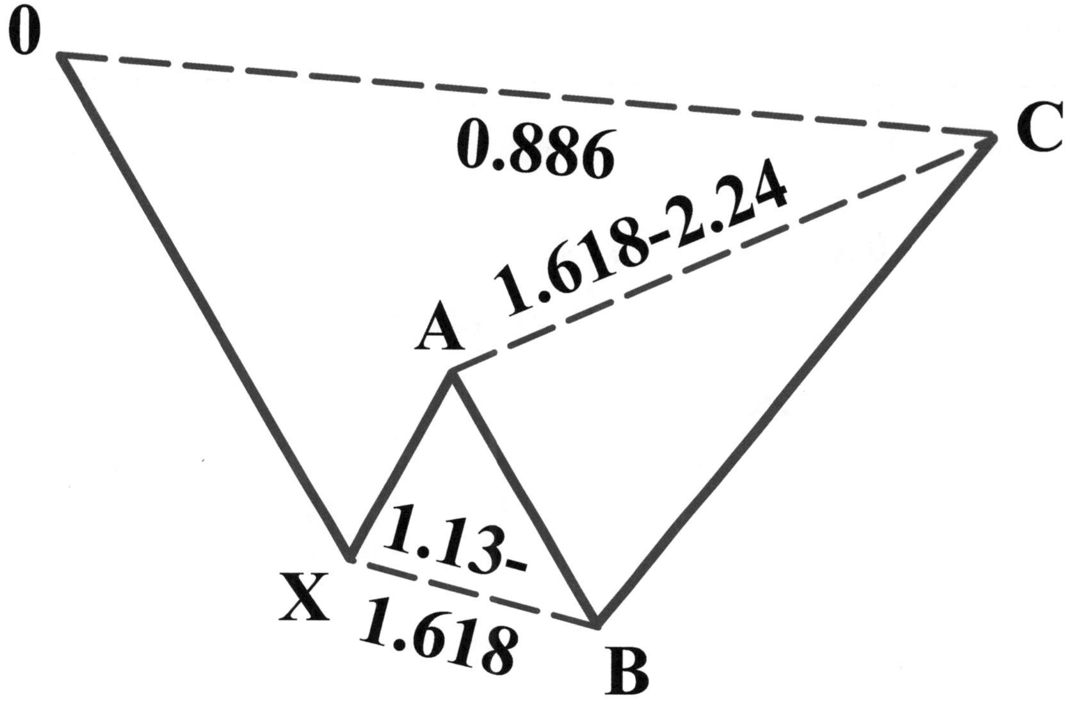

Figure 2.13

Philadelphia Gold and Silver Index (^XAU): Daily Bearish Harmonic Impulse Wave @ 0.886 Retracement

The next example of the XAU—Philadelphia Gold and Silver Index—shows an ideal Bearish Harmonic Impulse Wave at an 0.886 retracement (see Figure 2.14). In fact, the impulsive nature of the AB leg and the extended BC leg manifested the ideal elements that the structure should possess—a sharp rally that converges with a distinct 0.886 retracement. This creates a unique technical situation that defines a precise PRZ of harmonic resistance.

Figure 2.14

Harmonic Impulse Waves Conclusion

Although many Harmonic Impulse Waves are merely the precursor of complex patterns, these formations can be defined well in advance to define profitable short-term trading opportunities. Furthermore, the identification of these structures helps to classify price action within an expected technical framework that adheres to specific ratios. The understanding of harmonic structures like these helps to decipher price action more precisely and to define the potential future trend direction more accurately. The minimum 1.618 extension requirement is an important technical aspect of the structure and helps to differentiate this setup from other invalid candidates. Although Harmonic Impulse Waves are not the same as the traditional M-type and W-type structures, they serve to distinguish random price moves and refine harmonic price action even more clearly.

Chapter 3

New Harmonic Patterns

The 5-0 Pattern

Although I have been aware of the structure for quite some time, the 5-0 pattern is a relatively new discovery within the Harmonic Trading approach. I have studied thousands of cases to define the best 5-0 structures. Although I will not cover execution or trade management strategies, the principles are the same as for all harmonic patterns and can be found in *Harmonic Trading: Volume One*. Although this new pattern possesses many characteristics that are consistent with all harmonic structures, several traits truly differentiate it from the rest.

The 5-0 pattern is a unique structure that possesses a precise alignment of Fibonacci ratios to validate the structure. Although the 5-0 is considered a retracement pattern, as the 50% retracement is the most critical number within the Potential Reversal Zone (PRZ), the measurements of the various price legs are slightly different than the Bat or the Gartley. The 5-0 is within the family of 5-point harmonic price structures. However, the required B point alignment for other patterns does not apply in the case of the 5-0. Rather, the 5-0 requires a minimum Extreme Harmonic Impulse Wave of at least 1.618—but not to exceed 2.24—at the C point to distinguish the setup. In addition, the 5-0 requires a Reciprocal AB=CD measurement to define the pattern's completion.

The basic premise of the pattern is to identify distinct reactions following the completion of a contrary trend. Valid 5-0 patterns typically represent the first pullback of a significant trend reversal. In many instances, the AB leg of the structure is a failed final wave of an extended trend. Within Elliott Wave terms, the AB leg may be a failed wave 3 of a corrective "abc" or a failed wave 5 of an entire completed trend. Although these are obvious similarities, from the Harmonic Trading perspective, it is important to examine the structure via its relative Fibonacci measurements to satisfy the pattern requirements. The 5-0 is an incredibly precise pattern that possesses only two numbers—the 50% retracement of the BC leg and the Reciprocal AB=CD. It is important to note that the measurements utilized to define the PRZ are different from all other harmonic patterns in two distinct ways: the structural completion point of the final leg and the calculation of the AB=CD pattern.

50% BC Projection Defines the Pattern's Completion Point

In most cases, the XA leg is the defining measurement of the pattern's completion, while the BC projection is normally a complementary number. In contrast, the 5-0 pattern utilizes the 50% BC retracement as the defining limit in the setup.

Reciprocal AB=CD

A Reciprocal AB=CD pattern is typically a shorter countermove of equal length within a longer trend. Each price segment is distinct and forms a structure that looks like a lazy "Z" or "S." The pattern resembles an Elliott Wave Zig-Zag structure but is distinguished by the assigned Fibonacci ratios.

Bullish Reciprocal AB=CD

The Bullish Reciprocal AB=CD possesses price segments that are equivalent and typically form a structure that marks the continuation of the primary trend (see Figure 3.1). Although I will discuss Reciprocal AB=CD patterns within well-established bullish channels later in the book, the structure works best in these situations.

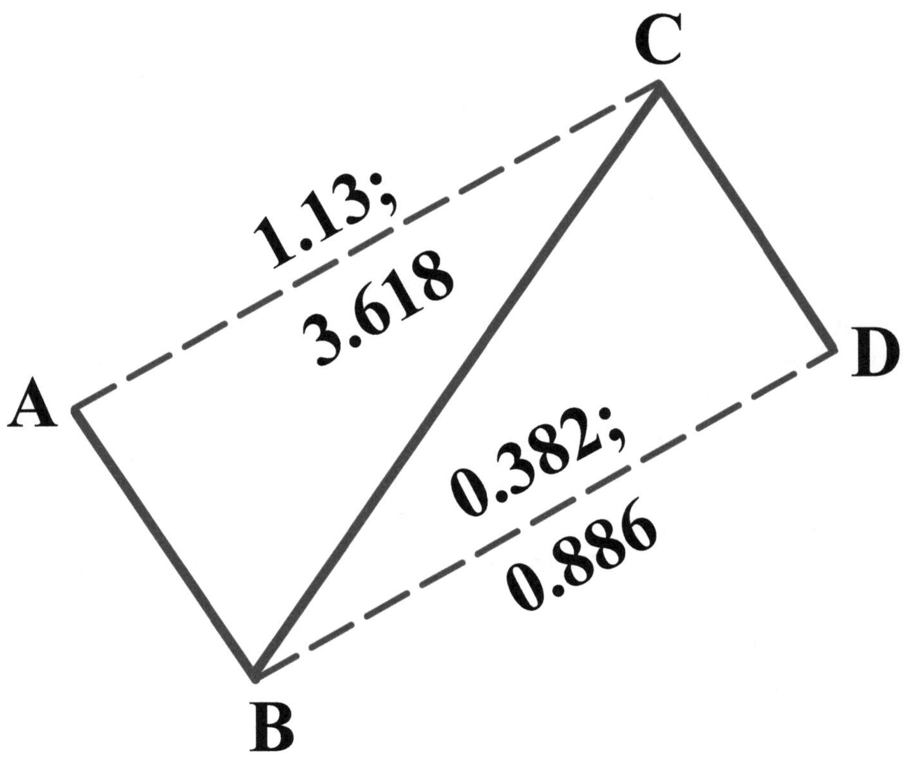

Figure 3.1

It is important to remember that the Reciprocal AB=CD is more of an approximation measurement that quantifies the general area where the primary trend will continue. In many situations, the AB leg of the Bullish Reciprocal AB=CD is normally the first corrective move in a newly established a trend. Although the CD leg will at least test the equivalent completion point in most cases, the PRZ of the Reciprocal AB=CD is not as precise as the regular bullish AB=CD pattern.

Fedex Corp. (FDX): Weekly Bullish Reciprocal AB=CD

The chart of Fedex Corp. illustrated in Figure 3.2 exemplifies the concept of a Bullish Reciprocal AB=CD, as the AB leg was the first corrective move within a longer-term bullish channel on the weekly chart. The stock reversed sharply after testing the equivalent CD leg that was approximately 15 points. The completion of the Reciprocal AB=CD was projected at 44.50, and it was complemented by the 0.618 weekly reciprocal retracement at 43.95. It is important to note that the reciprocal retracement was established by the prior 1.618 AB projection, and it triggered the corresponding completion of the CD leg at the 0.618 retracement.

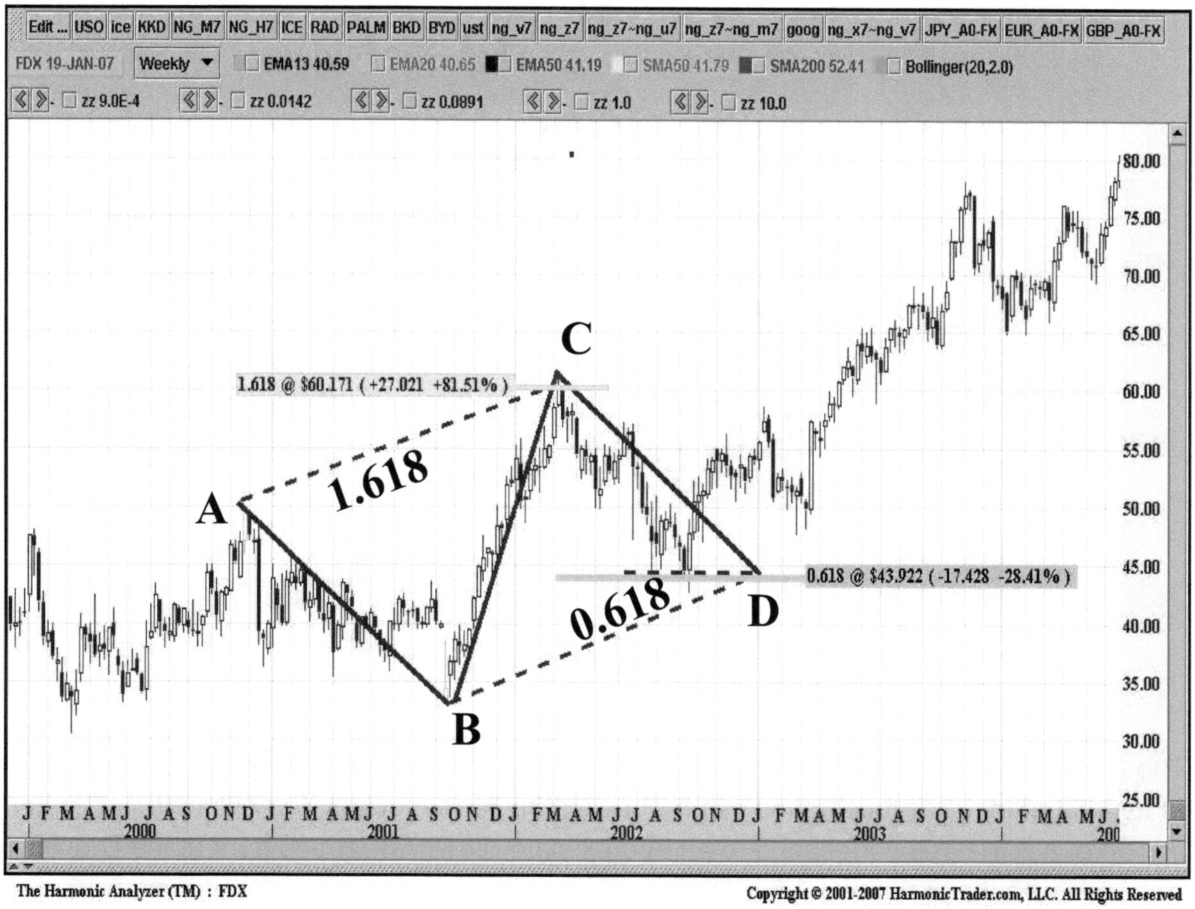

Figure 3.2

This weekly chart clearly exemplifies the ideal structure of the Reciprocal AB=CD pattern. Again, it is important to look for patterns that utilize a clear prior corrective move early within the newly established bullish trend. FedEx possessed a sharp pattern on this weekly chart over the course of two years. The strong reversal precisely at the PRZ was a clear indication that the new bullish trend was about to resume. Patterns such as these form on weekly, daily, and intraday charts in the same fashion.

Bearish Reciprocal AB=CD

In the same manner as the bullish version, the Bearish Reciprocal AB=CD, illustrated in Figure 3.3, must possess a distinct structure. Again, the AB leg is typically the first corrective move within a new downtrend. Although the projected completion represents a general approximation of the continuation of the primary trend, the price action in this area will reverse shortly after testing the entire zone in the valid setups.

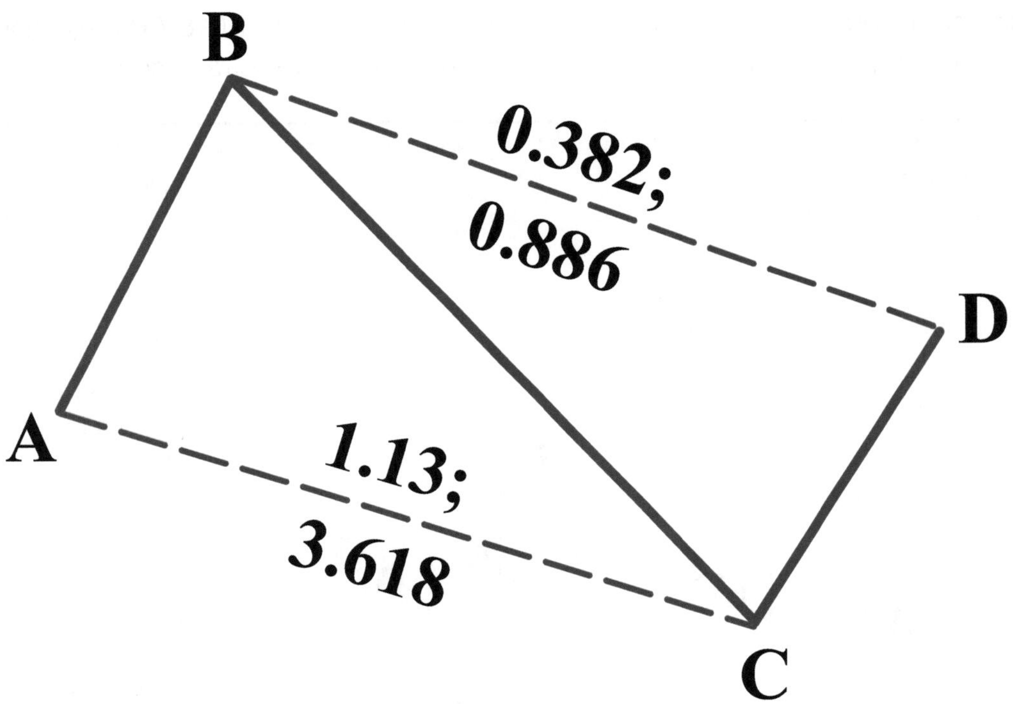

Figure 3.3

The CD leg is equivalent and completes at the reciprocal retracement of AB. It is important to be mindful of the reciprocal ratios established by the AB projection. For example, a C point extension of a 1.618 will correspond to an approximate 0.618 AB retracement at the D point. In combination with the reciprocal AB=CD completion point, the reciprocal ratio serves to confirm the potential resistance of the pattern.

Baker-Hughes (BHI): Weekly Bearish Reciprocal AB=CD

Baker-Hughes formed this distinct Bearish Reciprocal AB=CD that possessed a distinct AB leg (see Figure 3.4). Although the CD leg was slightly longer than the 26-point AB leg, the 70.7% Reciprocal Retracement Ratio served to confirm the area near the completion point of the pattern as important short-term resistance.

Figure 3.4

Again, it is important to remember that the completion point of the pattern represents a minimum approximation of potential harmonic resistance. Therefore, the reciprocal ratio is important in these situations to confirm the completion point.

Basic 5-0 Requirements

Although the pattern incorporates 5 points within the structure (X, A, B, C, D), the initial price leg (0) can start from the beginning of any extended price move. However, the initial point (X) must possess a specific alignment with respect to the A and B point. The X, A, B formation of the structure is usually some type of Extreme Harmonic Impulse move. The XA projection that defines the B point ideally must not exceed a 2.24. Any extension greater than a 2.24 will negate the structure, as smaller impulse moves are preferred. Again, this is the failed wave 3 or wave 5—in Elliott Wave terms—that establishes the rest of the structure.

- ***Look for initial impulsive reversal at X, A, B points that possesses a 1.13-1.618 extension.***
- ***The AB projection must possess a minimum 1.618 extension at the C point but not exceed 2.24.***
- ***The D point is defined by the 50% BC retracement and the Reciprocal AB=CD pattern completion.***

The BC leg is the longest price length of the structure that must be at least a 1.618 extension of the AB length, but it must not exceed 2.24. This tight range of 1.618–2.24 is a defining element of the structure. If the 1.618 AB minimum extension is not reached, the structure is not a valid 5-0. After the BC leg has reversed from that zone, the 50% retracement is measured from the B point to the C point. In addition, the Reciprocal AB=CD is projected from the C point (an equivalent length of the AB leg) to complement the PRZ.

Although the 5-0 pattern is not a typical M- or W-type price structure, the same principles within the Harmonic Trading approach are applied to these situations. The Reciprocal AB=CD helps define the general area, while the 50% retracement pinpoints the precise range of the harmonic zone. The following illustrations and examples will clearly explain these concepts.

The Bullish 5-0 Pattern

The Bullish 5-0, illustrated in Figure 3.5, starts at the 0 point, representing an extended down leg to begin the pattern at X. The initial point (X) acts as the low of this prior substantial decline. After a quick reactive bounce to the A point, the structure abruptly continues the decline, only to find support slightly past the prior low at X. This is the failed wave 3 or wave 5—in Elliott Wave terms—that establishes the rest of the structure.

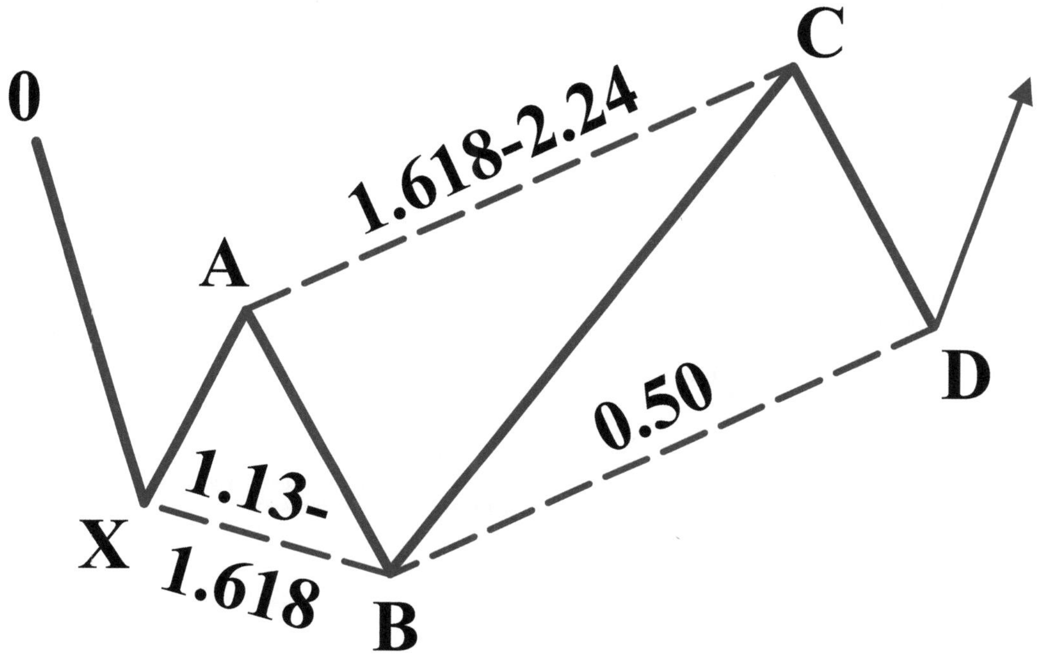

Figure 3.5

The important limits from a Harmonic Trading perspective require that this X, A extension be at least a 1.13 but not greater than a 1.618. After that impulsive failed wave is established, the BC leg rallies to at least a 1.618 extension of the AB length, but it does not exceed 2.24.

Again, this tight range of 1.618–2.24 is a defining element of the structure. If the 1.618 limit is not reached, the structure is not a valid 5-0. After the BC leg has reversed from that zone, the bullish 50% retracement is measured from the B point to the C point. In addition, the Reciprocal AB=CD is projected from the C point (an equivalent length of the AB leg) to complement the PRZ. It will take some time to identify this structure, but the obvious characteristic is the failed down wave followed by a precise 1.618–2.24 extension. At that point, it is important to calculate the 50% retracement level with the Reciprocal AB=CD and study the price action in the PRZ.

Eurodollar (EUR_A0-FX): 5-Minute Bullish 5-0 Pattern

This chart of the Euro demonstrates the effectiveness of the pattern in shorter-term situations (see Figure 3.6). After declining steadily throughout the previous day, the price action completed a failed down wave that nominally took out the prior session's low before rallying sharply to the 1.618 projection of the AB leg.

Figure 3.6

The Euro rolled over to retest the 50% level before resuming the uptrend. The Reciprocal AB=CD complemented the 50% retracement at the 1.3910 level, defining a precise area to get long.

Standard & Poor's 500 Trust (SPY): Daily Bullish 5-0 Pattern

This chart of the S&P 500 Spider is another example of an ideal Bullish 5-0 pattern (see Figure 3.7). On this daily chart example, the SPY ETF possessed a distinct Bullish 5-0 pattern that exemplifies the ideal nature of the pattern.

Figure 3.7

Starting with an impulsive AB leg with a 1.13 extension, the ETF formed an ideal extended BC leg that reversed at the 2.0 projection of AB. The price action reversed sharply after testing the PRZ of the pattern.

NASDAQ 100 March 2010 Mini-Contract (NQ_H0): 60-Minute Bullish 5-0 Pattern

Figure 3.8 shows a distinct 5-0 pattern on the 60-minute chart that reversed sharply after testing the entire PRZ.

Figure 3.8

This chart is remarkable due to the pattern pinpointed the intraday support. The price action formed the proper alignment of ratios for the structure, stabilized in the PRZ, and reversed immediately after testing the completion point of the pattern. These characteristics are the ideal signs of a valid reversal for any timeframe. The key is to focus on the price action following the completion of the pattern.

Standard & Poor's 500 June 2009 Mini-Contract (ES_M9): 15-Minute Bullish 5-0 Pattern

This chart of the ES was illustrated in advance (see Figure 3.9). The structure was distinct, and the 50% retracement was calculated at 936. In addition, the Reciprocal Bullish AB=CD was projected to complete in the same area.

Figure 3.9

This 60-minute chart exemplifies the ideal structure for the 5-0, especially with the distinct 2.0 impulse projection. Like a magnet, the price action steadily declined to the 50% level of that extreme extension to complete the pattern. The chart in Figure 3.10 shows the price action, as the ES approached the PRZ at 1113.

Standard and Poor's 500 June 2009 Mini-Contract (ES_M9): 15-Minute Bullish 5-0 Pattern Potential Reversal Zone (PRZ)

The black line represents the Bullish Reciprocal AB=CD completion point, and it converges at the same level as the 50% retracement. After a sharp decline into the PRZ, the price action was able to stabilize. After some consolidation, the ES held its ground above the initial test of the completion point.

Figure 3.10

This is an excellent example that possessed ideal price action in a reversal from a valid Bullish 5-0. The structure was distinct, the alignment of Fibonacci numbers was satisfactory, and the price action reversed precisely in the zone. Although it will take time to identify these situations, 5-0 opportunities like these occur frequently in the financial markets. Although a "clean" reversal from a single test of a PRZ is ideal, it is more common for price action to retest this pivot area a second or even multiple times before reversing significantly.

Bullish ab=cd within CD Leg of 5-0 Pattern

Although the 5-0 pattern requires only two harmonic numbers to define the PRZ, there are many situations where a smaller ab=cd pattern will form in the CD leg of the Reciprocal AB=CD (see Figure 3.11). These are unique situations because the ab=cd is usually distinct, and their structures can be effective in complementing the other numbers of the 5-0 pattern.

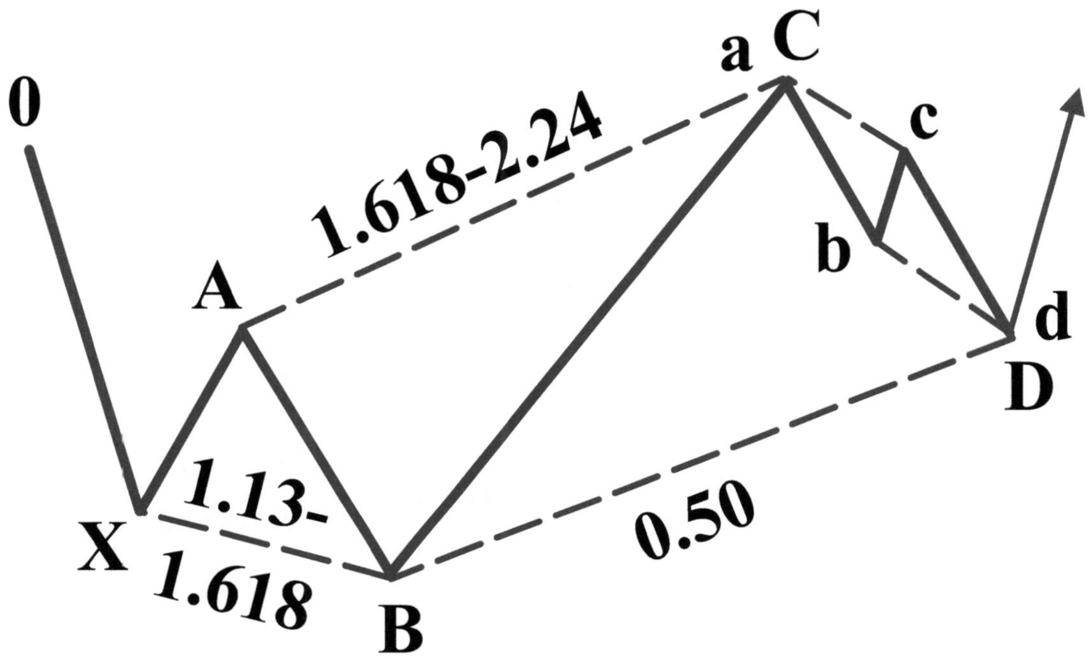

Figure 3.11

Although the other numbers in the pattern are more significant in defining the completion of the setup, the smaller ab=cd acts as an effective structural signal that validates many successful reversals. Furthermore, I believe that a Bullish 5-0 with a smaller ab=cd is a technically more significant harmonic structure than a pattern without one.

Japanese Yen (JPY_A0-FX): 60-Minute Bullish 5-0 with Bullish ab=cd

This chart of the Yen shown in Figure 3.12 is an excellent example of multiple AB=CDs converging at the completion of the 5-0 pattern. Although the completion of the smaller ab=cd was slightly above the other harmonic numbers, the addition of this pattern helped to confirm the entire area as a valid PRZ.

Figure 3.12

This example shows an ideal structure that possesses a distinct convergence of the 50% retracement and the Reciprocal AB=CD completion, as well. In particular, the impulsive 2.0 extension is another aspect of this example that can be found in most valid 5-0 patterns. The BC leg established the entire structure for the eventual completion at the D point. In addition, the pattern completed just above the psychological 90-level. Such round numbers can add to the validity of a setup, especially when they occur within close proximity of a PRZ.

Adobe Software (ADBE): Daily Bullish 5-0 Pattern

The example of Adobe Software shown in Figure 3.13 exhibits an ideal structure that possessed a distinct combination of harmonic ratios to validate the pattern. Clearly, the initial AB leg that completed at a 1.13 retracement was the primary clue of a valid structure. After making a critical low at the $31.50 level (B point), the stock surged to the 2.0 extension.

ADBE 25-MAR-09 HarmonicAnalyzer (TM) v6.05 Copyright © 2001-2008 HarmonicTrader.com, LLC. All Rights Reserved

Figure 3.13

Adobe promptly reversed at that extreme impulse extension and formed a distinct Reciprocal AB=CD that converged with the 50% retracement just under the $38 area. This example underscores the importance of a distinct structure that ideal 5-0 patterns must possess.

The Bearish 5-0 Pattern

The Bearish 5-0, illustrated in Figure 3.14, starts at the 0 point, representing the low of an extended rally up to the initial point of the pattern at X. The initial point X sets up the failed breakout area, where the rally from the A point to the B peak, nominally takes out the prior high at X. Again, this is the failed wave 3 or wave 5—in Elliott Wave terms—that establishes the rest of the structure.

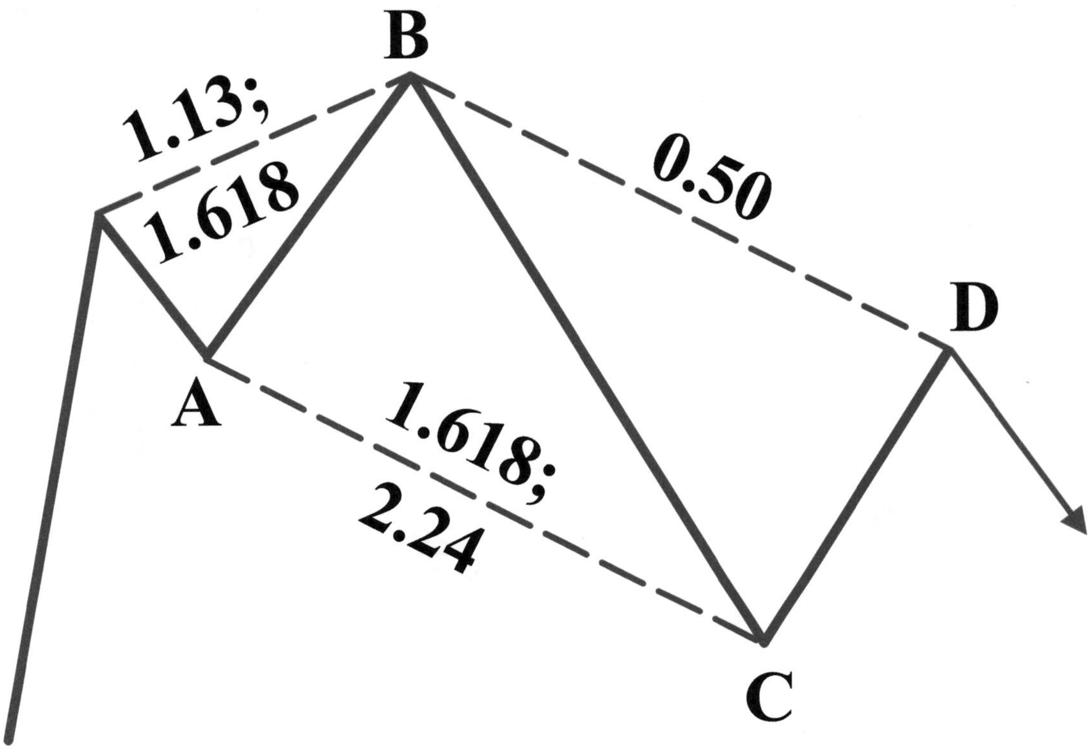

Figure 3.14

Remember, this X, A extension must be at least a 1.13 but not greater than a 1.618. After that impulsive failed wave is established, the BC leg declines to at least a 1.618 extension of the AB length, but it does not exceed 2.24. Again, this tight range of 1.618–2.24 is a defining element of the structure. If the 1.618 limit is not reached, the structure is not a valid 5-0. After the BC leg has reversed from that zone, the bearish 50% retracement is measured from the B point to the C point. In addition, the Bearish Reciprocal AB=CD is projected from the C point (an equivalent length of the AB leg) to complement the PRZ.

AMEX Oil Index ($XOI): 5-Minute Bearish 5-0 Pattern

Figure 3.15 is a fantastic intra-day example of a Bearish 5-0 structure that possessed the ideal Fibonacci alignment to validate the pattern. After a long rally, the index made an initial peak at the X point, pulled back to point A, and reversed sharply at the B point, establishing the failed wave of the 5-0 structure.

Figure 3.15

The chart in Figure 3.16 of the price action in the PRZ clearly shows the sharp reversal following the test of the 50% level. The Bearish Reciprocal AB=CD complemented the 50% retracement and defined a tight range just above the psychological 1100 level. The $XOI tested the 50% level and stalled immediately. After completing the Reciprocal AB=CD, it started to reverse.

AMEX Oil Index ($XOI): 5-Minute Bearish 5-0 Pattern Potential Reversal Zone (PRZ)

It is important to mention the C point on the chart in Figure 3.16. The mandatory 1.618 requirement was met in this case, but it was close. If the C point had not tested the 1.618 or fell just shy, it would have invalidated the structure.

Figure 3.16

Unlike other patterns, the 5-0 allows no discretion outside the prescribed parameters for the structure. Although such strict application reduces the number of potential trading candidates, it serves to distinguish the best opportunities.

Standard & Poor's 500 September 2009 Mini-Contract (ES_U9): 5-Minute Bearish 5-0 Pattern

This 5-minute chart in the ES shows another ideal intra-day structure with a perfect 50% retracement, calculated at 1030 with the completion of the Reciprocal Bearish AB=CD slightly below this level (see Figure 3.17).

Figure 3.17

The following chart of the price action in the PRZ clearly shows the sharp reversal following the entire test of the 5-0 resistance (see Figure 3.18). The Bearish Reciprocal AB=CD complemented the 50% retracement and defined a tight intra-day range. The ES rolled over sharply after testing the entire range of the harmonic resistance. This example required some consolidation before reversing, but such situations underscore the importance of waiting for the entire PRZ to be tested before executing the trade. In this case, the 5-0 pattern pinpointed the 1030 area as the ideal price level for the completion of the setup.

Standard & Poor's 500 September 2009 Mini-Contract (ES_U9): 5-Minute Bearish 5-0 Pattern Potential Reversal Zone (PRZ)

This Bearish 5-0 possessed an ideal reversal and downside continuation, which is a common trait of valid structures (see Figure 3.18). The best trading opportunities usually provide a quick indication of the validity of the reversal.

Figure 3.18

In this case, the ES stalled exactly at the entire range harmonic numbers and rolled over shortly thereafter. Again, this example demonstrates the importance of waiting for the entire range to be tested before executing the trade. Despite the brief consolidation required to resolve the setup, the 5-0 pattern accurately pinpointed the intra-day reversal. Whether it's a 1-minute, 5-minute, 60-minute, daily, or weekly chart, the principles remain the same, as clear opportunities like these will present themselves on all time frames.

Dow Jones Industrial Average ($INDU): 1-Minute Bearish 5-0 Pattern

The 1-minute chart in Figure 3.19 shows a distinct Bearish 5-0 that stalled immediately after testing the harmonic resistance and reversed precisely at the 10,175 level. Setups such as these form regularly, as 5-0 patterns can mark important intra-day continuation points. In this case, the Dow Jones Industrial Average reversed sharply after testing all of the numbers in the PRZ of this pattern.

Figure 3.19

The Bearish 5-0 pattern is an excellent harmonic structure that typically possesses a precise PRZ. Most valid reversals exhibit definitive price action that continues decidedly lower after testing the entire PRZ. It is important to note that the 50% retracement is typically the most significant harmonic resistance level within the PRZ. As this 1-minute example of the Dow Industrials demonstrates, the index reversed quickly after completing the pattern. Clearly, the 5-0 is an effective tool within the Harmonic Trading arsenal, but it is even more accurate when the structure possesses a smaller ab=cd pattern in the CD leg.

Bearish ab=cd within CD Leg of 5-0 Pattern

Although the 5-0 pattern requires only two harmonic numbers to define the PRZ, there are many situations where a smaller ab=cd pattern will form in the CD leg of the Reciprocal AB=CD (see Figure 3.20). These are unique situations because the ab=cd is usually distinct, and the structure can be effective in complementing the other numbers of the 5-0 pattern.

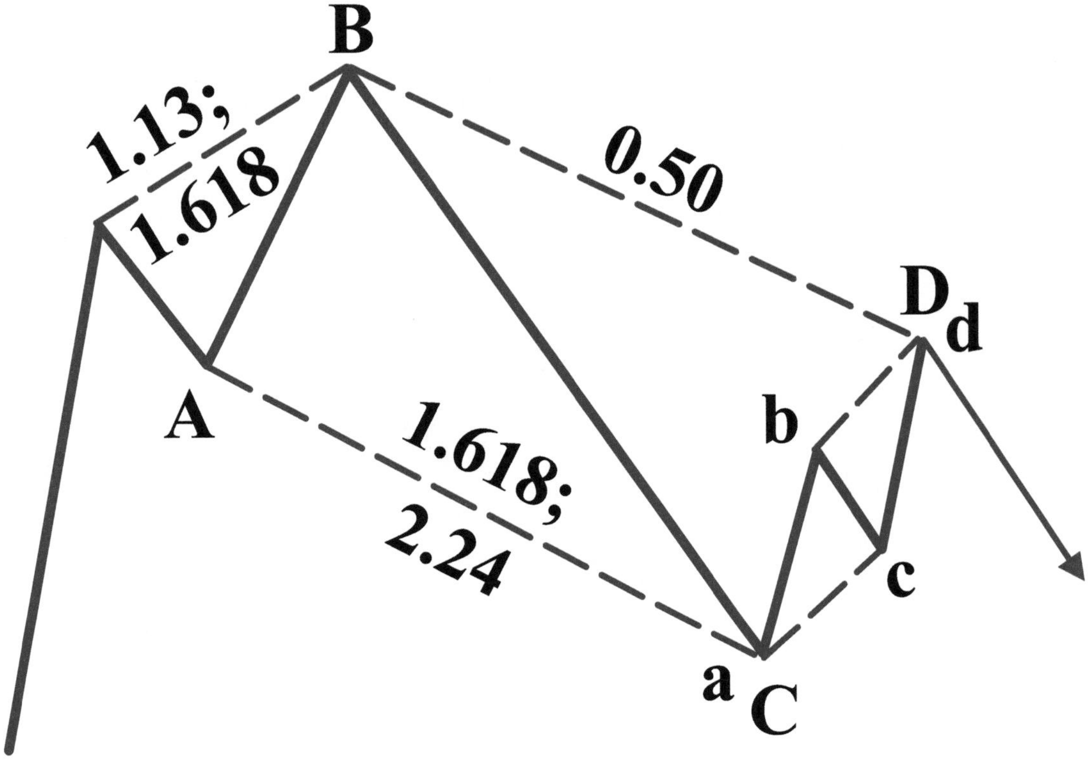

Figure 3.20

Although the other numbers of the pattern are more significant in defining the completion of the setup, the smaller ab=cd acts as an effective structural signal that validates many successful reversals. Furthermore, I believe that a Bearish 5-0 with a smaller ab=cd is a technically more significant harmonic structure than a pattern without one.

Natural Gas March 2010 Contract (NG_H0): 15-Minute

This 15-minute chart of the March 2010 Natural Gas contract shows a distinct Bearish 5-0 that possessed a smaller Bearish ab=cd within the CD leg (see Figure 3.21). The addition of the smaller ab=cd was a key signal that this pattern would yield a valid reversal.

Figure 3.21

The structure was distinct on this 15-minute chart. The sharp reversal precisely at the completion of the pattern was a clear sign of the strength of this harmonic resistance. The following chart shows the price action in the PRZ (see Figure 3.22).

Natural Gas March 2010 Contract (NG_H0): 15-Minute Bearish 5-0 Pattern Potential Reversal Zone (PRZ)

The Natural Gas March 2010 Contract reversed immediately after testing all of the numbers in the PRZ. The Bearish 5-0 possessed four harmonic numbers in a tight range (see Figure 3.22). The addition of the smaller ab=cd pattern served as an important confirmation point within the PRZ. Furthermore, the fact that the smaller ab=cd pattern completed above the actual 50% level helped to indicate that the price action would reverse in the upper range of this area.

Figure 3.22

It is important to note that the PRZ of the 5-0 pattern should possess a precise reversal such as the one in this example. In fact, most valid reversals from 5-0 patterns should occur immediately after the entire zone has been tested.

5-0 Pattern Violations

More than any other pattern, the structure of the 5-0 presents a unique opportunity when the price action violates the PRZ. As with all 5-0 patterns, the best setups depend upon a distinct alignment of ratios within the structure. Therefore, when attempting to execute a trade based upon a failed setup, it is still imperative to look at those candidates that possess the most distinct structures.

Bullish 5-0 Pattern Violations

Despite the failure of the pattern, these situations offer a specific opportunity to execute a trade that follows the predominant trend. In this case when the 5-0 pattern fails, the price action typically declines decidedly lower. In many cases, the breakdown in the price action usually declines to at least the relative 0.886 retracement beyond completion of the pattern. The illustration in Figure 3.23 shows the ideal PRZ of a 5-0 pattern.

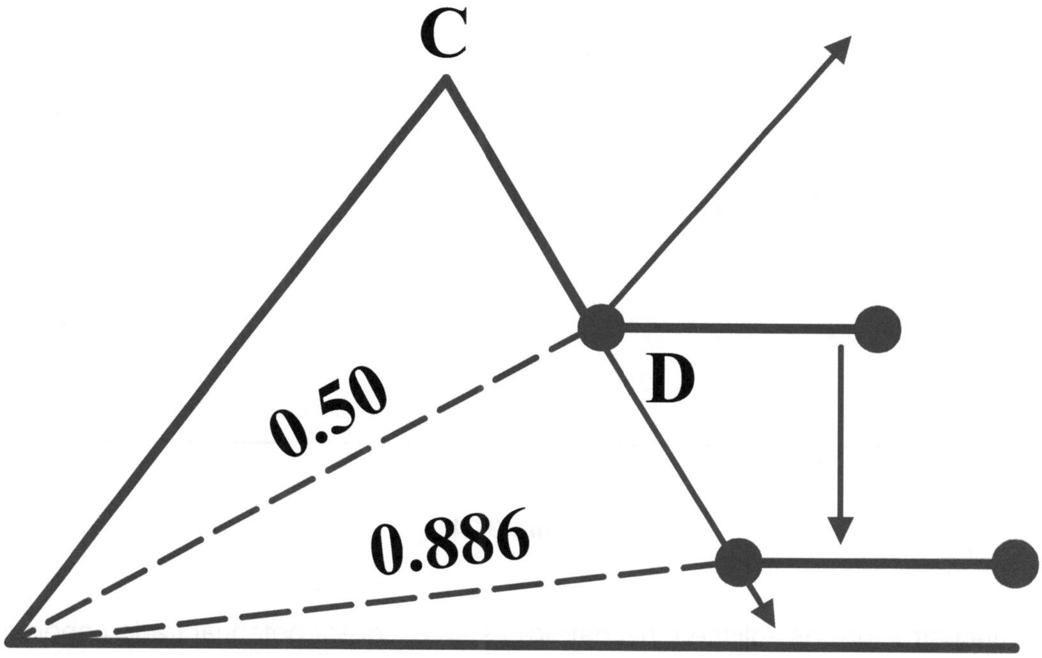

Figure 3.23

When the 50% retracement area has been exceeded, the breakdown of price action frequently signals a trade opportunity. It is important to note that the trade opportunity does not develop until the entire PRZ has been tested and price action has clearly violated the initial test. Although this is more of a general guideline than a specific rule, the breakdown typically extends to the 0.886 retracement at a minimum. Regardless of whether the initial starting point of the 5-0 pattern is violated, this unique technical zone creates an opportunity to sell after this violation with a minimum target of the imminent 0.886 retracement.

General Motors (GM): Daily Failed Bullish 5-0 Pattern

This daily chart of General Motors clearly demonstrated how a failed Bullish 5-0 pattern led to a downside continuation to the 0.886 retracement—and beyond (see Figure 3.24).

Figure 3.24

The distinct structure established this pattern as an excellent potential trade opportunity. Although GM stabilized initially as it approached the PRZ, the stock eventually declined sharply after testing the entire range of support and violated the setup. In fact, the failure of this daily pattern was technically significant, as it marked an acceleration of the long-term downtrend that eventually resulted in the demise of the company.

General Motors (GM): Weekly Failed Bullish 5-0 Pattern Potential Reversal Zone (PRZ)

The enlarged chart in Figure 3.25 of the price action in the failed Bullish 5-0 PRZ clearly shows how the stock declined dramatically after violating the projected harmonic support.

GM 01-JUN-09 HarmonicAnalyzer (TM) v6.05 Copyright © 2001-2008 HarmonicTrader.com, LLC. All Rights Reserved

Figure 3.25

It is important to study the example of GM because the price action follows a typical pattern—if you will—when the PRZ is violated. Most violations will experience some type of nominal reaction on the first test of the PRZ. However, price action that fails to continue to the upside and clearly lags will typically signal that a failure is imminent. The trigger for the failure occurs when the PRZ is violated after all the numbers are tested. Although this model can vary depending upon the situation, the example of General Motors illustrates the ideal situation.

Bearish 5-0 Pattern Violation

In much the same manner as the Bullish 5-0 violation, the bearish situation offers a specific opportunity to execute a trade on the breakout above the PRZ, attempting to capitalize on the continuation of the predominant trend (see Figure 3.26). In this case, when the 5-0 pattern fails, the price action typically rallies decidedly higher. In many cases, the breakout in the price action usually rallies to at least the following 0.886 retracement beyond completion of the pattern. The next illustration shows an ideal violation of the 5-0 PRZ.

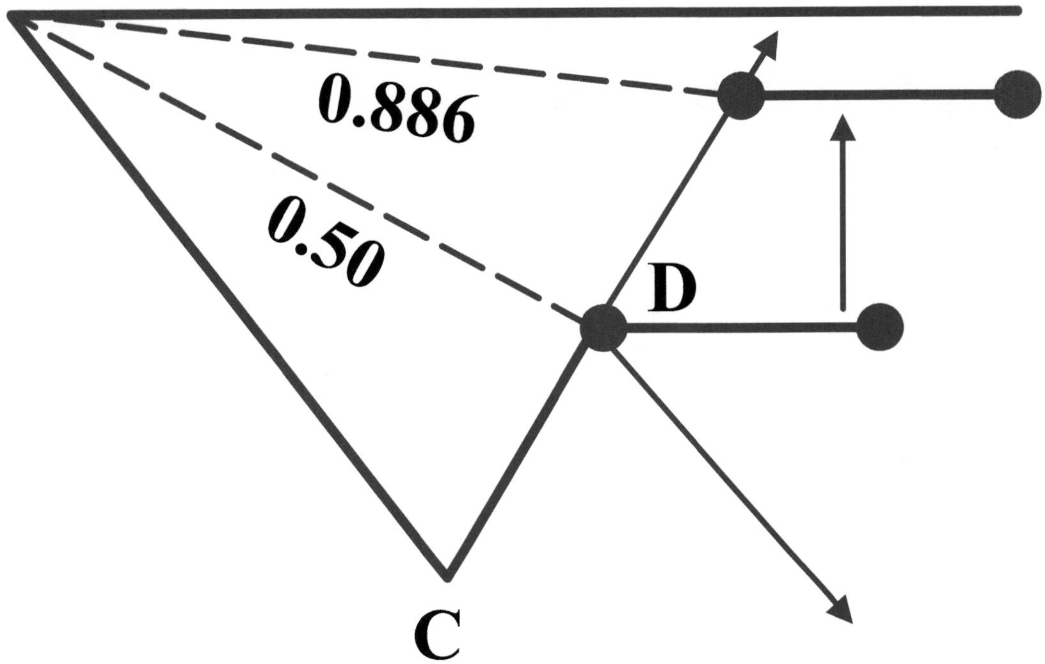

Figure 3.26

When the 50% retracement area has been exceeded, the breakout above this area is the decisive signal for the trade. It is important to note that the trade opportunity does not develop until the entire PRZ has been tested and the price action has clearly violated the initial test. Although this is more of a general guideline than a specific rule, the breakout typically rallies to test the 0.886 retracement at a minimum. Regardless of whether the initial starting point of the 5-0 pattern is violated, this unique technical zone creates an opportunity to buy this violation with a target of the critical 0.886 retracement.

Intercontinental Exchange (ICE): Daily Bearish 5-0 Pattern Violation

After an extended decline, ICE formed a fantastic Bearish 5-0 pattern on the daily chart (see Figure 3.27). This is another situation where the price action experienced a nominal reaction on the first test of the PRZ. The stock stalled in this PRZ for a few weeks before breaking out to the upside. Again, the trigger for the failure occurs when the PRZ is violated on the second test. In this case, ICE accelerated to the daily 0.886 shortly after violating the pattern.

Figure 3.27

This example provided a great deal of evidence of the impending failure. Although the stock pulled back slightly on the initial test of the pattern completion, the price action held firmly in this area and slowly "drifted" higher. This is another ideal situation where the decisive price action violated a distinct pattern and marked an important continuation in the predominant trend of the stock. ICE rallied sharply to the 0.886 and gave a nice 20-point pop within a month after the pattern violation.

Alternate Bat Pattern

The origin of the Alternate Bat pattern resulted from many frustrated failed trades of the standard framework. The standard Bat pattern is defined by the B point that is less than a 0.618 retracement of the XA leg. Typically, the best structures employ a 50% retracement at the midpoint. Although there is room for interpretation to incorporate other ratios in the standard Bat pattern, I began to notice a peculiarity in those M- and W-type structures that possessed a 0.382 retracement or less at the mid-point (B). These variations frequently resulted in an eventual completion that was slightly beyond the expected 0.886 retracement of the standard framework. In many cases before I became aware of this alternate alignment, I would execute trades at the 0.886 retracement only to close the trade for a loss due to the lack of a reversal in the projected harmonic area. After slightly exceeding the initial point at X of the pattern and triggering my stop loss, many of these reversals would turn shortly thereafter, usually at the 1.13 extension of the structure.

Again, the defining element of these situations was directly attributed to those M- and W-type structures that possessed a retracement that was a 0.382 or less at the midpoint. It took some time to differentiate the structures, but the more I was "whipsawed" by these patterns the more I realized that further differentiation was required in these cases. Although the special situations for this pattern will be covered in greater detail later in this material, it is important to understand that such specification is required to differentiate these similar structures. It can be frustrating to try to trade these two types of patterns without differentiating their structures.

Although the Alternate Bat employs a 1.13 XA extension as a defining element of the PRZ, the 0.886 retracement is still a consideration within this range of harmonic numbers, as it serves as a *minimum* requirement for this pattern to be valid. In essence, the Alternate Bat typically completes in the area beyond the 0.886 retracement, but it should not exceed the 1.13. In fact, valid reversals in this pattern frequently reverse precisely at this level. The BC projection is typically an extreme harmonic number that complements the 1.13 extension. Although the Alternate AB=CD pattern is included in the standard Bat, this PRZ normally possesses just two harmonic measurements to define the completion of the pattern. In combination with a minimum 0.886 retracement, the Alternate Bat possesses several critical structural elements to define excellent trade opportunities.

The Alternate Bat pattern is an extension structure that is mostly utilized in combination with other technical factors to define specific trading opportunities. I will outline the application of the Alternate Bat in these situations—in particular, the RSI BAMM. In addition, the structure must possess the prescribed alignment of ratios to validate the pattern, as this dictates the eventual execution of the potential trade opportunity.

Alternate Bullish Bat Pattern

The Alternate Bullish Bat pattern, illustrated in Figure 3.28, is a specific M-type structure that utilizes a 1.13 XA extension, as the defining support level in the PRZ. The BC projection utilizes an extreme harmonic ratio that is at least a 2.0 extension but more frequently appears as a 2.618 or 3.14.

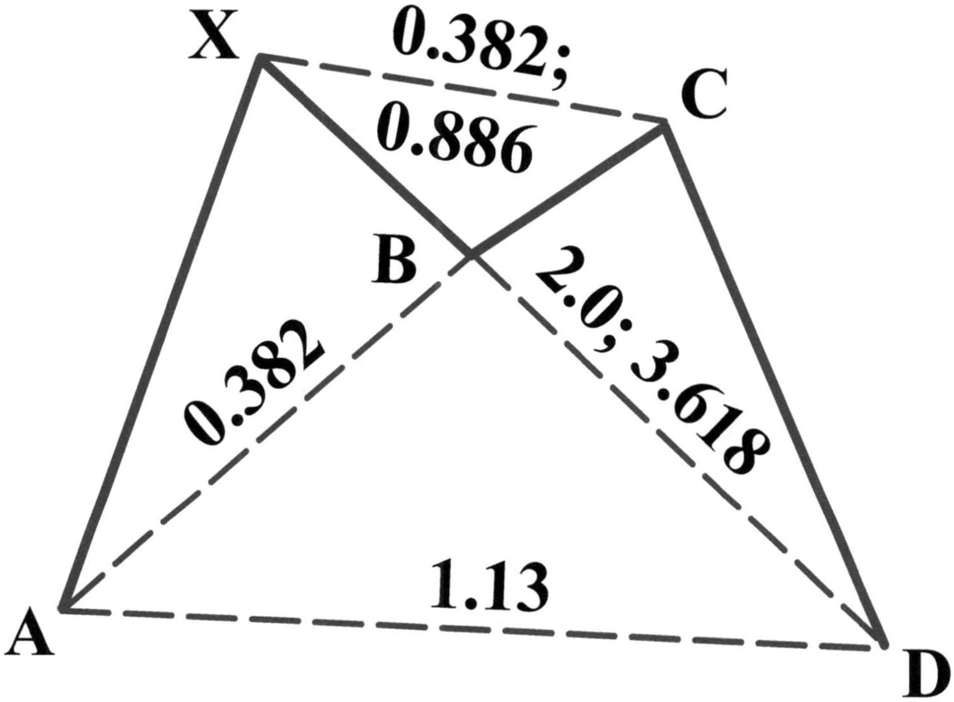

Figure 3.28

Although the Bullish AB=CD is not included in this setup, the 0.886 retracement serves as a minimum support level to help define the completion of the pattern, while the convergence of the 1.13 XA and extreme BC projections pinpoint the PRZ. Again, the 1.13 XA extension should not be exceeded, as most valid reversals rally shortly after testing this area.

Dow Jones Industrials ETF (DIA): Weekly Alternate Bullish Bat Pattern

In this example, the Dow Diamonds possessed a distinct M-type structure that possessed a 0.382 mid-point (see Figure 3.29). The alignment established the structure as an Alternate Bat pattern instead of the standard version.

Figure 3.29

This structure was remarkable due to the size of the pattern. The Diamonds developed over the course of seven years on this weekly chart. The 1.13 extension marked the critical low of the 2008 bear market. The convergence of the 1.13 XA and the 3.14 BC projection pinpointed the long-term support.

Eurodollar (EUR_A0-FX): 5-Minute Alternate Bullish Bat Pattern

The Euro possessed a distinct Alternate Bullish Bat on this intra-day chart that reversed sharply after testing both numbers that converged in the same exact area to define the PRZ (see Figure 3.30). This is another case where the structure of the Alternate Bat pattern indicated a deeper retest of the initial support point and marked the ultimate reversal for the price action.

Figure 3.30

If this unique differentiation did not exist, the execution in this situation would have likely been stopped out for a loss, as the price action would have violated the 0.886 retracement and the initial point X before the eventual reversal. However, the 0.382 retracement at the pattern's mid-point clearly indicated that the price action would dip slightly below the initial point at X to the 1.13 extension.

Alternate Bearish Bat Pattern

The Alternate Bearish Bat pattern, illustrated in Figure 3.31, is specific W-type structure that utilizes a 1.13 XA extension, as the defining resistance level in the PRZ. The BC projection utilizes an extreme harmonic ratio that is at least a 2.0 extension but more frequently appears as a 2.618 or 3.14.

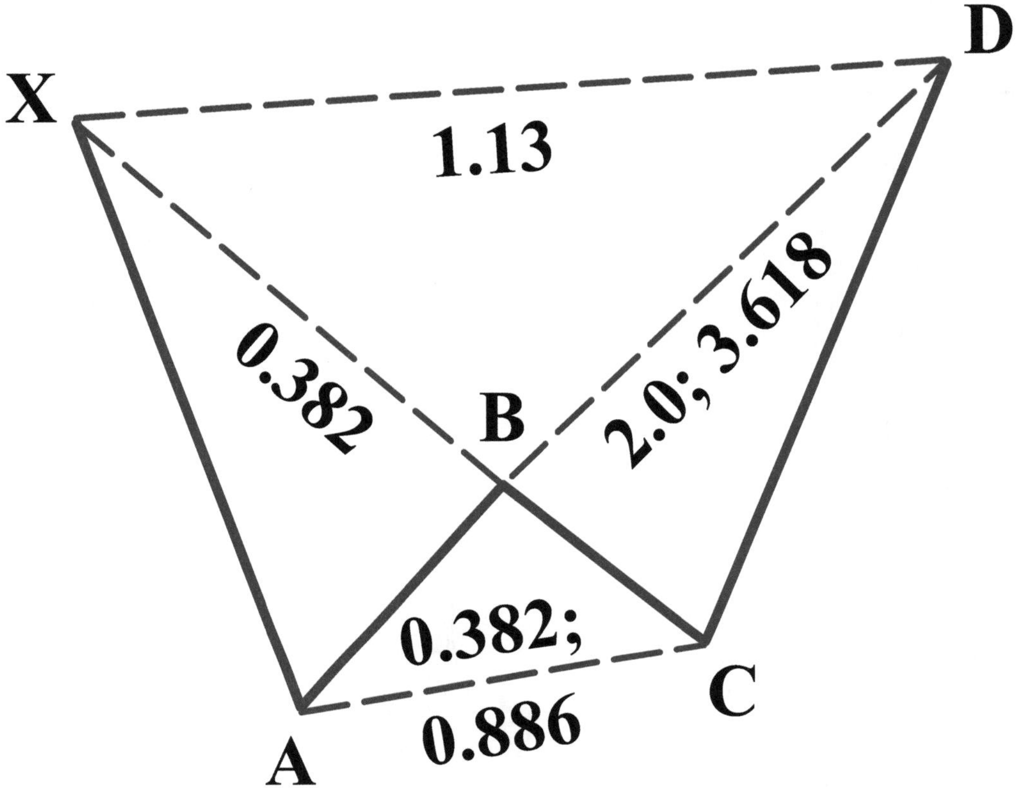

Figure 3.31

Although the Bearish AB=CD is not included in this setup, the 0.886 retracement serves as a minimum resistance level to help define the completion of the pattern, while the convergence of the 1.13 XA and extreme BC projections pinpoint the PRZ. Again, the 1.13 XA extension should not be exceeded, as most valid reversals start to decline shortly after testing this area.

Eurodollar (EUR_A0-FX): 5-Minute Alternate Bearish Bat Pattern

This Alternate Bearish Bat in the Euro shown in Figure 3.32 exemplifies the structure of the pattern. The 0.382 retracement at the midpoint (B) was the indication of an extended 1.13 XA projection as the defining harmonic resistance level in the PRZ.

Figure 3.32

This is another case where the extreme BC projection effectively complemented the 1.13 XA extension to define the precise area for the pattern completion and eventual reversal. Both extensions defined the 1.4440 area as an excellent short-term selling opportunity.

Nike (NKE): Daily Alternate Bearish Bat Pattern

The daily chart in Figure 3.33 shows a distinct Alternate Bearish Bat that reversed decisively after the stock tested the completion point of the pattern. The W-type structure possessed two numbers that converged in the same area. Both extensions defined the PRZ as the make-or-break harmonic resistance. The 0.382 retracement at the mid-point of the pattern distinguished the setup and indicated a complete retest of the prior peak of the trend. This structural element defined the upper range of the harmonic resistance and pinpointed the eventual completion of the setup at the 1.13 XA extension.

Figure 3.33

Although this trade may have been a challenging execution since the stock reversed immediately after completing the pattern, the 1.13 projection was the optimal entry point for the short position. The PRZ was clearly defined, as the extreme BC leg complemented this area just above the initial point at X. Also, this underscores the importance of the 0.886 as a minimum technical level in the completion of the alternate version of the pattern. Although the price action reversed quickly after hitting the 1.13 XA extension, the differentiation of structures in situations like these prevents an early entry and helps to optimize trading decisions. In this case, the ideal entry for the trade was just above the standard Bat PRZ, as the low B-point in the pattern's structure indicated an eventual reversal slightly above this area. Although these two types of Bat patterns appear similar, such understanding and comprehension immensely improves executions and reduces overall risk by pinpointing reversals as precisely as possible.

New Harmonic Patterns Conclusion

The new patterns presented in this chapter help to further the existing identification strategies within the Harmonic Trading approach. The 5-0, Reciprocal AB=CD, and the Alternate Bat are slightly different in structure than the existing array of patterns. Furthermore, these patterns should be employed only in specialized situations, as they require precise conditions to validate their structures.

Patterns such as the Alternate Bat continue to underscore the importance of exact specification within the Harmonic Trading approach. Although the standard version and the Alternate Bat look similar, the critical differentiation at the pattern's mid-point clearly identifies the proper corresponding execution area and filters out many inherently flawed trading opportunities. In this case, the 1.13 extension dramatically improves the accuracy of the overall Bat pattern setup. Furthermore, such differentiation broadens the general comprehension of price action with respect to M- and W-type retracement patterns.

These patterns are among the most precise within the entire Harmonic Trading arsenal. Although many of these situations require new measurement techniques, the same principles are still applied to each situation. As is the case with all harmonic patterns, the exact alignment and precise rules that define each structure is critical in determining the best trading opportunities.

Chapter 4

Harmonic Patterns Relative to the Trend

Patterns with the Trend

When analyzing patterns within a defined trend, it is important to be mindful of the general principle that all patterns are primarily signposts of potential future price action. Regardless of what type of pattern may form, a complete structure represents some type of corrective price action within the context of the larger trend. Such patterns provide clear signals of continuation points that confirm the predominance of the existing trend. These formations are critical because they can indicate execution areas within well-established trends that otherwise might seem futile.

There are many situations where a well-established trend has persisted for such a long time that a potential opportunity may seem to have passed long ago, only to experience price action that continues in the predominant direction for a substantially greater move. Many times I have analyzed a particular chart that possesses a well-defined trend and passed on the potential opportunity because it seems that I was late in the move. For example, a stock that has rallied from $10 to $50 a share has increased 500% and may seem to possess limited upside. From a psychological perspective, it can be difficult to convince yourself that there is a great deal of further gain only to watch the stock rally from $50 a share to $100 or more. In situations like these, the formation of complex harmonic patterns within the limits of the established trend can act as a signpost or signal of a significant continuation at hand. Furthermore, the Potential Reversal Zone (PRZ) of the pattern within the trend can serve to measure and pinpoint where these continuation areas complete.

AB=CD Patterns as Continuation Signals within Established Trend Channels

AB=CD patterns within established channels are typically utilized in conjunction with other measurement techniques to define the approximate continuation area for the predominant channel. The simplest structure within established trend channels is an AB=CD pattern. In fact, many AB=CD patterns serve as a minimum requirement before a trend can continue in its predominant direction. Although distinct complex patterns frequently provide more accurate PRZs, a simple AB=CD pattern in combination with the limits of a trend channel is typically sufficient enough to define a continuation opportunity.

Bullish AB=CD Patterns as Continuation Signals within Established Trend Channels

Bullish AB=CD patterns frequently act as a significant continuation signal within the uptrend channel (see Figure 4.1). In combination with the rising trend line support, the pattern's completion serves as a minimum requirement from a harmonic perspective to trigger a long position within the context of the channel.

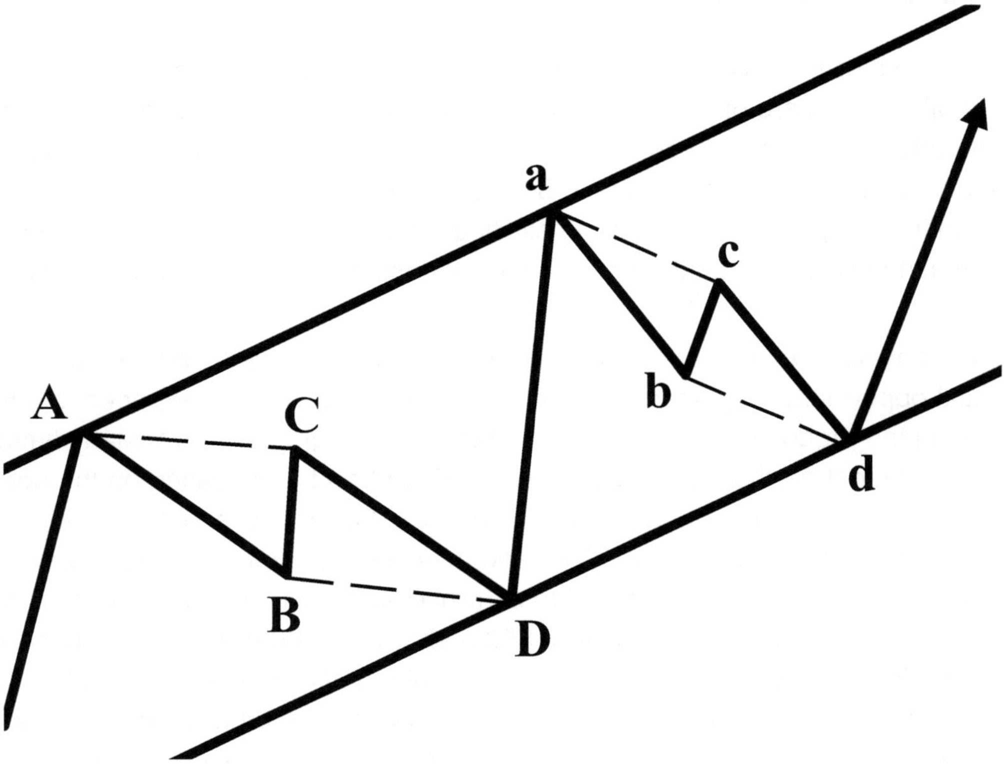

Figure 4.1

Regardless of how far the trend has progressed, a small correction within a larger bullish move represents an opportunity to execute at the completion of a harmonic pattern with the power of a strong predominant bias favoring further upside. Quite simply, executing a trade in such a manner attempts to put "the wind to your back" and to capitalize on the continuation of a distinct bullish trend.

NASDAQ Composite (^IXIC): Daily

Throughout 2004–2005, the NASDAQ Composite formed three distinct Bullish AB=CD patterns on the daily chart within the context of the predominant bullish trend (see Figure 4.2).

Figure 4.2

In each case, these daily Bullish AB=CD patterns acted as distinct continuation signals of the predominant trend. Although the price action nominally exceeded the completion point of each pattern, the PRZ clearly pinpointed the continuation of the bullish trend. In combination with the support line of the channel, the completion point of each AB=CD pattern served as an effective entry point to get long within this long-term trend.

NASDAQ Composite (^IXIC): Daily
Bullish AB=CD #1: Completed August 2004

The first Bullish AB=CD pattern completed in August 2004, as shown in Figure 4.3. Although the price action sold off sharply as it tested the completion point of the pattern, the bullish trend resumed after briefly exceeding the PRZ.

Figure 4.3

NASDAQ Composite (^IXIC): Daily Bullish AB=CD #2: Completed April 2005

The second Bullish AB=CD completed in April 2005 and resulted in the continuation of the primary uptrend (see Figure 4.4). The price action reversed more precisely from the PRZ than the setup from the prior August, and it rallied significantly higher after completing the pattern.

Figure 4.4

NASDAQ Composite (^IXIC): Daily Bullish AB=CD #3: Completed October 2005

The third Bullish AB=CD pattern within this 18-month time frame completed in October 2005, as shown in Figure 4.5. The price action exceeded the completion point of the pattern but reversed quickly after testing the entire PRZ. Moreover, the completion point for the pattern served as the defining support level for the continuation of the predominant uptrend, as the price action failed to test the rising channel. Situations such as these underscore the importance of pattern completions to indicate the continuation of a predominant trend.

Figure 4.5

Bearish AB=CD Patterns within Trend Channels

Bearish AB=CD patterns frequently act as effective continuation signals within established downtrend channels, as illustrated in Figure 4.6. Also, Bearish AB=CD patterns in combination with the declining trend resistance serve as a minimum requirement from a Harmonic Trading perspective to trigger a short position within the context of the channel.

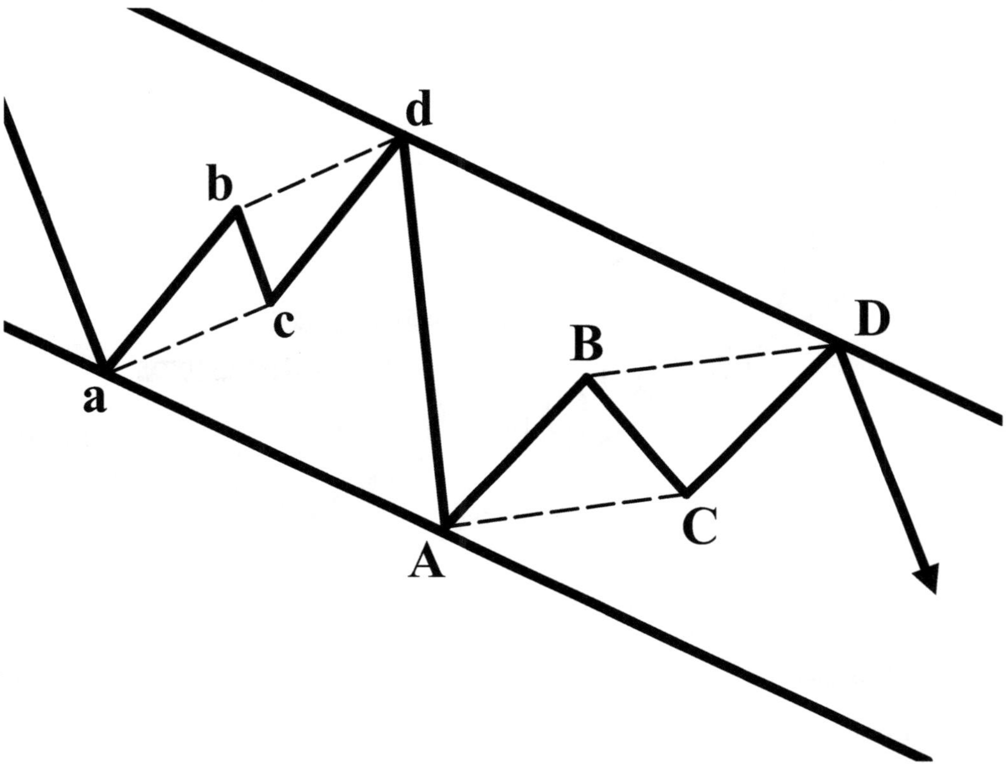

Figure 4.6

Sometimes, these situations may be difficult to execute because the trend has persisted for quite some time. Although the price action may seem to not have much farther to go, Bearish AB=CD patterns that materialize in these situations are extremely effective structural signals of significant trend continuations.

Toll Brothers (TOL): Weekly Bearish AB=CDs

The example of Toll Brothers in Figure 4.7 illustrates the principle of the Bearish AB=CD pattern acting as a critical continuation signal, regardless of where it develops within the context of the weekly trend channel.

Figure 4.7

The interesting thing to note about the completion of these patterns is that they occurred more than halfway from the stock's all-time peak. Although these patterns completed at the mid-point of the bearish trend, they were extremely effective in marking the continuation of the stock's long-term decline.

Bullish Reciprocal AB=CD Patterns within Trend Channels

Bullish Reciprocal AB=CD patterns are most effective when they are present within established uptrend channels. In fact, the AB leg often is the first corrective leg within a new bullish trend (see Figure 4.8).

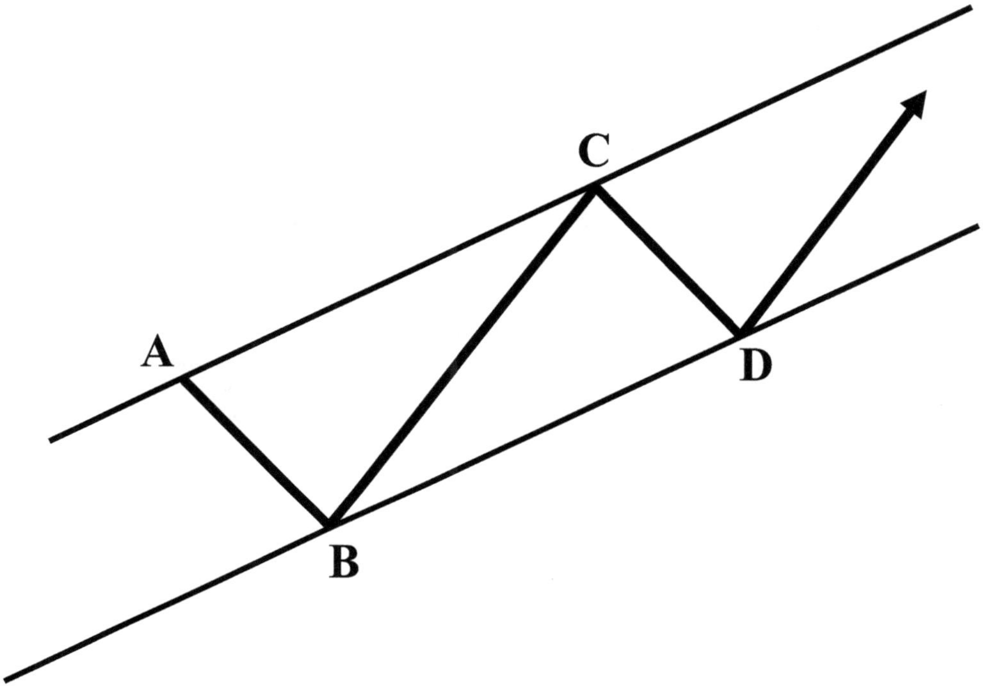

Figure 4.8

It is important to note that the completion of the Reciprocal AB=CD pattern is more of an approximation than an exact reversal point. Ideally, it is essential that the CD leg test the equivalent completion point. However, it is common for the price action to exceed this area before eventually resuming the predominant uptrend. Although the Reciprocal AB=CD may not yield as precise a PRZ as other patterns, it is effective as an approximation measure that complements other technical readings to define important continuations of predominant bullish trends.

Disney (DIS): Daily Bullish Reciprocal AB=CD Patterns within Trend Channels

The chart of Disney in Figure 4.9 clearly demonstrates the concept of an approximated completion point of the Reciprocal AB=CD pattern within the established bullish trend.

Figure 4.9

In this case, the stock consistently reversed at two-point corrective declines within this established bullish channel on the daily chart. Although the stock exceeded the two-point limit, the price action reversed after briefly exceeding the completion point of the CD leg in each case.

Bearish Reciprocal AB=CD Patterns within Trend Channels

In much the same manner as the bullish version, Bearish Reciprocal AB=CD patterns within established trend channels provide excellent approximation points of corrective moves (see Figure 4.10). When such repeated corrective price action manifests itself, the estimated measurement technique is effective as long as the established bearish channel remains intact.

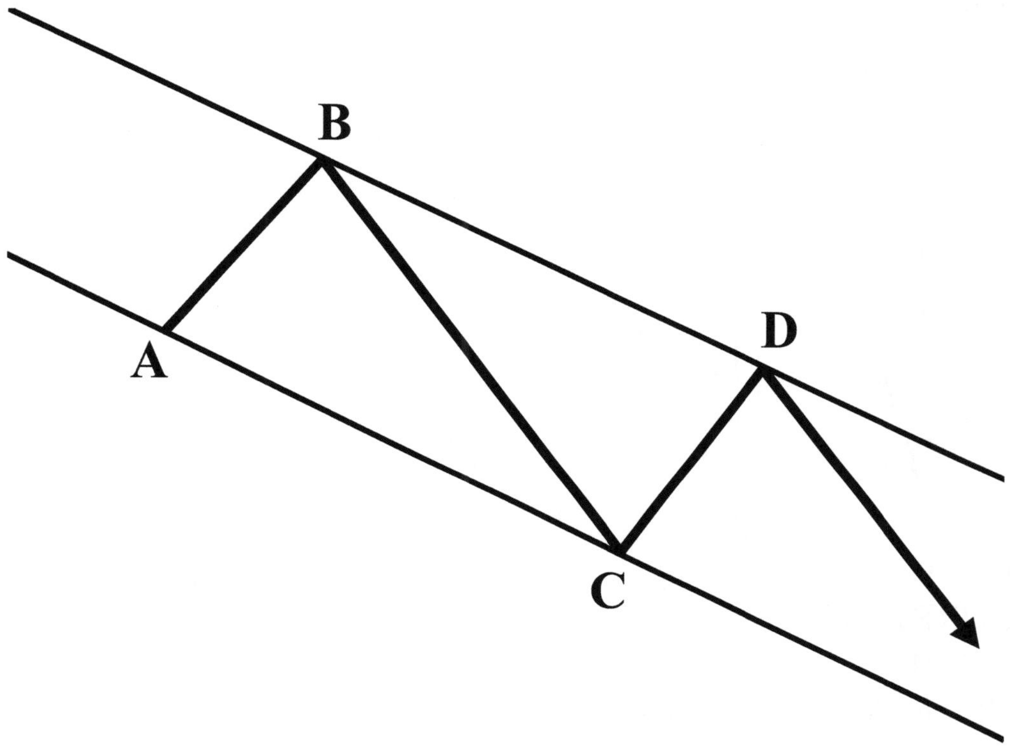

Figure 4.10

Well-established bearish channels frequently provide sharp reactions within their respective downtrend. But it is important to note that the completion of the Reciprocal AB=CD pattern is more of an approximation than an exact reversal point. Ideally, it is important to see the CD leg test the equivalent completion point. However, in many cases, the price action exceeds this area before ultimately resuming the predominant bearish trend. Although the Bearish Reciprocal AB=CD may not yield as precise a PRZ as other patterns, it is effective as an approximation measure that complements other technical readings to define important continuations of predominant bearish trends.

Standard & Poor's 500 Index (^GSPC): Weekly Bearish Reciprocal AB=CD Patterns within Trend Channels

One of the most interesting aspects of the bear market of 2008 was the continual corrective rallies within the established downtrend that were approximately 200 points each. The chart in Figure 4.11 clearly shows the weekly bearish channel that possessed the repeating Reciprocal AB=CD patterns.

^GSPC 16-FEB-10 HarmonicAnalyzer (TM) v6.05 Copyright © 2001-2008 HarmonicTrader.com, LLC. All Rights Reserved

Figure 4.11

Beginning with the first corrective wave in 2000 (A), the S&P 500 repeatedly bounced approximately 200 points each time it tested the lower range of its weekly channel.

Complex Patterns within Trend Channels

There are many cases when complex patterns form within well-established channels, signaling the continuation of the primary trend. Although many of these patterns do not possess distinctive high and low points, they are valid structures due to the proper alignment of harmonic ratios. These situations can sometimes be difficult to analyze because the patterns that form within the trend channels can seem insignificant. Sometimes, price action that adheres to the proper alignment to validate a harmonic pattern may even be difficult to see within the context of the larger trend. But these patterns possess even greater implications when they are located within the constraints of established trend channels.

There are two types of patterns to consider within channels. Retracement patterns such as a Gartley or a Bat typically develop in areas of consolidation in conjunction with the constraints of the channel. Extension patterns such as a Crab, a Butterfly, or an Alternate Bat frequently possess more extreme price action, as these structures include some type of extension to validate the setup. In this manner, the predominant trend will possess a few minor yet sharp corrective moves that will "threaten" the existing channel constraints.

Bullish Retracement Patterns within Bullish Trend Channels

Bullish retracement patterns such as a Gartley or a Bat typically develop in areas of consolidation in conjunction with the constraints of the channel. Figure 4.12 shows a Bullish Gartley, but either retracement pattern can be applied to these situations.

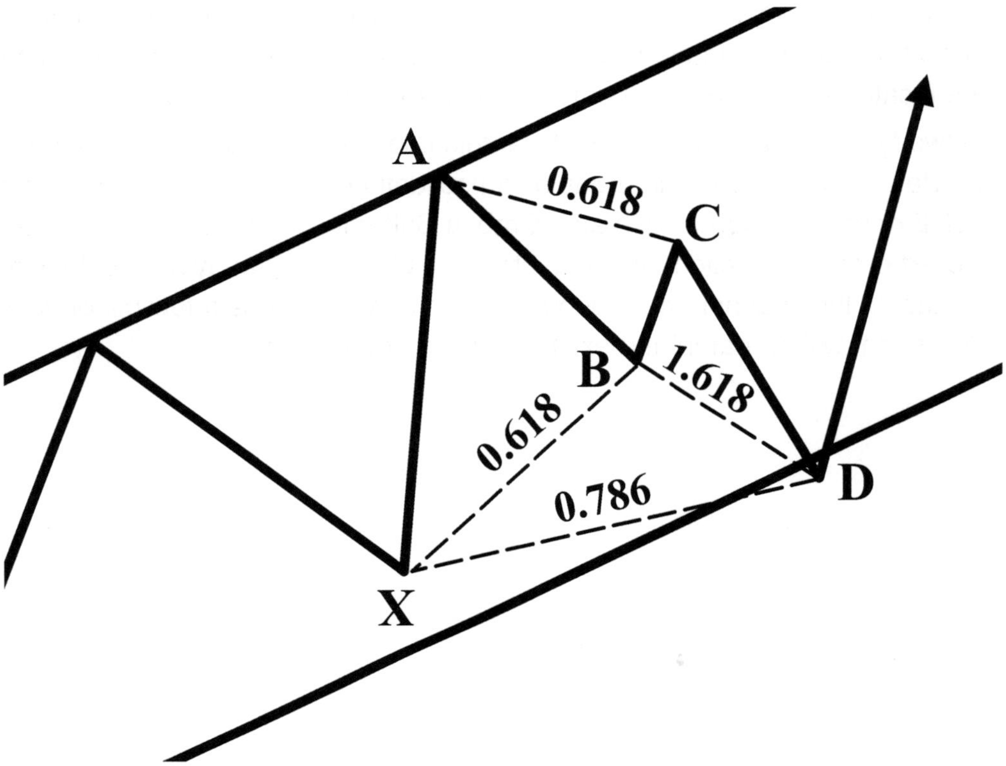

Figure 4.12

Chicago Mercantile Exchange (CME): Daily Bullish Gartley in a Bullish Trend Channel

The first example of the Chicago Mercantile Exchange shows an extended rally on the daily chart (see Figure 4.13). The Bullish Gartley that formed within this well-established channel completed several hundred points higher than it was the year prior.

Figure 4.13

This is a case where the pattern may seem to be developing at a point that is too far along within the bullish trend. Quite simply, since the stock has rallied several hundred points in the prior year, it might be difficult to believe that this pattern would yield a significant continuation of the predominant trend. However, the Bullish Gartley did just that, as the stock rallied another hundred points within a few months after completing this pattern.

Chicago Mercantile Exchange (CME): Daily Bullish Gartley in a Bullish Trend Channel

The enlarged chart in Figure 4.14 of the Bullish Gartley within the uptrend channel clearly shows a distinct harmonic pattern, despite the fact that the stock rallied as much as it did prior to this setup completing.

Figure 4.14

The example of CME clearly presents the concept of looking toward harmonic pattern completions as continuation signals within established trends. In this case, the Bullish Gartley was distinct and completed at the lower end of the support channel. The price action reversed sharply after testing all the numbers in the PRZ. When patterns like these develop within the context of an established bullish trend, these setups frequently are technically significant signals with respect to the overall direction of the stock.

Bullish Extension Patterns within Bullish Trend Channels

Bullish extension patterns such as a Crab, a Butterfly, or an Alternate Bat typically possess more volatile corrective price action yet remain within the constraints of the established channel. Figure 4.15 illustrates a Bullish Crab, but any of the extension patterns can be applied to these situations.

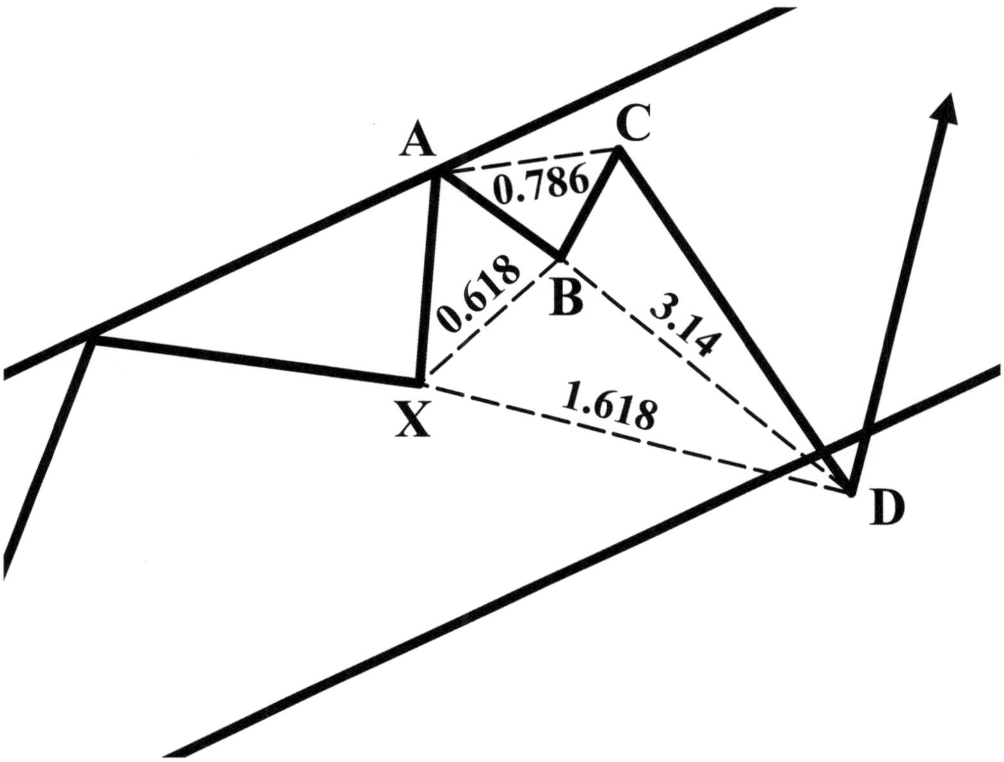

Figure 4.15

Although extension patterns usually encounter more volatile price action, these setups offer unique trading opportunities. In many of these cases, the PRZ sits just below the lower range of the bullish channel, often resulting in volatile price action as the pattern completes.

British Pound (GBP_A0-FX): 15-Minute Bullish Crab in a Bullish Trend Channel

The example of the British Pound in Figure 4.16 shows a Bullish Crab that completed just below the lower range of the trend channel. This pattern exemplifies the potential strength of a reversal that completes at critical trend channel support.

Figure 4.16

The pattern completed at 1.6325 area, despite the fact that this was a few pips below the support line of the trend channel. Although this may have seemed as if the channel was going to break down, the distinct Bullish Crab clearly indicated that the price action was testing a critical continuation area of the primary trend.

Bearish Complex Patterns within Downtrend Channels

Bearish retracement patterns such as a Gartley or a Bat typically develop in areas of consolidation in conjunction with the constraints of the primary downtrend channel. When these patterns complete at or slightly above the upper trend channel line, they present a unique opportunity to execute trades at the completion of distinct harmonic patterns that have the benefit of the primary trend complementing the resistance area.

Bearish Complex Retracement Patterns within Downtrend Channels

Again, bearish retracement patterns such as a Gartley or a Bat typically develop in areas of consolidation in conjunction with the constraints of the channel. Figure 4.17 illustrates a Bearish Gartley, but either retracement pattern can be applied to these situations.

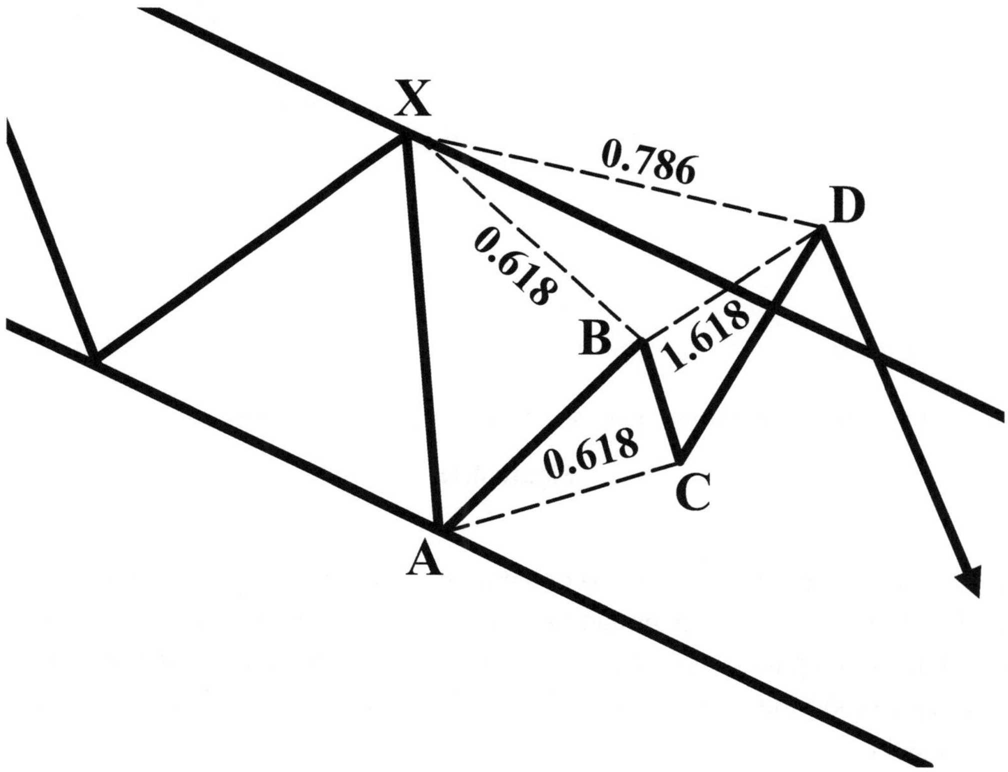

Figure 4.17

Australian Dollar (AUD_A0-FX): 15-Minute Bearish Gartley in Bearish Trend Channel

In Figure 4.18, the Aussie $ formed a Bearish Gartley after declining steadily over the previous few sessions. The price action held firmly within the bearish channel and formed a distinct pattern that marked the dramatic continuation of the established downtrend.

Figure 4.18

Despite exceeding the top range of the downtrend channel, the price action sold off sharply after completing the pattern. This example demonstrates the effectiveness of bearish patterns as critical continuation signals within established channels. In fact, patterns like these that complete slightly beyond the constraints of the established downtrend frequently can provide significant reversals.

Bearish Complex Extension Patterns within Bearish Channels

Bearish extension patterns such as a Crab, a Butterfly, or an Alternate Bat typically possess more volatile corrective price action yet remain within the constraints of the established channel. Figure 4.19 illustrates a Bearish Crab, but any of the extension patterns can be applied to these situations.

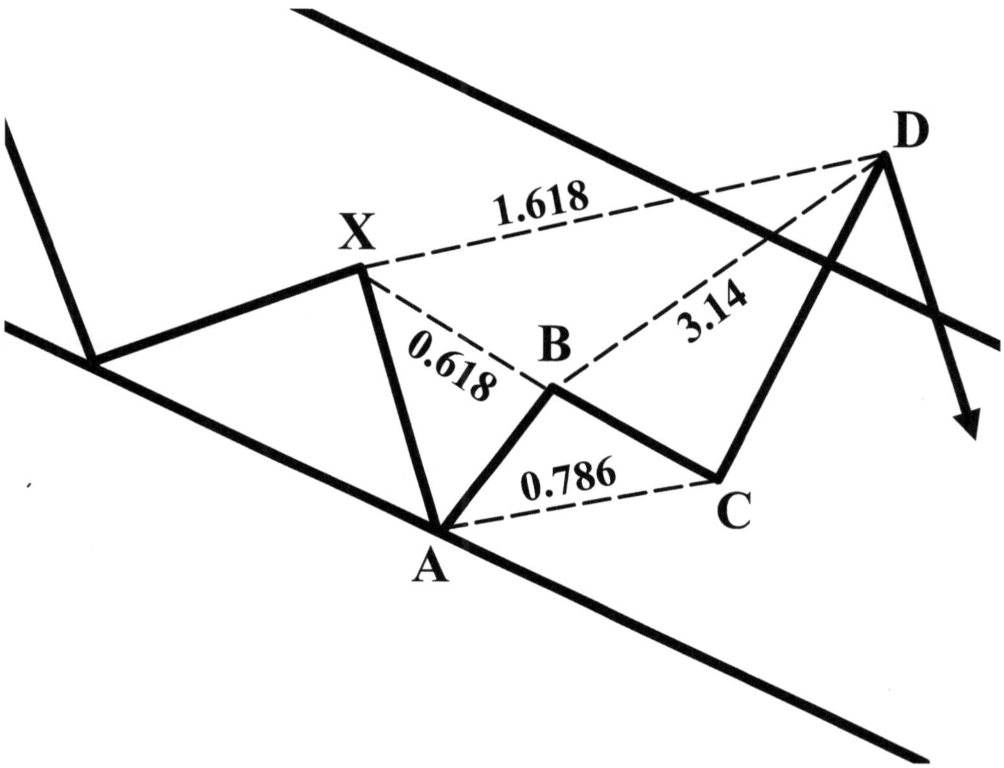

Figure 4.19

Although extension patterns frequently experience more volatile price action, these setups offer unique trading opportunities. In many of these cases, the PRZ sits just above the upper range of the bearish channel, often creating volatile price action as the pattern completes.

Apple (AAPL): 5-Minute Deep Bearish Crab Pattern within a Bearish Channel

Apple formed a Deep Bearish Crab within a defined downtrend (see Figure 4.20). In fact, the stock declined steadily within a defined range that contained the price action before it formed the pattern that marked the significant continuation. The Deep Bearish Crab that developed at the top range of this trend channel clearly illustrates the importance of harmonic patterns as "signposts of future price action.

Figure 4.20

The stock completed the Deep Bearish Crab, as it retested the top range of the channel. Apple stalled at this resistance and sold off sharply following the reversal.

Apple (AAPL): 5-Minute Deep Bearish Crab Pattern within a Bearish Channel

The enlarged chart in Figure 4.21 clearly shows the combination of the top range of the downtrend channel and the pattern's PRZ converging to define critical harmonic resistance in the $212 area. Again, this pattern signaled yet another continuation in the persistent bearish trend on the daily chart.

Figure 4.21

Apple demonstrated the importance of patterns that form in the direction of the trend. Well-defined trend channels should be clear and confine price action in a precise range. Within these constraints, patterns can form to signal the strength of the price action and identify optimal entry points for trade executions that attempt to follow in the direction of the predominant trend.

Failed Patterns Against the Trend

There are many cases where distinct harmonic patterns form within an established channel but they are challenged by the predominant trend. For example, a bullish pattern that forms within a defined bearish trend channel can present a challenging situation from a technical perspective. If the bullish pattern yields a valid reversal and the price action can rally beyond the downtrend channel, the PRZ would represent a critical support point. However, if the price action continued to decline and violate the bullish pattern, this area might be regarded as another continuation of the established downtrend. Again, this is a situation where harmonic patterns must be regarded as signposts of potential future price action. These setups—whether they fail or not—are critical make-or-break pattern completions that reveal a vast amount of technical information within a few price bars of its realization. Although a failed pattern might not yield the initial desired result of a valid reversal, such price action often signals a significantly deteriorating technical state of the primary trend and it must be respected.

Bullish Failed Complex Pattern Against the Trend

The overwhelming failure of patterns that act as clear continuation signals was exemplified in the historical examples of the bear markets of both 2000 and 2008. The violated Monster Bullish Gartley and the failed weekly Bullish 5-0, respectively, were two historic examples of this phenomenon. Both situations personally ingrained the significance of these failures for me as a vital element of the Harmonic Trading approach (see Figure 4.22). Although it is easy to spot the best examples in hindsight, the importance of such failures must be considered in real-time situations as opportunities unto themselves. The failure of a pattern's anticipated completion commonly indicates that something technically more significant is developing, especially when the trend is well defined. In fact, these types of continuation trades can yield decisive moves that offer accelerated declines following brief consolidation periods.

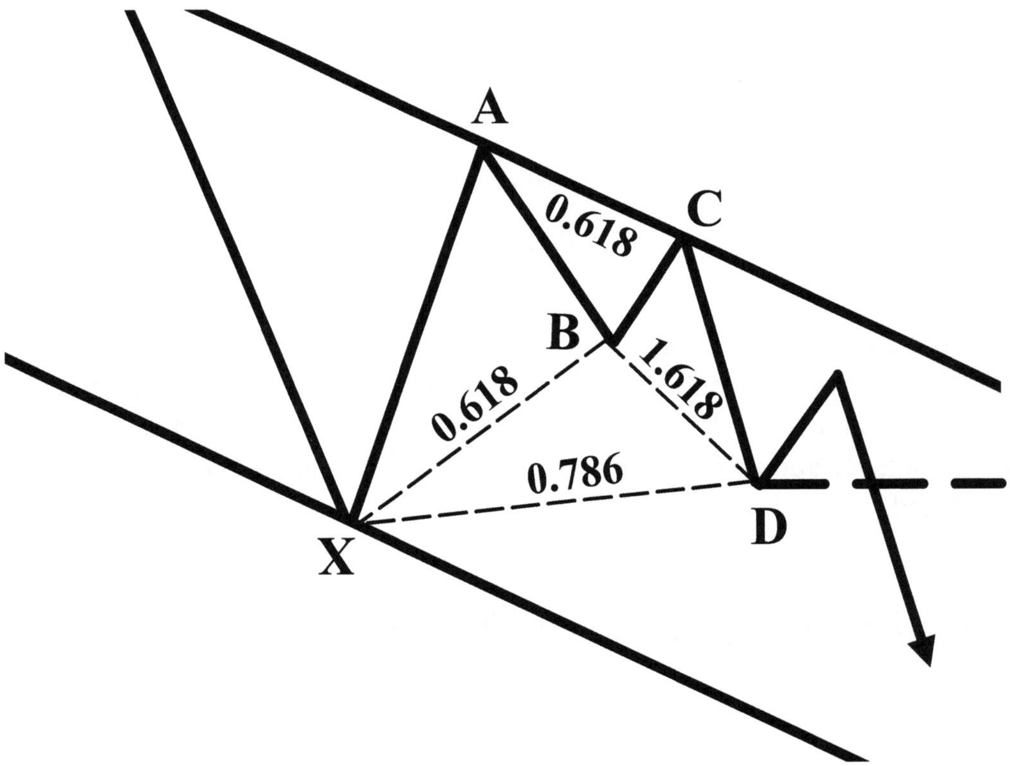

Figure 4.22

Standard and Poor's 500 June 2009 Mini-Contract (ES_M9): 5-Minute Bullish Gartley in a Bearish Trend Channel

The intra-daily chart of the S&P 500 June 2009 mini-contract clearly illustrates the concept of a failed bullish pattern within an established downtrend (see Figure 4.23). In the case the ES, the price action declined steadily for the entire session before forming the Bullish Gartley.

Figure 4.23

After a brief period of consolidation, the trend continued lower, violated PRZ, and dropped another 1% after the pattern's failure. The dramatic sell-off exemplifies the type of accelerated action that can be expected after a pattern is violated.

Standard and Poor's 500 June 2009 Mini-Contract (ES_M9): 5-Minute Bullish Gartley Potential Reversal Zone (PRZ) in a Bearish Trend Channel

The enlarged chart of the Bullish Gartley PRZ in Figure 4.24 clearly shows the decisive downside continuation that resulted following the failure of the pattern.

Figure 4.24

This is another case where the obvious failure of a bullish harmonic pattern within the context of an established downtrend acted as a critical continuation signal. Again, the continuation signal is triggered in these situations when the price action exceeds the PRZ and follows through to the downside within a few price bars after the violation.

Failed Bearish Patterns in a Bullish Trend Channel

Failed bearish patterns within an established bullish channel typically signal an important continuation of the predominant trend. Again, failed harmonic patterns in these situations underscore their importance as continuation signals. This technical information is usually critical to the future direction of the price action, as bearish pattern failures within an established channel can lead to an acceleration of that trend.

Although Figure 4.25 only shows a retracement pattern, the same principles apply to extension structures. However, Bearish Gartley and Bearish Bat patterns typically yield the best moves following a decisive failure of their respective PRZ.

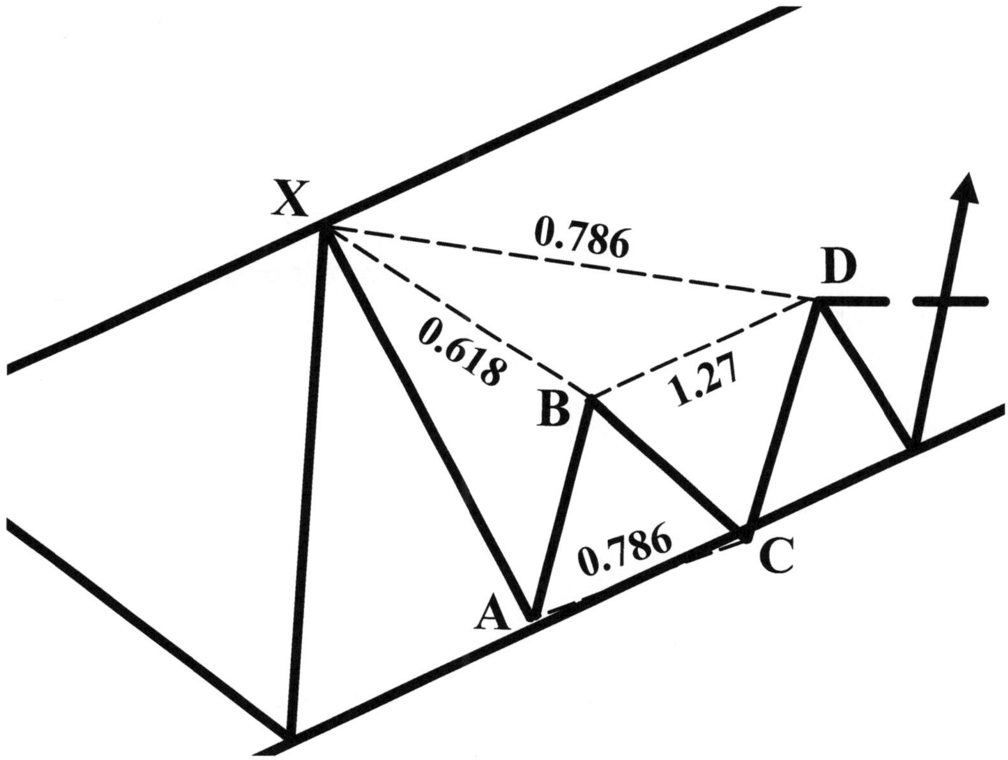

Figure 4.25

Dow Jones Transportation Average ($TRAN): Daily Failed Bearish Gartley Pattern in a Bullish Trend Channel

After rallying for quite some time, the Dow Jones Transportation Average formed a distinct Bearish Gartley within the constraints of an established bullish channel (see Figure 4.26). Although the pattern yielded an initial reversal, the price action quickly rebounded and rallied above the PRZ.

Figure 4.26

This example demonstrates how a distinct pattern can define critical technical levels within an established trend. In this case, the violation of the Bearish Gartley in the Dow Transports marked an important breakout and upside continuation of the predominant trend.

Dow Jones Transportation Average ($TRAN): Daily Failed Bearish Gartley Potential Reversal Zone (PRZ) in a Bullish Trend Channel

The enlarged chart of the pattern's PRZ in Figure 4.27 shows how the price action reversed nominally on the initial test of this area. The index consolidated in the PRZ for a short while before continuing higher.

Figure 4.27

The decisive breakout above the prior harmonic resistance established by the pattern was the technical entry point within this setup. Although not all failed patterns will possess such decisive price action, as is the case with the Dow Transports, most valid continuations will adhere to the predominant bias established by the primary uptrend.

Harmonic Patterns Relative to the Trend Conclusion

When analyzing harmonic patterns relative to the trend, it is important to keep in mind the general principle that patterns are primarily signposts of potential future price action. Regardless of what type of pattern may form, a completed structure represents some type of corrective price action within the context of the larger trend and provides significant information regarding the potential future price direction.

These patterns rely on precise ratio alignments within the constraints of an established trend to define the potential continuation points. These formations are critical because they can indicate execution areas within well-established trends that otherwise might be overlooked. Also, harmonic patterns provide reliable technical signals, regardless of the extent that a trend has persisted.

Not to be overlooked in its own merit, failed harmonic pattern PRZs define the exact price level within the overall predominant trend for the entry of a trade. Although a pattern's completion may not yield the anticipated result of a change in trend, the price action in this area will typically offer evidence of the strength of the move well in advance. Furthermore, the PRZ of a pattern that completes within an established trend can clearly outline the make-or-break price level for the entry point of a trade. The immediate action after a pattern completes often can provide an enormous amount of technical information regarding the state of the future price action unlike any other methodology.

The analysis of harmonic patterns relative to the trend is an important consideration when looking to execute a trade. Regardless of the time frame, price action has a tendency to adhere to certain channels. Although this is not the case with all price action, situations that exhibit defined channels can present clearer trading opportunities, especially when harmonic patterns are present.

Chapter 5

BAMM Theory

BAMM = Bat Action Magnet Move

BAMM is an abbreviation for *Bat Action Magnet Move.* The essence of this theory is based upon the primary tenet of Harmonic Trading that not all patterns are the same, as specific "technical entities" in the form of harmonic patterns define unique trading situations. In *Harmonic Trading: Volume One*, I discussed "The Great Gartley Controversy," which explains the importance of exact alignments of Fibonacci ratios with respect to price structures. My differentiation of similar pattern structures led me to discover the importance of respecting exact alignments. Specifically, the Bat pattern, which requires a different alignment of Fibonacci ratios than the general Gartley pattern, consistently guided my trade executions at different price levels. In doing so, I was able to differentiate price structures and define the best trading opportunities.

The essence of this argument focuses primarily upon the location of the mid-point (B) within the pattern structure. In my interpretation of the Gartley, the mid-point is required to occur at a 0.618 retracement of the XA leg. I realized that any B point with a retracement less than a 0.618—specifically a 50% or less retracement—resulted in a completion point that was closer to the initial starting point at X. This variation became known as the Bat pattern.

With this understanding, I was able to differentiate various M- and W-type price structures and have a better understanding of the potential future direction of the price action. In the Bat structure, when the CD leg exceeded the B point, I was confident that the price action would test the 0.886 retracement of the XA leg. There were many times where I would identify this situation in advance, watch this phenomenon develop, and see the price action reach this target. As these situations became more apparent, it dawned on me to begin playing these moves by capturing the segment of the CD leg instead of waiting for the ultimate completion of the larger pattern. Like a magnet, the Potential Reversal Zone (PRZ) of the Bat pattern frequently provided clear direction of where the price action was headed. Hence, the BAMM—Bat Action Magnet Move—was born.

The Magnet Effect

One of the greatest experiences with the Harmonic Trading techniques is the first time that you identify a potential pattern, observe the price action, test the PRZ, and reverse precisely from that projected area. For many people, this type of experience is when the harmonic lightbulb turns on. I've received numerous e-mails from many people who describe this exact sequence of events. From that point forward, people tend to never look at the financial markets the same way again.

But, what is this experience? I remember when I first started to differentiate the various M- and W-type structures, I became excited the more I was able to differentiate various harmonic setups. In most cases, I was able to recognize these situations well in advance. For example, pattern developments in the various major indices in my advisory reports, especially the S&P 500, were identified months if not more than a year in advance. How was this possible? Time and time again, there were distinct harmonic patterns forming on many long-term charts that eventually came to fruition. As I tracked these situations, I realized in all patterns there was a distinct point where the potential completion of a harmonic pattern would be triggered. Regardless of the pattern, the price action frequently was drawn to the distinct harmonic zone. In my opinion, this technical phenomenon was defined by the relative structure of the overall price action as it entered the final CD leg of the pattern.

Although this phenomenon did not occur in every situation, a majority of these circumstances where distinct harmonic patterns would develop, enter into the final CD leg, and ultimately test all of the numbers in the PRZ. Regardless of whether the pattern completion was valid, the zone from the point the CD leg is triggered until it tests the completion point of the pattern continually presented a fantastic trading opportunity to capitalize on the predominant trend and the magnet effect of the harmonic price action.

Harmonic Breakouts and Breakdowns

I soon realized that these situations were unique technical breakouts and breakdowns that were defined by their relative harmonic ratio alignments. In the same fashion as harmonic patterns, these structures possessed precise technical conditions to define these unique situations. Also, these specific harmonic breakouts or breakdowns enabled me to develop pattern-specific rules for each trading opportunity. After refining the details for these setups, the execution and the management of these trades became easier to handle.

Depending upon the ratio alignment, the trigger of the final leg of the structure occurs when the price action of the CD segment exceeds the prior B point. Whether the price action is a breakout or a breakdown, the extent of this move can be projected with a large degree of certainty as long as the entire structure satisfies all of the necessary elements to validate the pattern. This classification creates a unique technical situation that requires many conditions to be valid before triggering a potential trade opportunity. Furthermore, these breakout and breakdown strategies attempt to capture a small segment of the price action relative to the larger pattern. Unlike many general technical strategies that attempt to capitalize on breakouts and breakdowns, this approach employs the advanced pattern identification techniques to differentiate these situations as unique. It is important to realize that these are special breakout and breakdown trading strategies that rely on many technical conditions to be present to validate the opportunity. Therefore, the technical considerations and price parameters are precisely defined, providing a more detailed framework to assess the trade opportunity.

As I mentioned previously, within the context of Harmonic Trading, the Bat pattern possessed these technical traits more clearly than any other setup. Time and time again, I was able to differentiate Bat versus Gartley patterns well in advance. As soon as the CD leg exceeded the B point, the final segment represented a fantastic opportunity to capitalize on the predominant trend—at least capturing the segment to the pattern's completion point. Of course, the Bat presented a larger zone, as the CD leg extended further beyond the B point, which was typically a 50% retracement or less, in this pattern and completed at the 0.886. Unlike the Gartley pattern, which utilized a 0.618 retracement and offered a smaller zone between the B point and the D point, the Bat became a reliable structure to employ these strategies. Hence, BAMM—Bat Action Magnet Move—best described this technical phenomenon. Harmonic breakout or breakdown might be a more appropriate technical term to describe this type of price action. However, the entire concept is encompassed within the dynamics of the Bat pattern.

Bullish BAMM Breakout

The illustration of the Bearish Bat pattern in Figure 5.1 shows the point where the BAMM is triggered. Utilizing the Bat pattern illustration, when the B point of a pattern is at a 50% level or less, the CD leg typically experiences a greater retracement of the XA move to the 0.886 level.

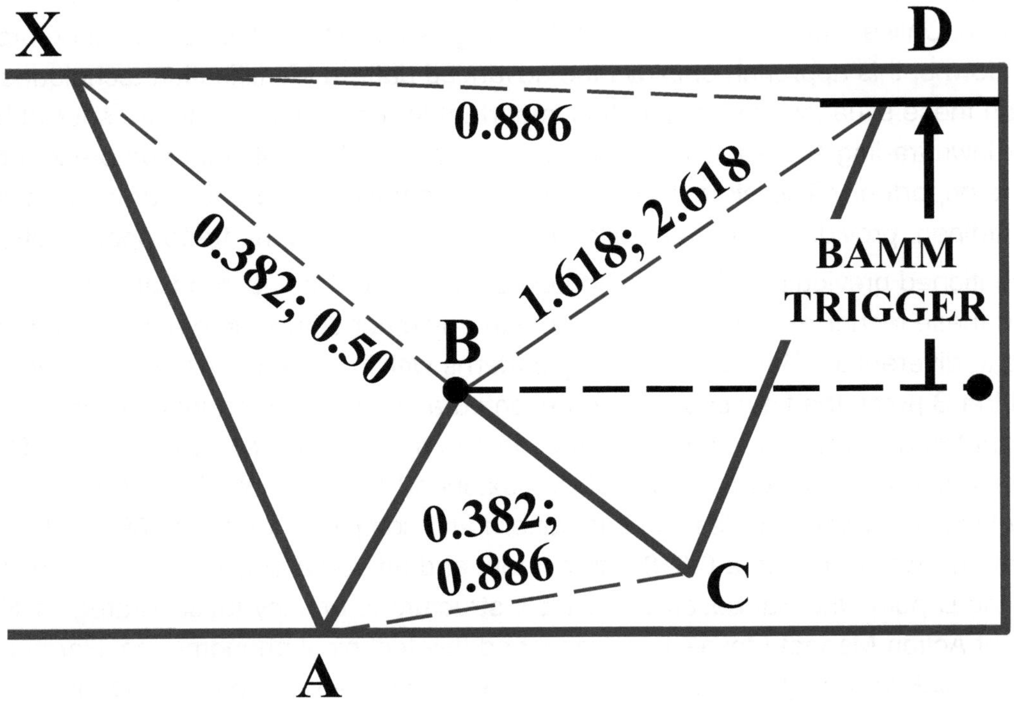

Figure 5.1

In the case of the Bearish Bat pattern, when the price action exceeds the B point in a breakout move, the segment of the CD leg typically extends toward the 0.886 retracement, which is usually complemented by other harmonic measurements. As a side note, it is important to point out that the Bearish Bat is utilized in the Bullish BAMM because the opportunity to get long on the breakout of the B point is striving to capture the segment to the completion of the pattern at the 0.886 retracement. Also, it is important to note that this technique typically employs shorter-term trading strategies within the context of a longer-term pattern. The ultimate goal is to capitalize on those smaller yet higher-probability price moves within the completion of a much larger pattern.

Standard & Poor's 500 Continuous Contract (ES_#F): Daily Bullish BAMM Breakout

In May 2006, the continuous mini-contract of the S&P 500 formed a distinct Bearish Bat pattern that was triggered when the CD leg exceeded the prior B point on its way to test all of the numbers in the PRZ (see Figure 5.2).

Figure 5.2

As the index rallied above the B point resistance, the price action triggered the BAMM, as the index decidedly rallied 40 points to close this gap. Clearly, the predominant trend of the daily action dictated the short-term bullish bias until the pattern was completed. Any intra-day trades during this time should have favored the long side until the BAMM completed. In this case, the larger daily trend clearly defined the short-term upside within the constraints of the pattern. This daily scenario clearly illustrates the BAMM concept and the ability of these "magnet moves" to decipher price action and define trading opportunities.

Bullish BAMM Breakout in the CD Leg

The BAMM phenomenon can be clearly witnessed upon close inspection of the CD leg. As the price action rallies above the B point, the "magnet effect" begins (see Figure 5.3).

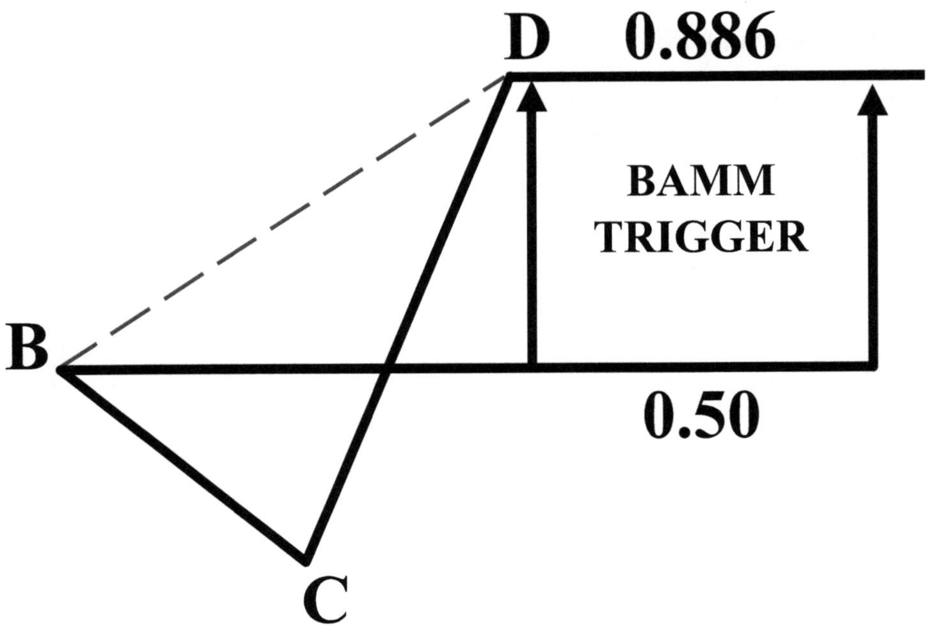

Figure 5.3

The most important technical aspect of this breakout is the clear continuation to the upside after the price action exceeds the B point. The breakout should continue convincingly until it tests the PRZ. Although not all price action rallies straight to the completion point of the pattern, the most valid situations exhibit decisive continuation. If not, it is best to cover those positions that tend to stall after the BAMM is triggered.

Standard & Poor's 500 Continuous Contract (ES_#F): Daily Bullish BAMM Breakout in the CD Leg

The enlarged chart in Figure 5.4 shows the price action in the CD leg of the Bearish Bat that exemplifies the ideal bullish continuation necessary to validate these trading opportunities. In this case, the ES rallied sharply on the harmonic breakout above the prior B point and proceeded to test the PRZ in a direct "magnet move."

Figure 5.4

Although the ES experienced a few down days along the way, the price action climbed steadily in this BAMM zone until all of the numbers in the pattern's PRZ were tested. This BAMM breakout defined a precise 40-point zone that was "under the magnet effect of the pattern." This clearly identified a bullish bias in this area until the pattern was completed. Technical information like this can immensely improve trading results, as the understanding of such harmonic phenomena will consistently identify the predominant market bias and identify those trades that seek to benefit from the established trend.

Bearish BAMM Breakdown

Figure 5.5 illustrates a Bullish Bat pattern that outlines the point where the BAMM is triggered. Utilizing the Bat pattern illustration, when a B point of a pattern is at a 50% level or less, the CD leg typically experiences a greater retracement of the XA move to the 0.886 level.

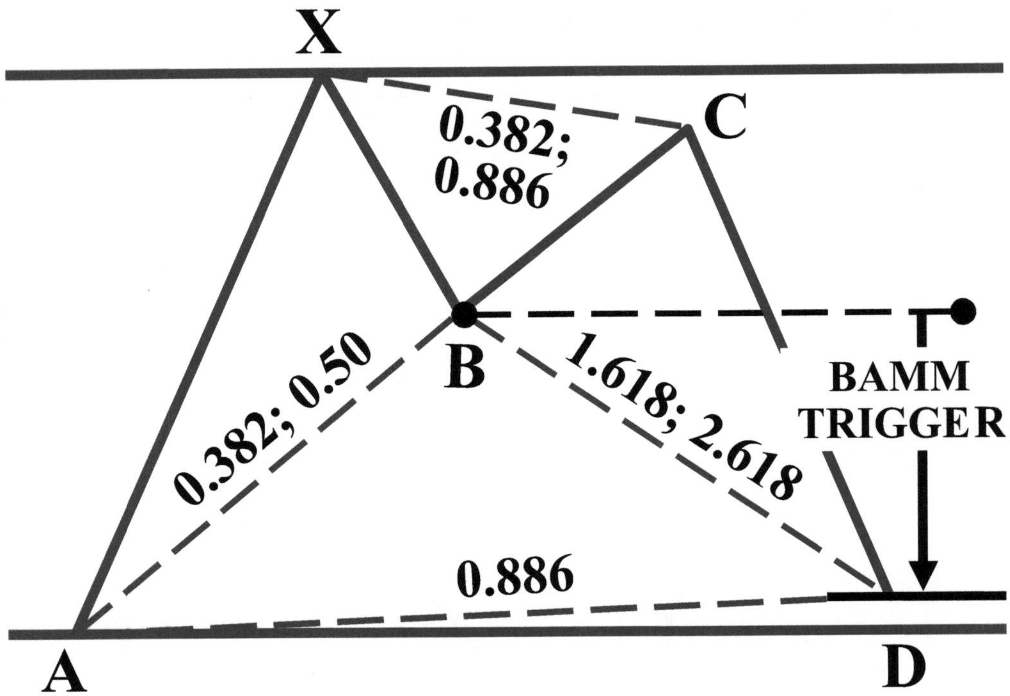

Figure 5.5

In the case of the Bullish Bat pattern, when the price action exceeds the B point in a breakdown move, the segment of the CD leg typically extends toward the 0.886 retracement. The 0.886 retracement is usually complemented by other harmonic measurements that help define the immediate PRZ. Again, it is important to point out that the Bullish Bat is utilized in the Bearish BAMM. The opportunity to sell on the breakdown of the B point is striving to capture the final segment that represents the completion of the pattern at the 0.886 retracement. Also, it is important to note that this technique typically employs shorter-term trading strategies within the context of a longer-term pattern. The ultimate goal is to capitalize on those smaller yet higher-probability price moves within the completion of a much larger pattern.

Eurodollar (EUR_A0-FX): Weekly Bearish BAMM Breakdown

For more than a year, the Euro formed this distinct Bullish Bat that started to break down sharply after violating the prior B point (see Figure 5.6). The BAMM was triggered when the CD leg exceeded the prior B point at 1.2750 on its way to test all of the numbers in the PRZ.

Figure 5.6

As the Euro broke down under the B point support, the price action triggered the BAMM. The index fell another 700 pips to close this gap and test the PRZ. Clearly, the predominant trend of the daily action dictated the short-term bearish bias until the pattern was completed. Any trades—intra-day or daily swing positions—during this time should have favored the short side until the BAMM completed. In this case, the larger weekly trend defined the short-term downside within the constraints of the pattern. This long-term weekly scenario clearly illustrates the BAMM concept, and the ability of these “magnet moves” to decipher price action and to define trading opportunities.

Bearish BAMM Breakdown in the CD Leg

The BAMM phenomenon can be clearly witnessed upon close inspection of the CD leg. As the price action declines below the B point, the "magnet effect" begins, as illustrated in Figure 5.7.

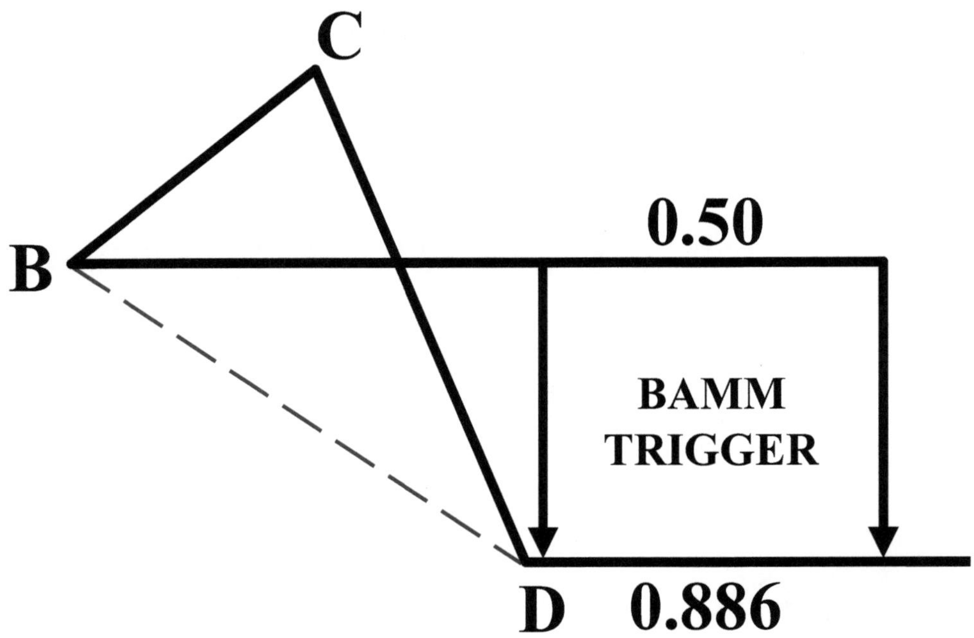

Figure 5.7

The most important technical aspect of this breakdown is the clear continuation to the downside after the price action exceeds the B point. The breakdown should continue convincingly until it tests the PRZ. Although not all price action declines straight to the completion point of the pattern, the most valid situations will exhibit decisive continuation. If not, it is best to cover those positions that tend to stall after the BAMM is triggered.

EuroDollar (EUR_A0-FX): Weekly Bearish BAMM Breakdown in the CD Leg

The chart in Figure 5.8 shows the price action in the CD leg of the Bullish Bat.

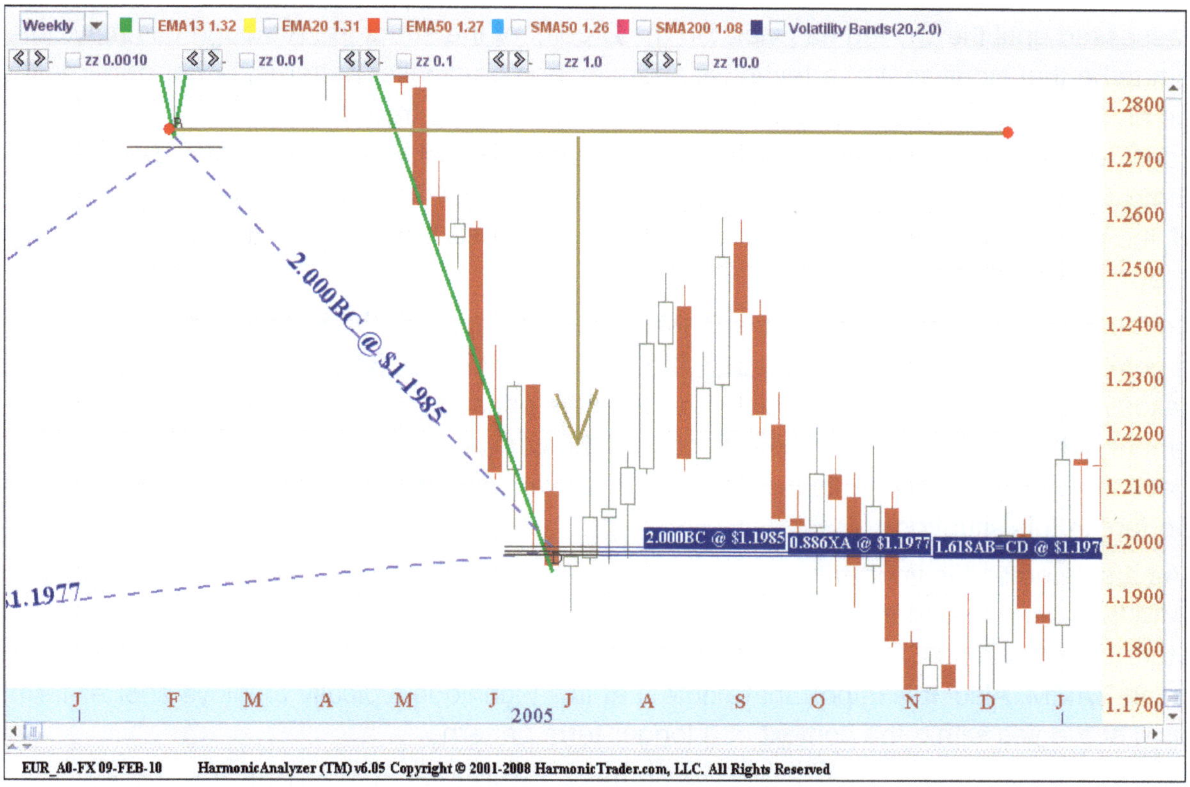

Figure 5.8

This chart shows the ideal continuation to the downside necessary to validate these trading opportunities. In this case, the Euro sank sharply on the breakdown below the prior B point at 1.2750.

The Euro exhibited the ideal price action in this example, and it clearly illustrates the "magnet effect" of the BAMM concept. In the case of the Euro, it sold off sharply through this BAMM zone until all of the numbers in the pattern's PRZ were tested. This BAMM breakdown defined a substantial 750-pip zone that was "under the magnet effect of the pattern" and accurately identified the predominant bearish bias until the pattern was completed. Again, technical information like this can immensely improve trading results, as the understanding of such harmonic phenomena will consistently identify the predominant market bias and identify those trades that seek to benefit from the established trend.

AB=CD BAMM

As outlined previously, the CD leg is the most powerful price segment that possesses substantial implications for trading opportunities within the BAMM framework. When analyzing the completion of an AB=CD pattern, the determination of the pattern's completion point cannot be assessed until the CD leg has violated the B point of the structure. Although this may not seem to be that significant of a technical phenomenon on smaller patterns, larger patterns in price and time can offer tremendous opportunities to execute trades within this AB=CD BAMM window with the profit objective clearly defined by the PRZ. Although the AB=CD BAMM technical phenomenon might be more appropriately called *AB=CD Magnet Move* or *AB=CD MM*, the principles embodied within the BAMM theory best describe the entire concept. Hence, the term is AB=CD BAMM.

In much the same manner that the BAMM principles apply to the Bat pattern when the mid-point retracement level is exceeded, the AB=CD BAMM capitalizes on the "harmonic breakout/breakdown" in distinct structures. Once the price action exceeds the B point, the segment of the CD leg typically extends toward the completion point of the pattern. The BC projection usually complements the setup, as the exact completion point of the pattern is most important in this situation.

As a side note, it is important to point out that the Bearish AB=CD is utilized in the Bullish BAMM because the opportunity to get long on the breakout of the prior B point is striving to capture the remaining CD segment to the completion of the pattern. The inverse is true for the Bearish BAMM. Also, it is important to note that this technique typically employs shorter-term trading strategies within the context of a longer-term pattern.

Again, the ultimate goal is to capitalize on those smaller yet high-probability price moves within the completion of a much larger pattern. Therefore, the point at which the CD leg exceeds the prior B point provides a gap that represents a highly probable area of acceleration. Like a magnet, the price action is pulled toward the completion point of the larger AB=CD pattern. Although complex harmonic patterns provide even greater confirmation of the completion of the structure, the important focus is on the area where the CD leg exceeds the prior B point to the completion zone.

Bullish AB=CD BAMM

In the case of the Bearish AB=CD pattern, the price action will typically accelerate on the breakout of the resistance level at the B-point, as illustrated in Figure 5.9.

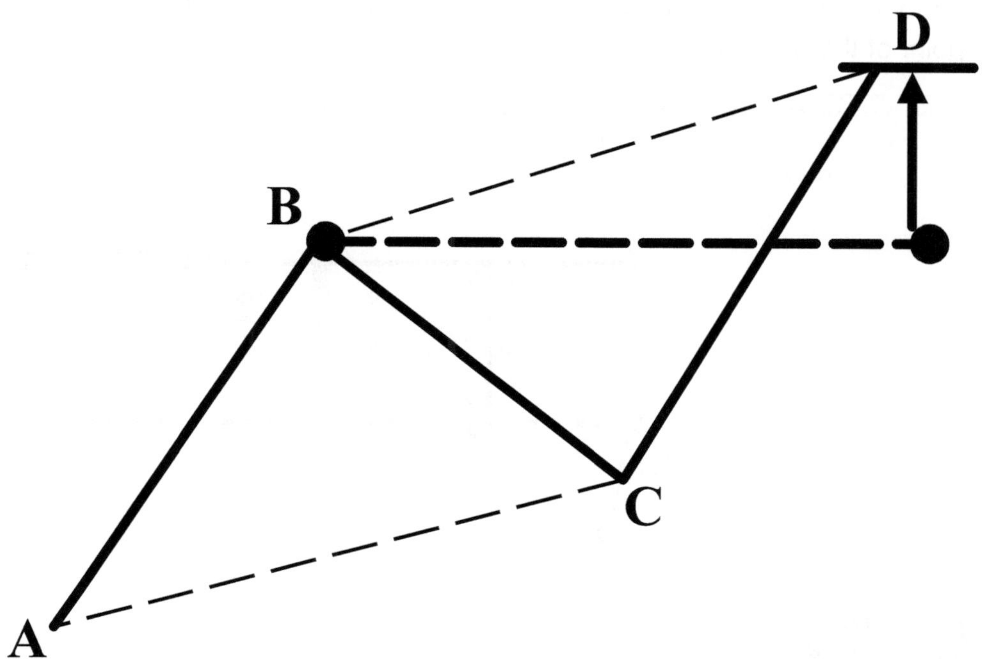

Figure 5.9

The most important technical aspect of this breakout is the clear continuation to the upside after the price action exceeds the B point. The breakout should continue convincingly until it tests the PRZ. Although not all price action rallies straight to the completion point of the pattern, the most valid situations will exhibit decisive continuation. If not, it is best to cover those positions that tend to stall after the AB=CD BAMM is triggered.

Home Depot (HD): Daily Bullish AB=CD BAMM

The weekly chart in Figure 5.10 shows a distinct Bearish AB=CD pattern that formed over the course of six months. The structure rallied above the prior B point and accelerated to the completion point of the pattern.

Figure 5.10

It is important to underscore the degree of confidence in the overall trend bias that these situations instill. Although this technical understanding does not dismiss effective trade management strategies to capitalize on these potential opportunities, the BAMM phenomenon offers a great deal of evidence about the state of the predominant trend and a reliable completion target for the price move. Defining these price constraints based from the BAMM conditions instills a great deal of confidence in the position, as all parameters are outlined in advance. In essence, these high-probability BAMM zones create tradable “windows” of price segments.

Home Depot (HD): Weekly Bullish AB=CD BAMM Breakout in the CD Leg

The enlarged chart in Figure 5.11 shows the weekly price action in the CD leg of the Bearish AB=CD. This chart shows the ideal upside continuation necessary to validate these harmonic breakout trading opportunities. In this case, Home Depot rallied decisively as it broke above the prior B point resistance just above $38.

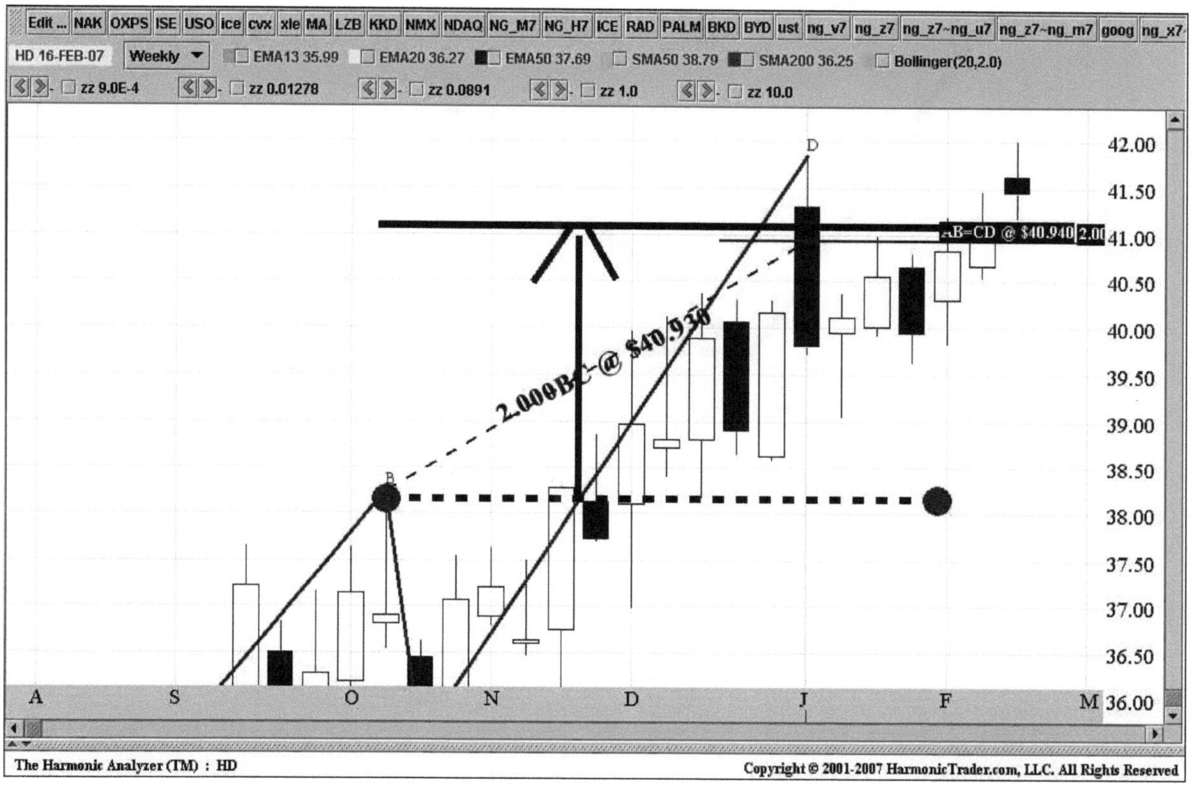

Figure 5.11

Although a 3-point breakout might not seem like a big deal, the true beauty of this concept is the understanding of the "magnet effect" of the price action as it completes the pattern and the high probability bias that this technical phenomenon engenders. In this case, the "harmonic breakout" on the weekly chart confirmed that the predominant trend would continue to the completion point of the pattern. Situations such as these create a reliable bias of the primary trend, which can optimize trading decisions by staying on the right side of the market.

Bearish AB=CD BAMM

In the case of the Bullish AB=CD, the price action will typically accelerate on the breakdown of the support level at the prior B-point, triggering a trade opportunity to sell on this continuation with a target completion at the pattern's PRZ (see Figure 5.12).

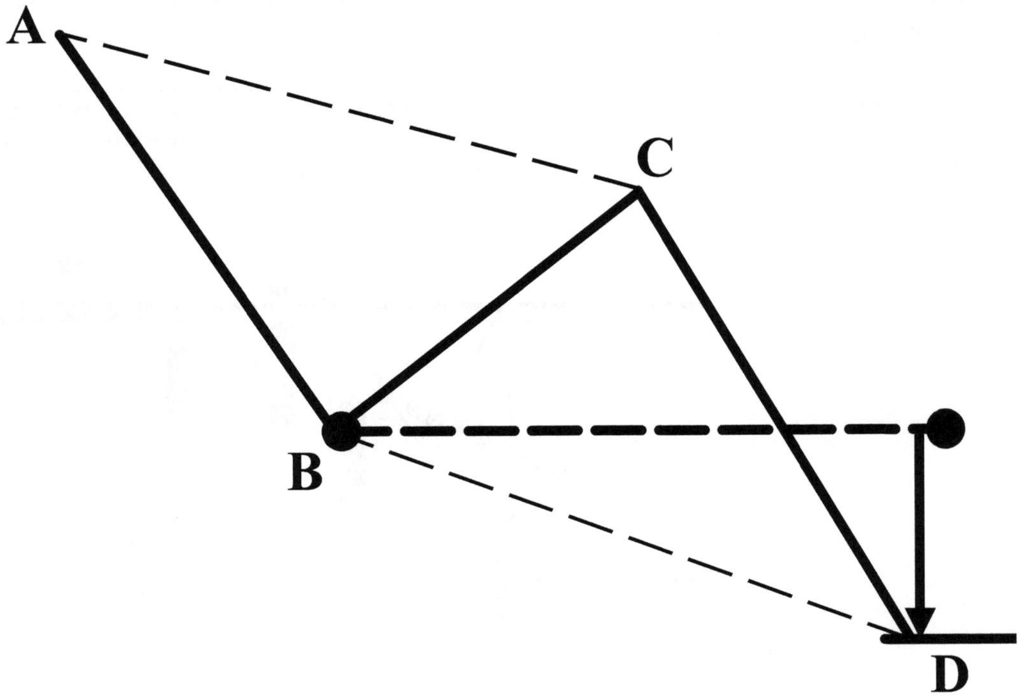

Figure 5.12

After the B point is violated, the trend should continue decidedly lower toward the completion of the pattern. Although the price action may not decline straight to the PRZ, the overall trend should maintain a steady descent to the harmonic numbers.

Disney (DIS): Daily Bullish AB=CD BAMM

The daily chart in Figure 5.13 shows the distinct AB=CD pattern that formed over the course of nine months. The structure broke down under the prior B point and accelerated to the completion point of the pattern.

Figure 5.13

Although the price action bounced about halfway to the ultimate completion of the pattern, the eventual bearish continuation and overall negative bias dictated the predominant trend until the harmonic support was tested.

Disney (DIS): Daily Bullish AB=CD BAMM

The enlarged chart in Figure 5.14 shows the price action in the CD leg of the Bullish AB=CD and the ideal continuation to the downside necessary to validate this trading opportunity. In the case of Disney, the stock accelerated to the downside after violating the B point.

Figure 5.14

The AB=CD BAMM is most effective when utilizing larger time frames to define the bias for a shorter-term move. In the case of Disney, the daily downtrend after the BAMM was triggered would have indicated that the predominant bearish bias would be maintained until the pattern was completed at a minimum. Therefore, the BAMM trigger would have dictated short positions at this time until the harmonic support was tested.

BAMM Conclusion

There are many situations where distinct structures seem to indicate their completion long before the reality. The ability to recognize harmonic price action within distinct structures is one of the greatest advantages of this methodology. Although not all harmonic patterns complete as expected, there are an overwhelming number of situations where this phenomenon reveals a great deal about the future potential price action well in advance.

There are many types of BAMM or "magnet move" phenomena that occur within many of the structures of harmonic patterns. The BAMM and AB=CD BAMM are two examples of special technical situations where the potential completion of a particular pattern is first recognized and effective strategies can be employed to capitalize on obvious harmonic price action. Other types of BAMM phenomena—such as "morphing" situations—can materialize where failed retracement patterns evolve into extension patterns. For example, there are many situations where a failed Bearish Bat turns into a Bearish Crab. Although these situations are not as precise as the BAMM and AB=CD BAMM, they represent another type of phenomenon that involves the acceleration of price action from one harmonic level to the next. Again, it is within these "windows of harmonic levels of support and resistance" where a great deal of technical information can be garnered and high-probability trade opportunities defined.

Chapter 6

RSI BAMM

As the bear markets of 2000 and 2008 demonstrated, the need for strategies that determine the overall bias is essential to develop a relative perspective on the position of any trade. For example, there is a significant difference between a long position, representing a continuation of the predominant bullish trend, as opposed to a brief correction within the overall downtrend. Despite the prevalence of distinct patterns that favor one side of the market or the other, the larger time frame and predominant trend will always dictate the extent of any move and the possibility for profit.

Technical Indicators

Larger trend considerations such as these were not the only new factors that helped determine the overall bias during these challenging bear markets. Other technical measures such as Relative Strength helped to confirm the extent of the predominant trend. Furthermore, these considerations have become increasingly more vital to the Harmonic Trading approach and in the determination of the overall validity of patterns as reliable structural signals.

Although indicators were not new to my analysis, as I frequently employed these studies and others such as Volume and Price Gap strategies, I must admit that I was not always as open-minded regarding their importance. When I initially started to define the Harmonic Trading approach, I employed simple trend lines, Volume, and a few other technical studies to complement my existing price pattern analysis. The main focus of this approach was always on the completion of price patterns. As I examined other complementary strategies to filter the pattern completions, I realized that indicators and oscillators provided significant technical signals that helped gauge the overall state of the price action.

Actually, I first discussed the dynamics of harmonic price action as it relates to the Trend, Volume, and Price Gap studies in *The Harmonic Trader.* In this book, I outlined trading strategies that analyzed patterns within the context of well-established trend channels, as well. In recent years, I investigated a variety of technical indicators, including Stochastics, Volatility Bands, MACD, and Relative Strength. Of all these measures, I have been looking for the technical measure that would reveal the extent of buying and selling relative to the predominant trend. Since price patterns often represent the structural end of a significant trend, it seems that it is most important to understand some type of relative measure that manifests the degree of buying and selling at critical harmonic areas. Although many technical indicators were advantageous in my research, within the framework of this approach, certain measures offered more relevant and reliable predictive information. From a harmonic pattern perspective, the structure is as important as where it completes relative to its prior price history. Therefore, the importance of the *relative* structural alignment led me to the Relative Strength Index (RSI), which provided that measure.

The integration of other technical studies, in particular RSI, was a significant evolution in my research. As a dedicated student of the financial markets, I have always believed it is important to embrace a gamut of market strategies to thoroughly understand market price action. Considering a variety of technical methods can provide greater confirmation of potential price action.

In fact, H. M. Gartley in his infamous book *Profits in the Stock Market*, emphasized such multiple confirmation strategies of technical methods, stating:

> ***"Patterns must be used in conjunction with other technical working tools. The study of tops and bottoms, to be of greatest value, must be combined, and used in conjunction with the study of other working tools, such as Trend Lines, Moving Averages, Gaps, and particularly Volume, as well as Dow Theory and the general market phenomena which we call 'Breadth-of-the-Market' studies."***
>
> (*Profits in the Stock Market* [Pomeroy, WA: Lambert-Gann Publishing, 1932], 221).

The evolution of the Harmonic Trading approach has led to a more integrative perspective that is congruent with Gartley's philosophy. Patterns—in this case, harmonic patterns—must be used in conjunction with other technical working tools. Of the vast array of indicators and oscillators available that I have researched, RSI represents the most effective measure in relation to the completion of harmonic patterns.

Although when talking about Relative Strength, sometimes people confuse the subject as relative to another index, such as the S&P 500. In this case, I'm talking about the Relative Strength measure that calculates the internal change of price movement, usually comparing the current price history with that of an average of a certain number of periods prior. (Typically, a 14-period average is calculated.) The readings of RSI measurements exhibit a number of unique technical traits in their own merit. For example, patterns that complete at extreme RSI readings can help to identify those special situations where the impending reversal signals the end of an extended trend. In many instances, I have noticed RSI readings that have formed similar complex structures in setups that possessed distinct price patterns. Even more compelling were situations where a Bearish Gartley, for instance, would develop on the price chart, while an indicator reading was showing a Bearish Three Drives structure. Both the price and the indicator reading structures completed at the same point within their own relative chart, serving to confirm the reversal. These are a few of the many distinct relationships that help to decipher price action within the context of harmonic price patterns. Furthermore, these unique phenomena can pinpoint the most critical turning points in the markets. Regardless of these obvious relationships, I was still looking for those exact situations where the dynamics of harmonic price patterns and technical indicators identified unique Potential Reversal Zones (PRZ).

Relative Strength Index (RSI)

The RSI was discovered by Welles Wilder in the 1970s. Wilder introduced RSI in his book *New Concepts in Technical Trading Systems*. In addition to the RSI technique, he introduced several other indicator and oscillator studies, including the Directional Movement Index (DMI). He presented a variety of unprecedented technical measurement strategies, but RSI is among his finest contributions to the field of Technical Analysis. Although it is properly categorized as a momentum oscillator, RSI is typically considered one of the more popular indicator studies available today.

The RSI was devised by Wilder as a means of calculating the change in momentum of price movement as it relates to a predetermined time period. The name Relative Strength Index is slightly misleading, as the RSI does not compare the relative strength of two markets, but rather the internal strength of the price action of an individual issue.

RSI is a price-following oscillator that ranges between 0 and 100. The RSI typically peaks above 70 and bottoms below 30, and it usually forms these readings before the underlying price chart. The RSI equation is derived by calculating the ratio of the average of X (number) price bars (days) day's closes up divided by the average of X (number) price bars (days) day's closes down. Although "X" can be any value, Wilder employed a 14-period factor in his computation. The equation is calculated as follows:

$$\text{RSI} = 100 - (100 / (1+\text{RS}))$$

$$\text{RS} = \frac{\text{Average of 14 (X) day's closes UP}}{\text{Average of 14 (X) day's closes DOWN}}$$

This equation quantifies the relative momentum of the current price action with that of 14 (X) periods ago. The extreme RSI readings provide excellent measures to the degree that the price action has persisted and the continued strength or momentum of the predominant trend. The true value of these readings occurs when the price and the indicator react at extreme areas. When the RSI tests an extreme overbought or oversold area at critical harmonic levels of support or resistance, the price action can reveal a great deal regarding the potential state of the predominant trend.

Divergence

The benefit of the RSI is most advantageous when compared to clear areas of support and resistance. *The key technical event occurs when the price and the RSI diverge.* In fact, in his book *New Concepts*, Wilder emphasized the importance of divergence:

> ***"Although divergence does not occur at every turning point, it does occur at most significant turning points. When divergence begins to show up after a good directional move, this is a very strong indication that a turning point is near. Divergence is the single most indicative characteristic of the Relative Strength Index."***
>
> (*New Concepts in Technical Trading Systems* [Greensboro, NC: Trend Research, 1978], 70).

I agree with Wilder. In fact, I believe that the RSI is the most reliable technical reading to reveal such divergence as it directly relates to price. Furthermore, the technical phenomenon of RSI divergence is particularly revealing when related to the completion of harmonic patterns.

As my research continued to explore this technical phenomenon further, I soon realized that the various RSI readings could be differentiated in much the same manner as harmonic patterns. I was able to define different types of extreme RSI readings and categorize these structures accordingly. This experimentation yielded significant technical information and helped to validate harmonic setups immensely.

RSI + BAMM = RSI BAMM

When applied to indicator readings, the BAMM concept differentiated various structures, especially in the extreme overbought and oversold RSI zones. The differentiated RSI readings at the completion of distinct harmonic patterns confirmed reversals and the overall validity of the setup in an unprecedented manner.

Although the BAMM principles could be applied to many technical studies, Relative Strength readings formed more distinct structures than any other indicator and provided the most reliable information in these divergent situations. As I continued to investigate the effectiveness of this strategy, one divergent technical situation, in particular, that I discovered worked unbelievably well within the Harmonic Trading approach.

RSI BAMM

The RSI BAMM is a method that examines the state of the indicator before considering the structure of the price action. As is the case with harmonic patterns, the RSI BAMM requires specific conditions to be met to validate a trade opportunity. Regardless of the extent of any price move or the structure that it forms, the RSI BAMM requires that a mandatory reading in the extreme overbought or oversold area occur to initiate the setup.

This condition creates an inherent problem within the Harmonic Trading approach, since the setup is dependent upon the RSI reading and not the price structure. For example, there are many instances where an extended predominant trend will seem to go on forever. Price action that enjoys a rally for quite some time may seem to never stop. Frequently, such well-established trends trade quite nicely within an upward sloping range and seem to be invincible. These situations can lull a trader into a complacent mindset, believing that the rally will last forever. However, the RSI reading can paint a different picture by assessing the relative extent of the price action. In other words, the RSI reading can indicate the degree of buying that has occurred. Although the RSI is an early signal, an extreme reading can serve as a potential warning sign of an impending reversal. When compared to the price action, clear areas of divergence can be defined.

I would like to take a moment and comment on a common misconception regarding indicators as a stand-alone technique for trading the markets. Many critics in the past have argued against the effectiveness of the RSI to be a reliable market signal. Some have argued that RSI does not possess credible technical information due to the fact that price action does not follow any consistent and predictable pattern following an extreme reading. Such universal application is not realistic, as anyone who really understands Technical Analysis knows this is not the proper analysis of such measures. All methods must be compared, contrasted, and analyzed with other approaches to determine the aggregate information provided from the price action. Whether to use trend lines, Stochastics, Candlestick reversal patterns, or any other method, it is imperative to have confirmation of multiple approaches to yield the most pertinent information for the best technical decision regarding any trade. In fact, in his book *New Concepts*, Wilder emphasized the importance of divergence:

> ***"The Relative Strength Index, used in conjunction with a bar chart, can provide a new dimension of interpretation for the chart reader. No single tool, method, or system is going to produce the right answers 100% of the time. A successful trader utilizes several different kinds of input into his decisions."***
>
> (*New Concepts in Technical Trading Systems* [Greensboro, NC: Trend Research, 1978], 70).

A Unique Technical Situation

Although the RSI BAMM involves many steps to validate this technical phenomenon and it might seem complex first, it is important to understand that this is truly a *unique technical situation*. The RSI BAMM is an advanced divergent condition where the RSI readings and harmonic pattern completions define extremely accurate technical levels and decipher the predominant trend in an unprecedented fashion. Although this advanced application of the basic tool that Welles Wilder developed decades ago does not appear in every market all of the time, when these conditions are present, the RSI BAMM is extremely accurate in defining precise levels of harmonic support and resistance. Furthermore, this technique quantifies the "indicative characteristic" of divergence in a manner that I believe even Wilder would find interesting.

I have accumulated a great deal of research on the various applications of the RSI. Starting with Wilder's original work and examining a variety of other material, I believe that the RSI BAMM is an unprecedented application of this technical tool. Although many of the strategies do include some of the simple concepts involved within the Wilder's original application—such as divergence, confirmation, and basic measurement techniques—the advanced application of the RSI with harmonic patterns represents uncharted territory for the Harmonic Trading approach, and for that matter, Technical Analysis.

The simple integration of the RSI represents a dramatic shift in the Harmonic Trading approach. Although the RSI BAMM may seem to stray from the principles of this methodology, the integration of the RSI adheres to the basic tenets of the Harmonic Trading approach. Fibonacci measurement techniques and pattern recognition strategies are still the primary basis that differentiate each situation and define the potential opportunity. I suggest to thoroughly study all aspects of this new strategy before attempting to implement it into real trading situations. Although the RSI BAMM requires many technical conditions to be met, pattern completions within this framework provide the significant trade signals and accurate evidence of the probable future price action well in advance.

Bullish RSI BAMM

The Bullish RSI BAMM begins with a complex reading in an oversold area under the 30 limit. Referring to the RSI BAMM illustration in Figure 6.1, the entire process requires several elements to validate this specific scenario. In much the same manner that the initial rules of harmonic pattern identification and differentiation may have seemed overwhelming, the RSI BAMM rules—albeit a bit complex upon first study—provide a coherent and comprehensive method for accurately measuring potential areas of divergence.

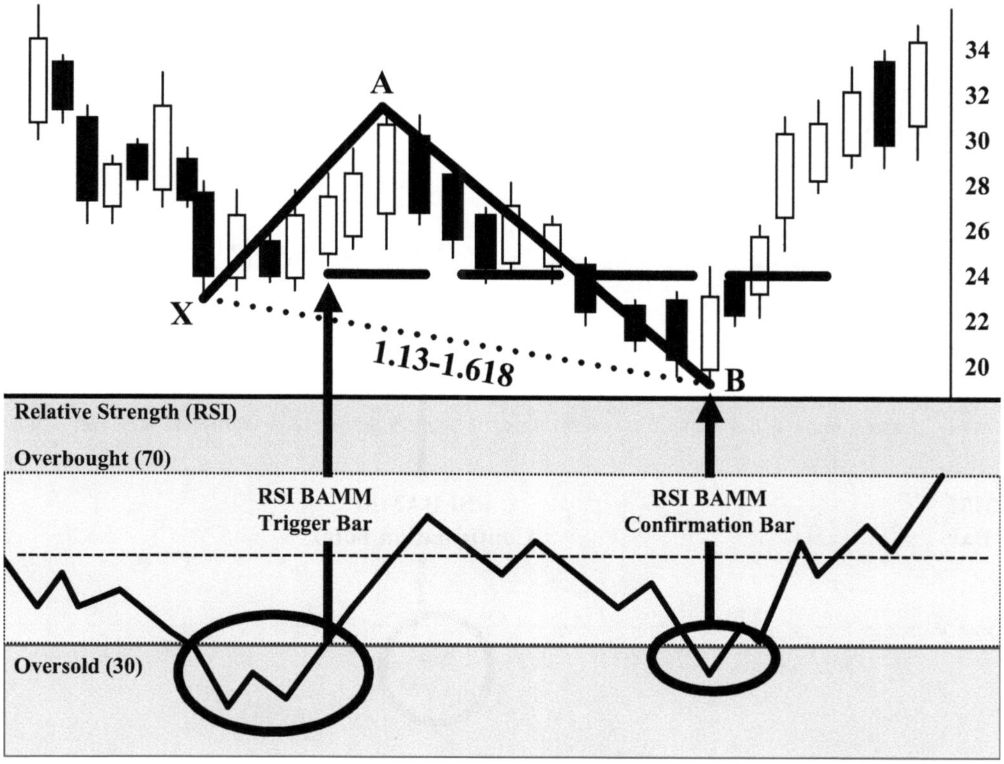

Figure 6.1

Obviously, the ideal situation does not occur every time. It is important to remember that the real application of the RSI BAMM principles requires a degree of flexibility. However, the ideal model does present all of the critical elements that clearly explain the effectiveness of this strategy. Furthermore, it is essential to maintain the patience to execute only those trades that possess all required elements that validate a trade signal based upon the rules of the Bullish RSI BAMM setup.

Despite its initial complexity, the RSI BAMM strategy in combination with harmonic patterns effectively validates PRZs and offers an enhanced level of precision and accuracy.

Chevron-Texaco (CVX): Daily Bullish RSI BAMM

The example of Chevron-Texaco in Figure 6.2 shows an excellent RSI BAMM setup on the daily chart. Figure 6.2 does not display all of the critical details of the RSI BAMM; rather, the Chevron-Texaco chart manifests all of the basic elements to validate this setup.

Figure 6.2

This example of Chevron Texaco shows a distinct RSI BAMM setup. The initial complex RSI formation established the beginning of the entire process, and the indicator completed the necessary steps to validate the setup. Although I will outline the advanced concepts later in this chapter, it is important to review this chart carefully because it truly exemplifies all of the ideal elements of the RSI BAMM.

Step 1: Initial RSI Test of Extreme Bullish Limit

In the Bullish RSI BAMM scenario, the first step is to identify price action that possesses an RSI reading in the extreme oversold zone below 30. As I mentioned previously, it is important to note that the 30 level for the oversold limit, as well as the 70 level to define the overbought area, were first outlined by Welles Wilder in his book *New Concepts and Trading Systems*. In addition, a 14-period average is calculated from his approach. Although this system utilizes the standard RSI measures, the indicator can be refined to utilize other levels and time periods to define the extreme Relative Strength levels. I leave that to you to research. I have experimented with other periods, and these results have yielded excellent confirmation signals. In general, the standard parameters above a 70 reading as overbought and below the 30 limit as oversold with a 14-period average serve as the best guidelines for the entire RSI BAMM approach. Besides, who am I to disagree with Welles Wilder?

Step 2: Complete a Bullish W-Type Complex RSI Structure

One of the reasons why the RSI BAMM is so effective is because it requires that the entire structure of the indicator form below the oversold 30 level before a trade signal can be generated. This is advantageous because the RSI structure can be distinguished while still allowing for enough time for the price action to set up correctly to validate the entire technique. The initial focus should be on the formation of the indicator reading in the entire extreme range rather than looking for a specific numeric level.

This is a mandatory requirement of the RSI BAMM, where all points of the W-type formation must take place below the 30 level. It is important to remember that this is an early signal, and the price action quite frequently will continue in the predominant downtrend after the W-type structure has formed. But, this marks the initial stage of the divergence setup, where the price action continues lower, while the RSI stabilizes and begins to move higher. However, due to the variety of indicator structures that form in the oversold area, it is important to differentiate the two types that form at RSI extreme levels.

Two Types of Bullish Indicator Structures

There are two general classes of W-type indicator structures that test the extreme oversold level—impulsive and complex. Most bullish indicator readings that are below 30 will be impulsive in nature and will not yield the required structure to be considered a valid RSI BAMM setup. However, valid complex structures that are correctly identified offer a tremendous technical advantage because they are particularly unique and represent a vital potential reversal area within the overall trend of the price action. The primary focus of the initial step is to identify a complex RSI W-type structure in the extreme oversold area under the 30-limit.

Bullish Impulsive Indicator Structures

A bullish impulsive indicator structure reflects price action that is experiencing a quick test of the extreme oversold support area, and it can typically reverse quickly without any consolidating price action (see Figure 6.3). Since the price action commonly reverses sharply in these cases, the indicator reading rallies above the extreme limit above 30 typically within 1 or 2 price bars of the initial test.

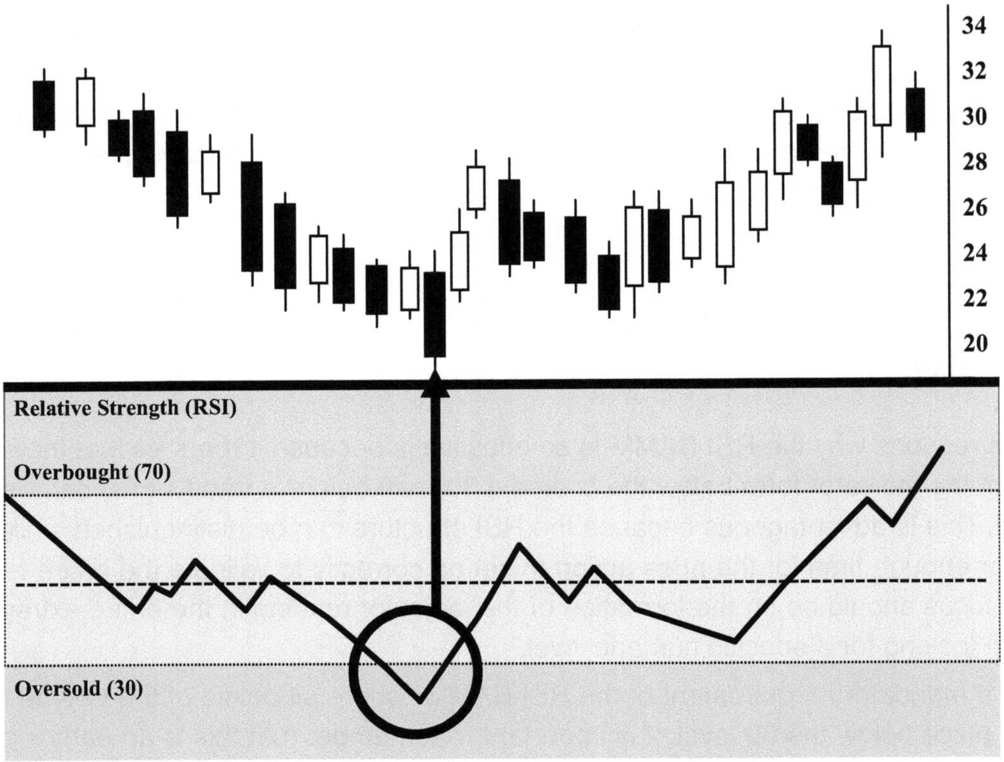

Figure 6.3

Although such impulsive formations may test the extreme bullish RSI level, it is important to focus on the nature of the indicator structure and not necessarily the exact numeric reading (as long as it is below the 30 limit). The exact indicator level is important in quantifying the extreme state of RSI, but the general indicator formation is the critical factor that serves as the essential trigger to validate a potential trade opportunity.

Chevron-Texaco (CVX): Daily Bullish Impulse Indicator Structure

In this example, Chevron-Texaco possessed an ideal impulsive structure (see Figure 6.4). It is important to note the sharp nature of the test of the extreme oversold area, as both the price action and the RSI reading reversed immediately after sinking below the 30 level.

Figure 6.4

Impulsive structures like these can be effective technical measures as they serve to confirm bullish patterns and other trading signals. However, it is important to note that the signals generated from extreme RSI readings do not constitute a comprehensive approach to trading the market. As I mentioned previously, I believe this is a common misconception in the application of the Relative Strength measure, and for that matter, most other technical indicators and oscillators. In my opinion, such technical measures must be utilized as a complementary methodology rather than as an exclusive approach. A Relative Strength reading below the 30 limit does not automatically signify a trade opportunity. In fact, certain extreme impulse structures can signal significant continuations of the predominant trend. These strategies will be covered later in the book. For now, it is important to keep in mind the two different types of structures. Furthermore, as is the case with all technical indicators, other methods must be employed to validate any potential trade opportunity on a multiple confirmation basis.

Bullish Complex Indicator Structure

A complex structure represents an indicator formation that initially exceeds the 30 level and forms a W-type pattern entirely in the extreme area, as illustrated in Figure 6.5. The complex structure typically remains below the oversold 30 limit longer than an impulsive formation.

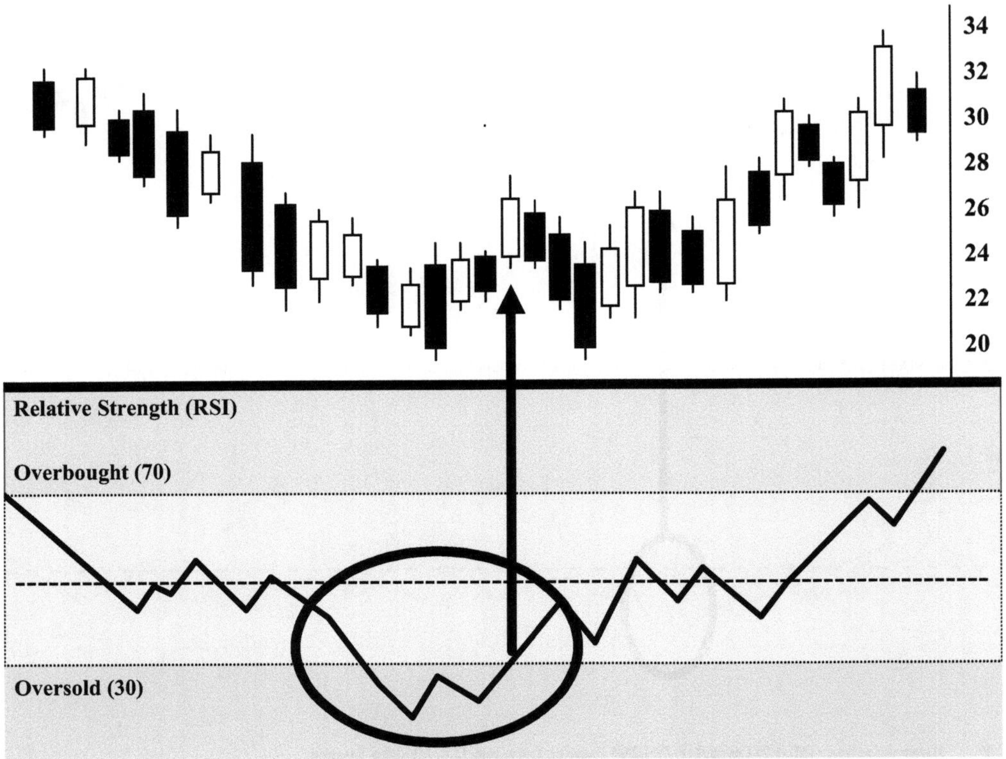

Figure 6.5

Despite representing a more significant technical condition than an impulsive formation, the bullish complex structure is usually an early trading signal. In fact, it is common for price action to continue to decline sharply in price, while the complex RSI structure is developing in the oversold range under the 30 limit. Although the advanced concepts will be clearly presented later in this chapter, it is important to keep in mind that a complex indicator reading is merely the starting point for the entire approach, not the defining event of the methodology. Furthermore, the complex formation establishes the beginning of the most critical aspect of the entire RSI BAMM methodology—divergence.

Chevron-Texaco (CVX): Daily Bullish Complex Indicator Structure

The chart in Figure 6.6 shows an excellent complex RSI structure, as the stock formed a distinct W-type pattern in the extreme oversold area under the 30 level.

Figure 6.6

It is important to note that the critical divergence stage begins after the completion of the complex Relative Strength reading. After a period of consolidation, the indicator stabilizes while the price action continues to decline. Although the price action may seem to be maintaining its current downtrend, valid complex bullish RSI structures usually trigger a reversal sooner rather later. However, these structures mark critical support levels well before a potential change in the overall direction, but this situation typically requires a secondary retest before completing the reversal.

Although a few other elements must fall into place for the Bullish RSI BAMM to be validated, the formation of a complex RSI structure triggers the starting point for the entire process. Again, this is an early signal, and it is critical to wait for the W-type structure to break above the

30 line to confirm its completion. After the complex RSI structure has been established, the other considerations of potential pattern completions and specific RSI BAMM harmonic measurements can be projected to determine the optimal reversal area. This leads us to our next step, which includes defining and measuring the price level that triggers this breakdown.

Step 3: Define the RSI Trigger Bar

After defining the complex RSI formation, the next step requires a measurement of the price area where the W-type indicator structure has completed. The price bar that causes the bullish complex RSI indicator reading to complete and to rally above the oversold 30-limit is known as the *RSI BAMM Trigger Bar*.

After identifying the RSI BAMM Trigger Bar, it is critical to mark the bottom of this price bar by drawing an extended line from the low, projecting the minimum RSI BAMM support level to the right of the chart (as is illustrated in Figure 6.7). This RSI BAMM Trigger Bar support line serves as a minimum technical level for the corresponding retest and the anticipated execution area of the completion of the final phase of the RSI BAMM.

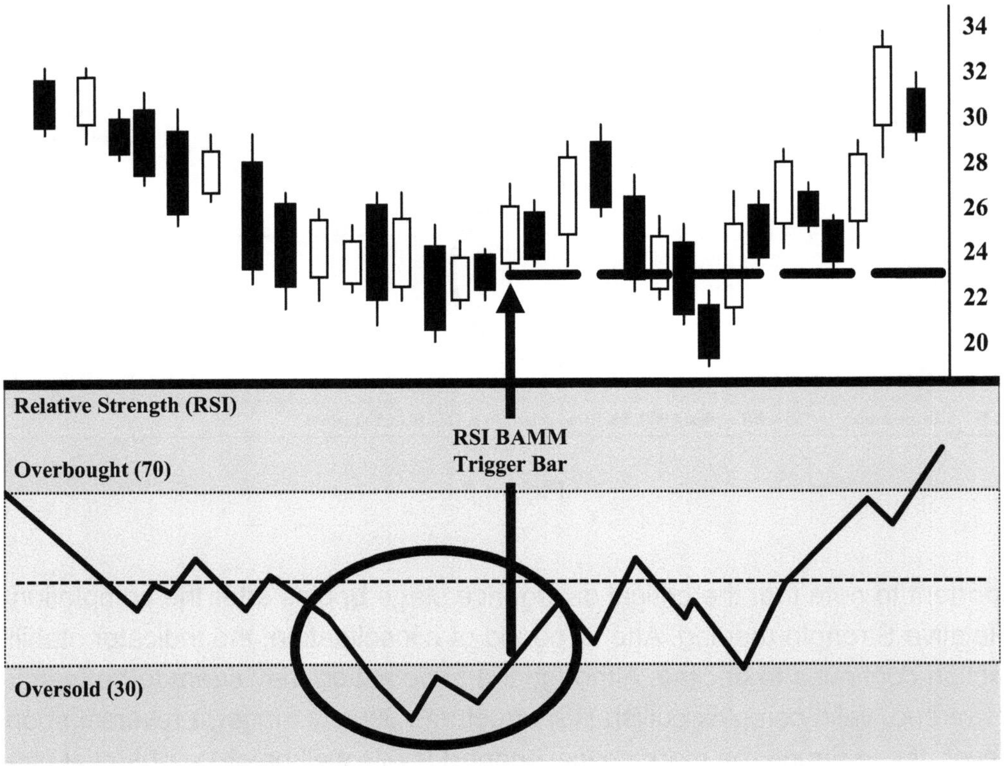

Figure 6.7

Chevron-Texaco (CVX): Daily RSI BAMM Trigger Bar

From a general perspective, the trigger bar as defined by the completion of the complex RSI structure denotes the starting point for the critical divergence phase that the entire methodology is attempting to define and quantify (see Figure 6.8).

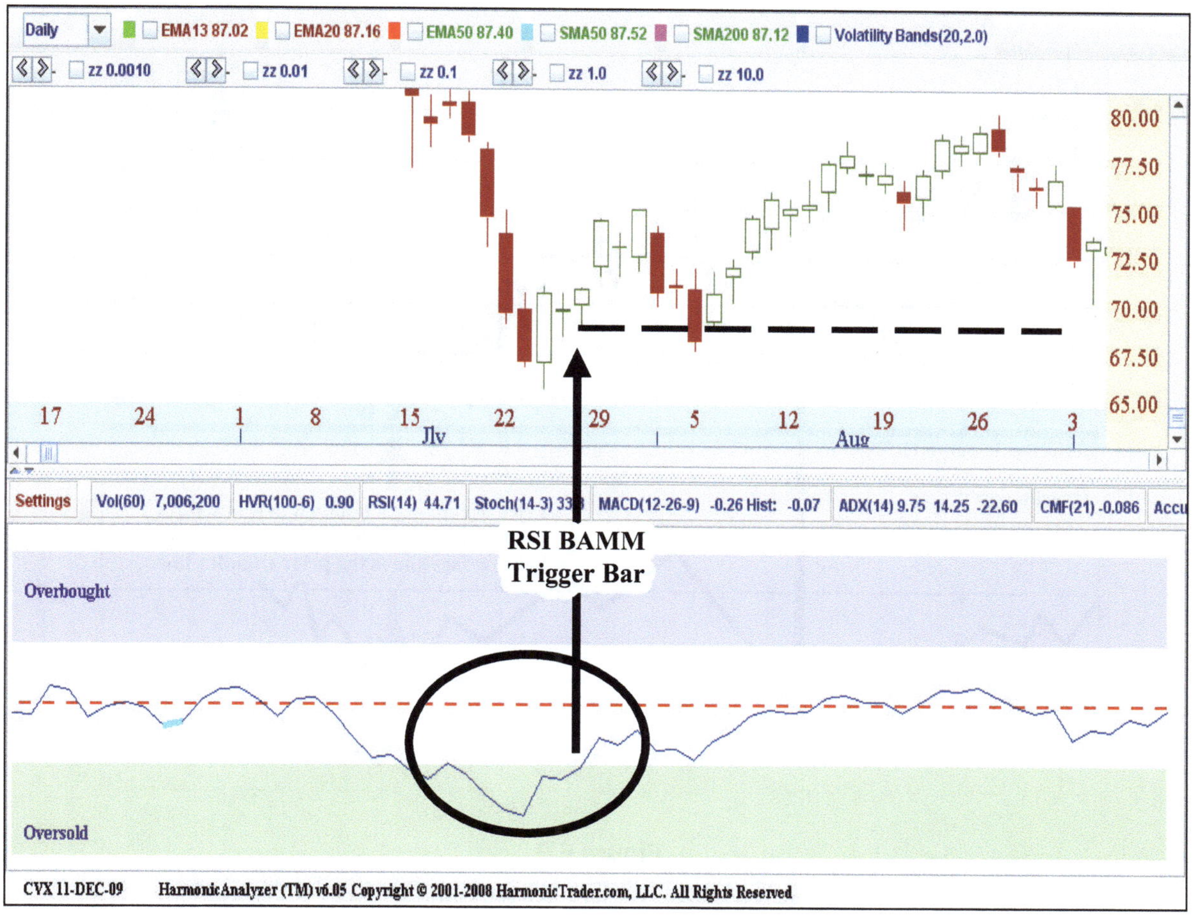

Figure 6.8

From a broader perspective, the RSI Trigger Bar can reveal a great deal about the validity of the setup and the state of the potential price action. For now, the most critical element of the RSI BAMM approach begins after the indicator has reversed from the oversold area by completing a complex W-type structure.

The position of the Bullish RSI BAMM Trigger Bar in relation to the prior extreme low point is critical. Although its significance will be further explained later in this section, it is important to remember that the Bullish RSI BAMM Trigger Bar typically will be the price bar that is the exact prior low of the current move or within a few intervals of the extreme low. The trigger bar is critical because it marks the completion point of the complex RSI structure. In essence, it is the price bar that completed the W-type structure and rallied the indicator reading above the oversold 30 level to generate a significant technical signal.

Step 4: Reaction of RSI and Price

After the initial pop following the completion of the complex RSI structure, the price and indicator begin to decline in tandem (see Figure 6.9). Frequently, this initial breakdown offers a distinct trading opportunity, but these strategies will be covered a bit later in this chapter. However, the initial breakdown still requires a few elements to be satisfied to realize the completion of the RSI BAMM.

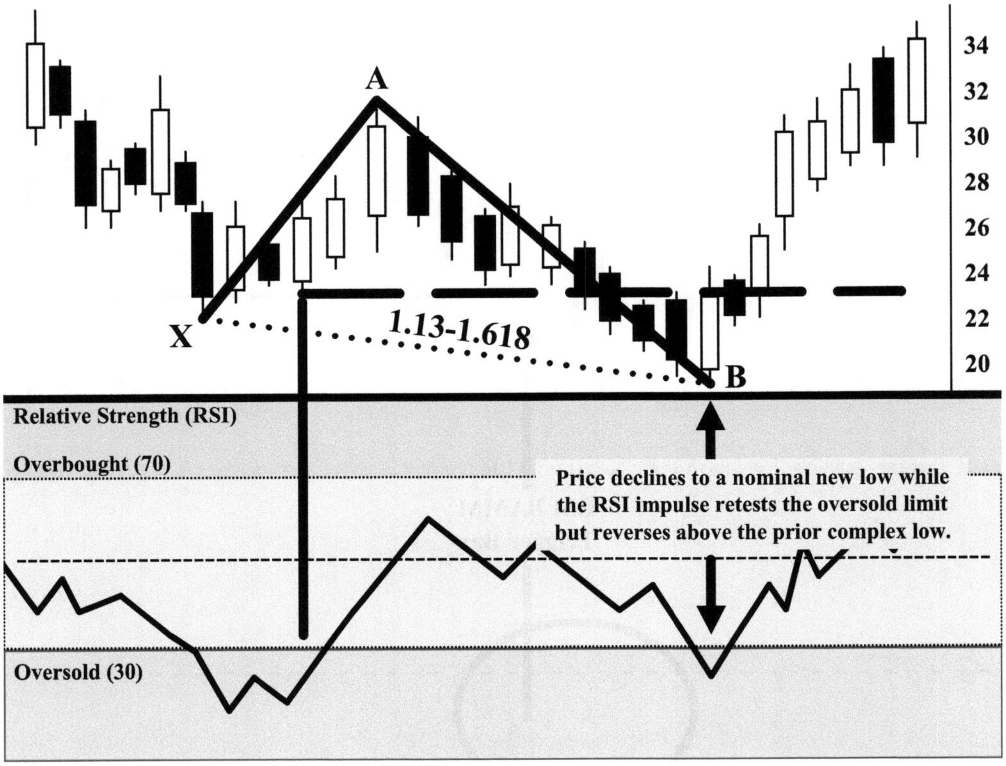

Figure 6.9

Chevron-Texaco (CVX): Daily Reaction of RSI and Price

After the RSI BAMM Trigger Bar has been established and the price action rallies following its completion, there will typically be a breakdown of this brief and sharp rally. In the case of Chevron-Texaco, the price action rallied sharply—establishing the first phase. After completing the RSI BAMM Trigger Bar, the price action and indicator reading began to roll over immediately after violating the brief yet sharp uptrend line (see Figure 6.10).

Figure 6.10

In all cases, when the price action rolls over after violating the uptrend line following the RSI BAMM Trigger Bar completion, the final phase of the entire RSI BAMM process begins. However, there is one condition for the initial reaction following the completion of the complex RSI indicator structure. This specific type of retest is a mandatory condition before the final stage of the RSI BAMM completion can be realized.

Specific Type of RSI Retest

This specific type of retest is one of the most critical aspects of the entire RSI BAMM methodology. *The RSI reading MUST retrace to at least the 50 level before the final retest can occur* (see Figure 6.11).

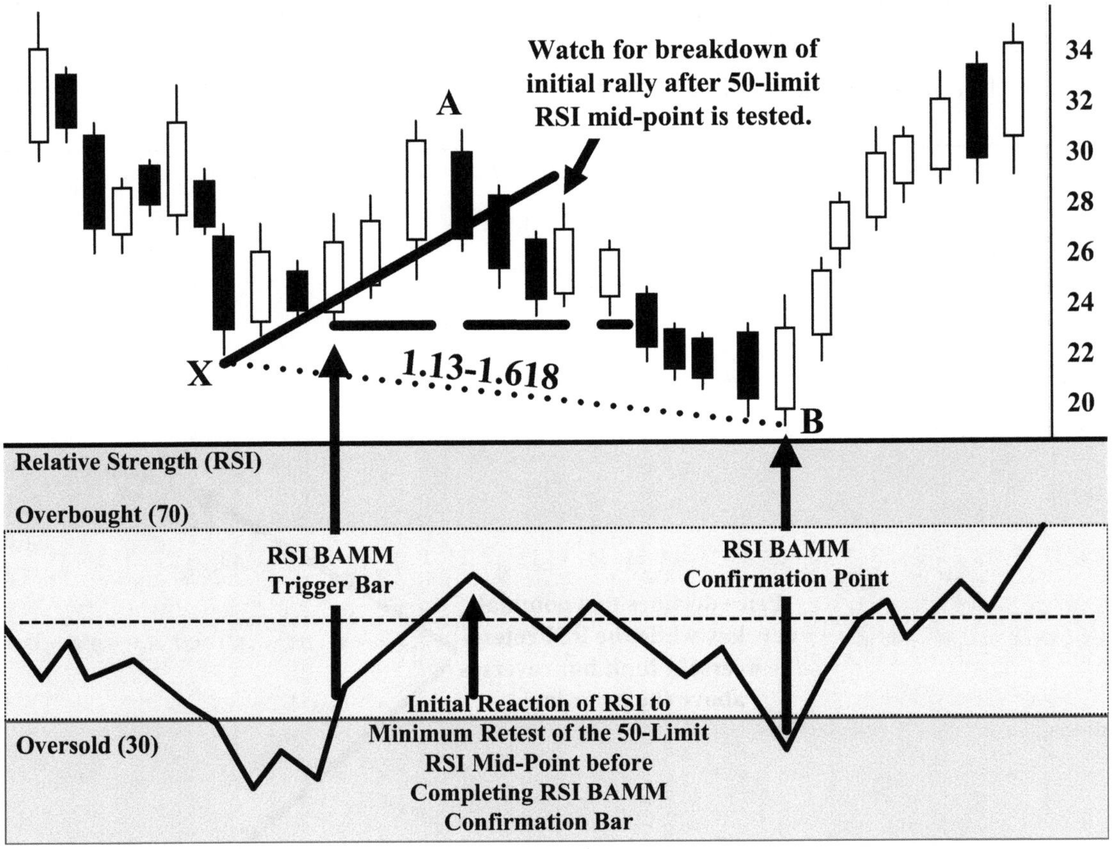

Figure 6.11

Although there is room for interpretation as the RSI reading may exceed the 50 level on this initial reaction, it serves as a minimum requirement to distinguish the most ideal situations. The mid-point retracement for the RSI reading is an important intermediate step that precedes the corresponding retest and the final phase of the RSI BAMM. This condition serves as a sufficient correction of the initial extreme RSI reading before establishing the final divergence. Let's look at the Chevron-Texaco example to illustrate this mandatory retest.

Chevron-Texaco (CVX): Daily RSI BAMM Trigger Bar

In the Chevron-Texaco example, the stock tested the minimum mid-point RSI line on the initial reaction after the completion of the complex RSI structure (see Figure 6.12). Although the stock required time to consolidate at this midpoint line before testing the Confirmation Point, the fact that it tested the mid-point line served as the minimum requirement to validate the RSI BAMM.

Figure 6.12

Again, it is important to note that the indicator reading may exceed the 50 level, but it must test this area at a minimum before completing the RSI BAMM Confirmation Point. In this example, Chevron-Texaco began to roll over after the first test of the RSI mid-point level but still required a period of time before resolving the divergent technical situation.

Step 5: The Final Phase—Divergence of RSI Versus Price

The final divergence stage begins after the RSI reading pulls back to at least the 50 mid-line. The short-term rally breaks down from the uptrend line of the initial reaction. The rollover of the initial rally leads to an eventual retest of the prior low. The price action *and* the RSI reading retest their relative prior support points in tandem. (The horizontal [dotted] line drawn from the low of the RSI Trigger Bar to the right of the chart defines the minimum resistance level for the completion of the RSI BAMM and the eventual entry of the trade [see Figure 6.13].) The important technical information of the entire approach is revealed in this retest. The best trading opportunities develop when distinct patterns complete at important retest points for the RSI. When patterns complete while the RSI stabilizes, these signs accurately validate successful reversals well in advance.

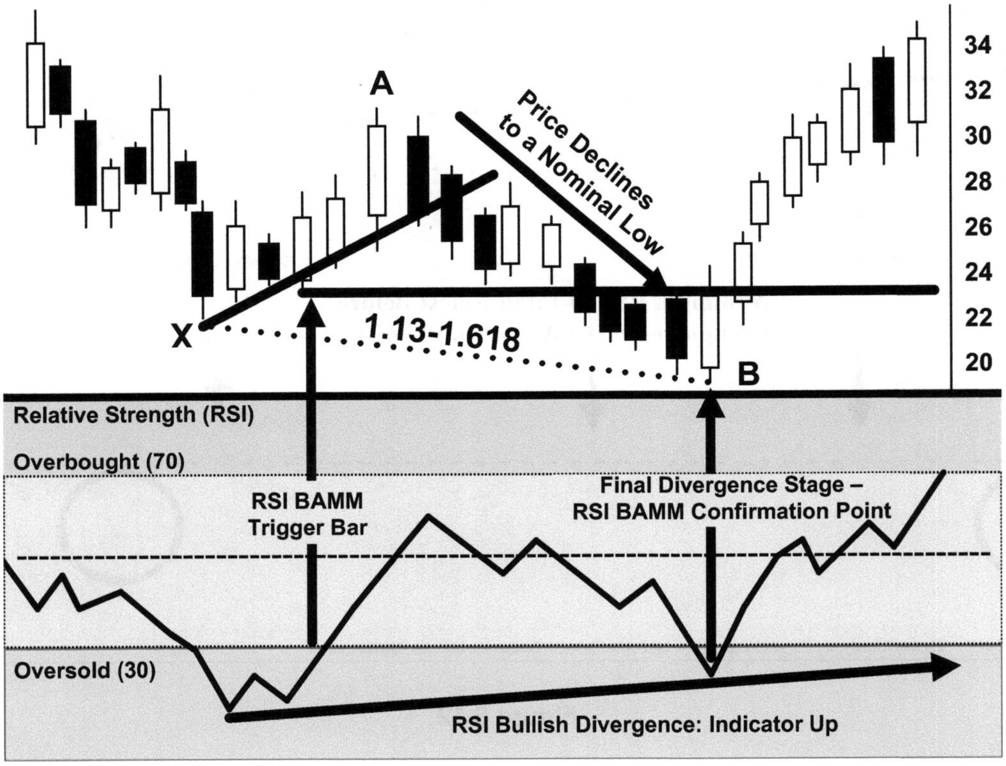

Figure 6.13

This is a situation where the Relative Strength reading is providing an early signal to the end of the predominant trend. Although this signal may be the end of the trend technically, the price action typically experiences one last decline to retest the support area, as established by the complex Bullish RSI structure. This final stage of the retest reveals a great deal about the strength of the predominant trend and the validity of the signal generated by the complex RSI structure. In essence, the price action diverges in a "last gasp" from the indicator reading.

Chevron-Texaco (CVX): Daily Divergence of RSI Versus Price

After Chevron-Texaco completed its reaction following the complex RSI BAMM structure, the final divergence stage was initiated. Clearly, the price action started to decline while the RSI reading stabilized (see Figure 6.14).

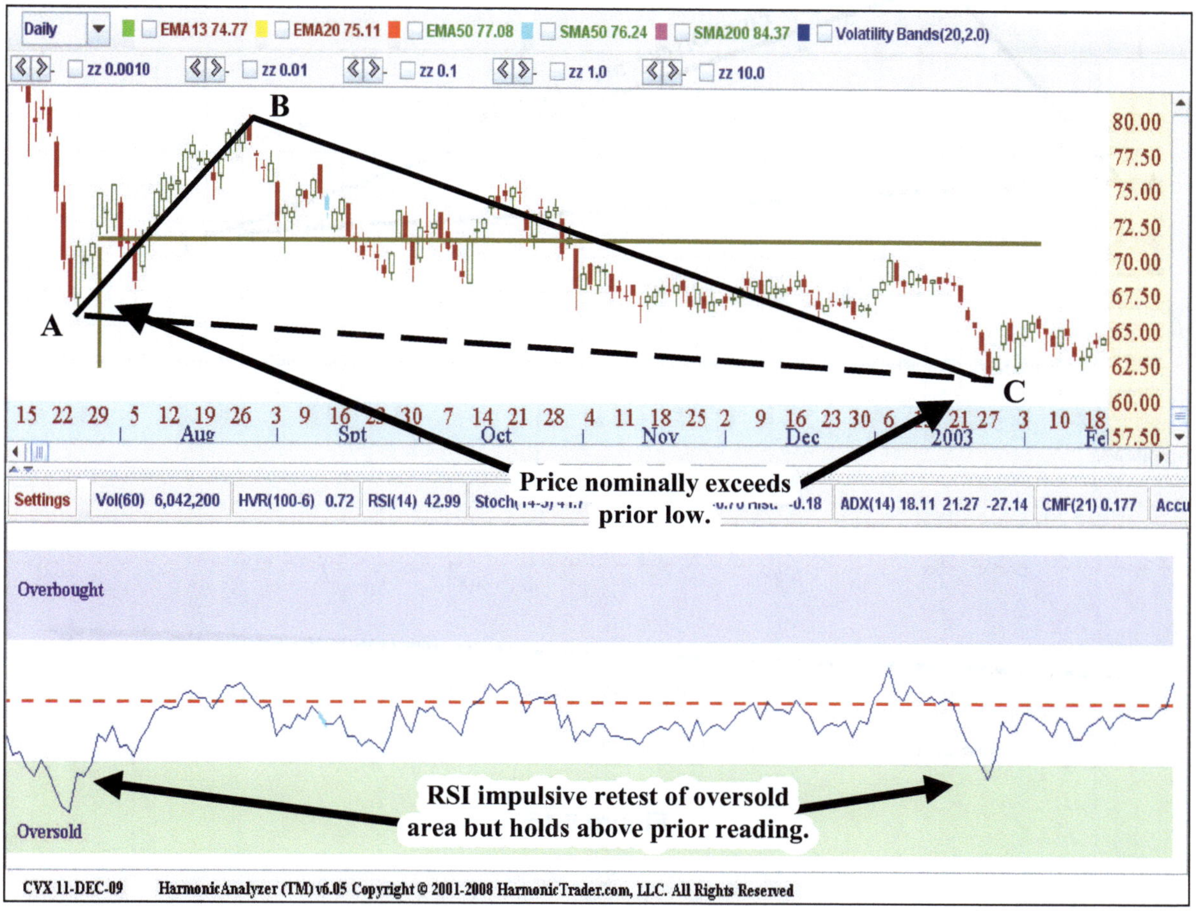

Figure 6.14

On the retest of the complex RSI structure, the ability of the indicator to test the extreme area while holding above the prior reading manifested the internal strength of this reversal zone. The price action rolled over to nominally sink below the prior low and retested the oversold area with an impulsive RSI structure.

This type of technical action is a perfect example of the RSI BAMM defining a critical divergence area. In fact, the phenomenon of this technical divergence is the most critical aspect of the entire methodology. Important clues and signals occur within this stage of the approach to validate these setups. Specifically, the price action should exceed the prior low nominally, while the RSI reverses above its prior reading and forming an impulsive retest of the oversold 30 limit. The critical point of the divergence can be seen in Figure 6.15 where the trend of the price action continues slightly lower while the trend of the RSI reading moves higher.

Figure 6.15

This final stage of the entire setup reveals the extent of divergence, where the Relative Strength reading of the trend indicates a reversal hand while the price continues to decline in a final dip. If the RSI structure is a valid support signal, typically the price action will reverse quickly after exceeding the initial prior low point. Although I will outline the advantages of utilizing Harmonic Trading techniques of pattern recognition and Fibonacci measurement strategies with the RSI BAMM Completion Point, it is important to examine this general technical phenomenon on its own.

This phase of the RSI BAMM defines the specific type of divergence that Welles Wilder described in his book *New Concepts in Technical Trading Systems*. However, the final phase of the RSI BAMM employs advanced strategies that refine this divergence to define unique and incredibly accurate trade opportunities. Specifically, pattern formations that converge with the RSI BAMM Confirmation phase offer remarkably important technical evidence of the state of the predominant trend and future probable direction.

Chevron-Texaco (CVX): Daily Bearish RSI BAMM Confirmation Bar

The enlarged chart in Figure 6.16 shows the bullish divergence between the RSI and the price. Clearly, the RSI stabilized as Chevron-Texaco declined to a nominal new low. After reversing from the RSI retest, the RSI BAMM Confirmation Point was completed and the reversal was triggered.

Figure 6.16

Step 6: Bullish RSI BAMM Confirmation Point: 1.13 Versus 1.618

In the development of the RSI BAMM, I was challenged for quite some time to discern the correct extension for the Confirmation Point. Although the difference between 1.13 and 1.618 may appear small, in real trading situations this gap frequently can be expensive. With respect to the primary tenets of Harmonic Trading and pattern identification, exact specification of technical measurement techniques is required to yield the most accurate information regarding the validity of any trading opportunity. Although these are general rules, I noticed a unique variation in the ultimate extension of the final divergence phase of the Bullish RSI BAMM.

The key factor depended upon the position of the Trigger Bar relative to the prior low. If the RSI BAMM Trigger Bar is a few price bars (typically 2–4) from the prior low, the execution of the trade will occur at the corresponding 1.13 extension. However, an RSI BAMM Trigger Bar that develops at the extreme low for the move will result in a 1.618 extension at the Confirmation Point.

As mentioned previously, the technical divergence that occurs in this step is the most important part of the entire approach because it gauges the price action at a critical "internal" point within the trend. Although the RSI BAMM structure may form in the indicator and indicate internal strength, the retest where the reading has stabilized and the price action has diverged offers an enormous amount of information regarding the technical state of the overall trend. Specifically, when the price declines below the initial low as the indicator reverses from an impulsive test of the oversold 30 limit, the Confirmation Point serves as a critical support level. Furthermore, this area validates the existence of any bullish patterns converging at either a 1.13 or a 1.618 extension. Although I will discuss the importance of pattern completions a bit later in this section, the prescribed RSI BAMM projection points define a precise technical window for a potential reversal. In combination with harmonic pattern recognition techniques, these methods complement each other immensely to pinpoint precise make-or-break technical levels. Simply stated, the key is to look for a harmonic pattern that completes in the same area and at the same time as the RSI BAMM Confirmation Bar. For now, it is important to review the basic rules for the measurement of the projected divergence—either 1.13 or 1.618—before discussing pattern completions in the final phase of the RSI BAMM.

1.13 Extension at Bullish RSI BAMM Confirmation Point

Although the general rule regarding the Confirmation Point extension differentiates the 1.13 and 1.618 ratios, the focus of the Trigger Bar should be on the extreme prior low. Essentially, if the Bullish RSI BAMM Trigger Bar is not the extreme price bar from the prior low, the 1.13 extension is utilized to quantify the minimum execution area for the trade. Typically, the RSI BAMM Trigger Bar that employs a 1.13 extension is either the third or fourth price bar from the extreme prior low. Without question, an extreme low price bar that comprises the RSI BAMM Trigger Bar will utilize a 1.618 extension. However, the 1.13 extension is merely a critical minimum price level at the RSI BAMM Confirmation Point (see Figure 6.17).

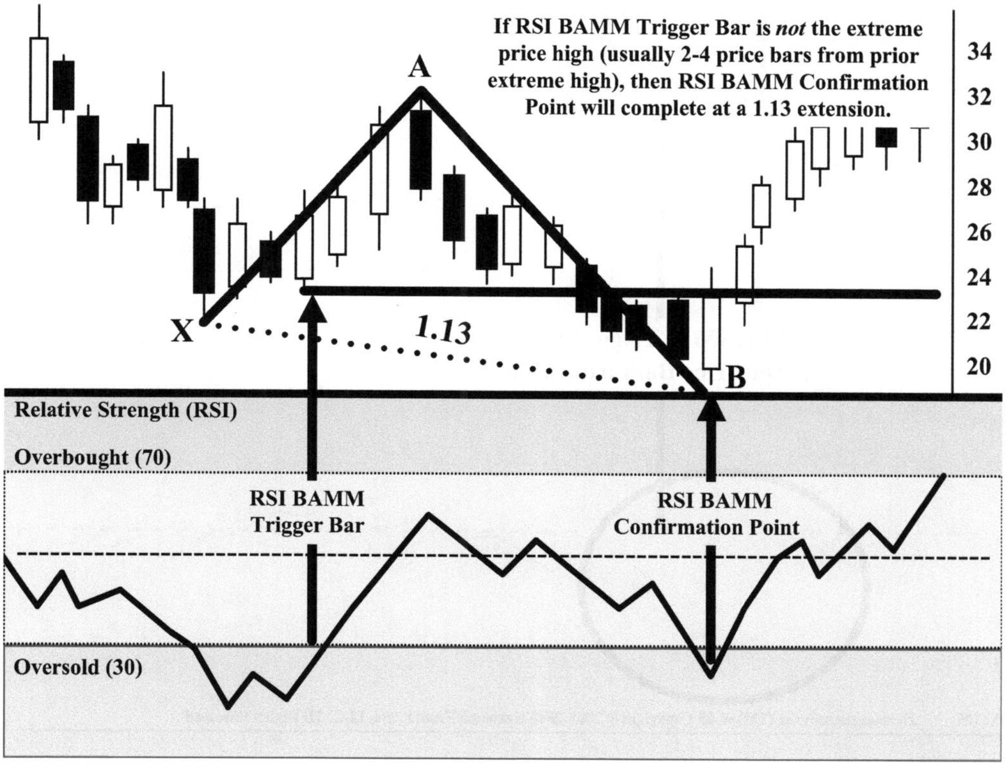

Figure 6.17

The completion of harmonic patterns may influence the ultimate execution point of the trade beyond the minimum target of the Confirmation Point in the case of a 1.13 extension. For example, a Bullish Butterfly may form in the final divergence leg and complete at a 1.27 projection, slightly past the 1.13 extension of the RSI BAMM Confirmation Point. In this situation, the completion of the harmonic pattern would be more significant and serve as the entry level for the trade. Although a test of the 1.13 extension should always be a minimum requirement for a trade to be triggered at the RSI BAMM Confirmation Point, the completion of a harmonic pattern in this area possesses greater significance and more distinct technical price levels to determine the validity of a potential trade.

Chevron-Texaco (CVX): Daily Bullish RSI BAMM Trigger Bar

In the Chevron-Texaco example shown in Figure 6.18, the RSI BAMM Trigger Bar is the third bar from the prior low. In these cases, the typical RSI BAMM Confirmation Point occurs at the 1.13 extension. Although there is room for interpretation, this example of the Chevron-Texaco shows an ideal situation.

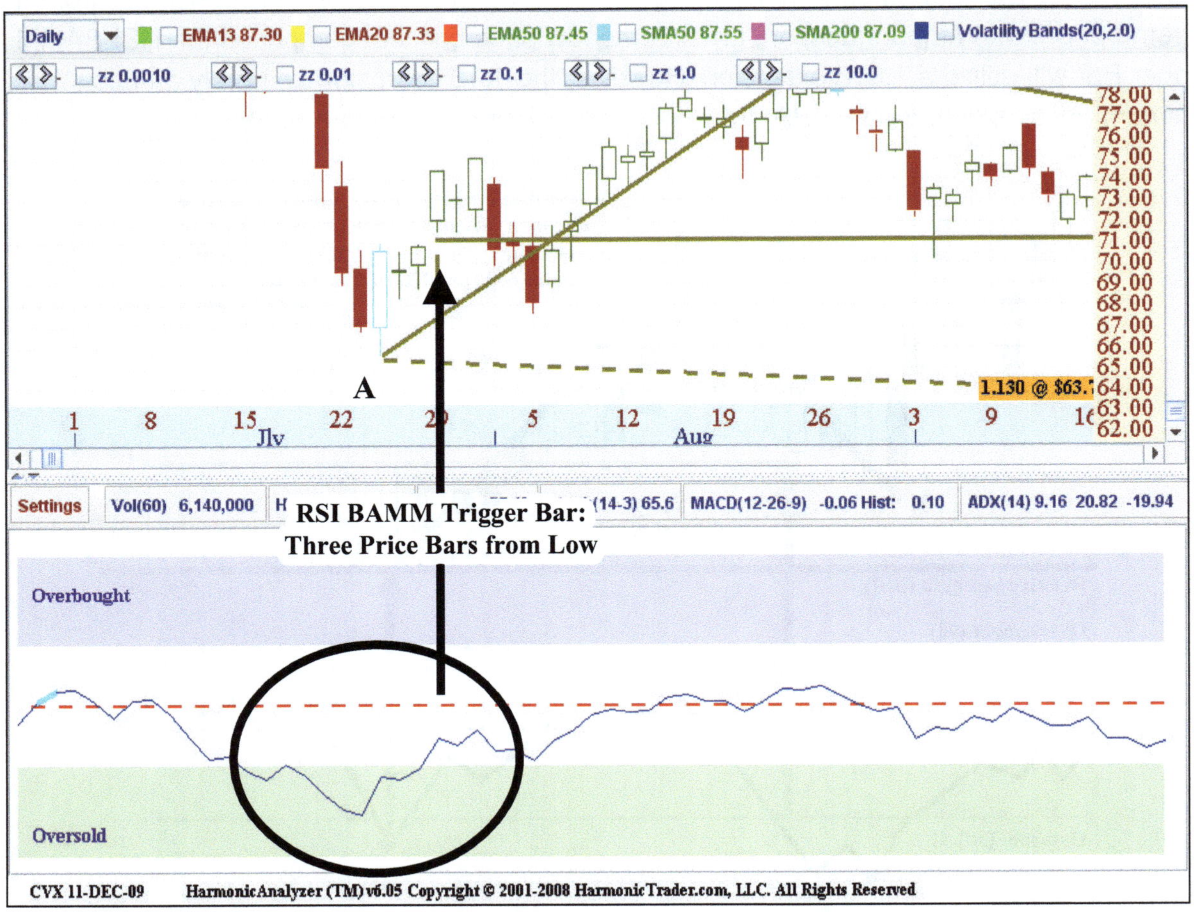

Figure 6.18

Unlike the case of the 1.618 extension, any situation that is not the extreme low will normally employ a 1.13 extension as the minimum RSI BAMM Completion Point.

Step 7: Trade Execution at the Bullish Pattern Completion and the Bullish RSI BAMM Confirmation Point

After establishing the necessary steps to define the final divergence phase of the Bullish RSI BAMM, the integration of harmonic patterns at the Confirmation Point represents the ultimate advancement of the entire Harmonic Trading methodology. Although the RSI BAMM Confirmation Point is generally differentiated by the location of the Trigger Bar as it relates to the prior low, the execution of the trade is defined by the completion of a distinct harmonic pattern in the PRZ.

The combination of these two methods in this manner yields precise levels of harmonic support and accurate entry levels for potential trades. However, there are a few important scenarios that must be regarded, as to know which patterns are to be applied to the appropriate RSI BAMM scenario. The primary focus should determine whether the RSI BAMM Confirmation Point will end at a 1.13 or a 1.618 extension.

Pattern Completion in 1.13–1.618 RSI BAMM Area

It is important to remember that the line drawn across the chart from the low point of the RSI BAMM Trigger Bar acts as a minimum support line for the entire setup. Although the two price levels of the 1.13 and the 1.618 define the entire area for the RSI BAMM, *the pattern that is completing within these constraints is the defining price range for the execution of a trade.*

The most important consideration involves the 1.13 and 1.618 RSI BAMM extensions to define which pattern is utilized at the Completion Point. If the 1.13 extension is triggered, there are several possibilities that may develop depending upon the price structure at the Completion Point. The most common and most effective pattern to define reversal points beyond the 1.13 extension is the Bullish Butterfly pattern. Although an Alternate Bat pattern is typically found completing exactly at the 1.13 extension and serves to define many excellent setups, there are other situations where a Bullish Gartley or a Bullish Bat develops to define the completion of the setup and execution of the trade. Regardless of the type, the completion of the pattern in relation to the RSI retest is the determining technical event that defines this situation.

The impulsive RSI retest must coordinate with the completion of the harmonic pattern at hand to validate the reversal. The completion of the pattern is the most important consideration in this zone, as long as the impulse RSI test has held above the prior reading's low. Although waiting for the RSI to test the overbought area may delay executions, it serves as an effective filter in the completion area of a pattern. Furthermore, this coordination represents the final point where the divergence of the RSI has completed and the price structure indicates the end of the trend.

Bullish Butterfly at 1.13 RSI BAMM Confirmation Point

In most cases, the Bullish Butterfly pattern forms at the 1.13 RSI BAMM Confirmation Point, as illustrated in Figure 6.19. Since the Bullish Butterfly employs a 1.27 XA extension, the completion of the pattern is going to be slightly below the 1.13 RSI BAMM Confirmation Point.

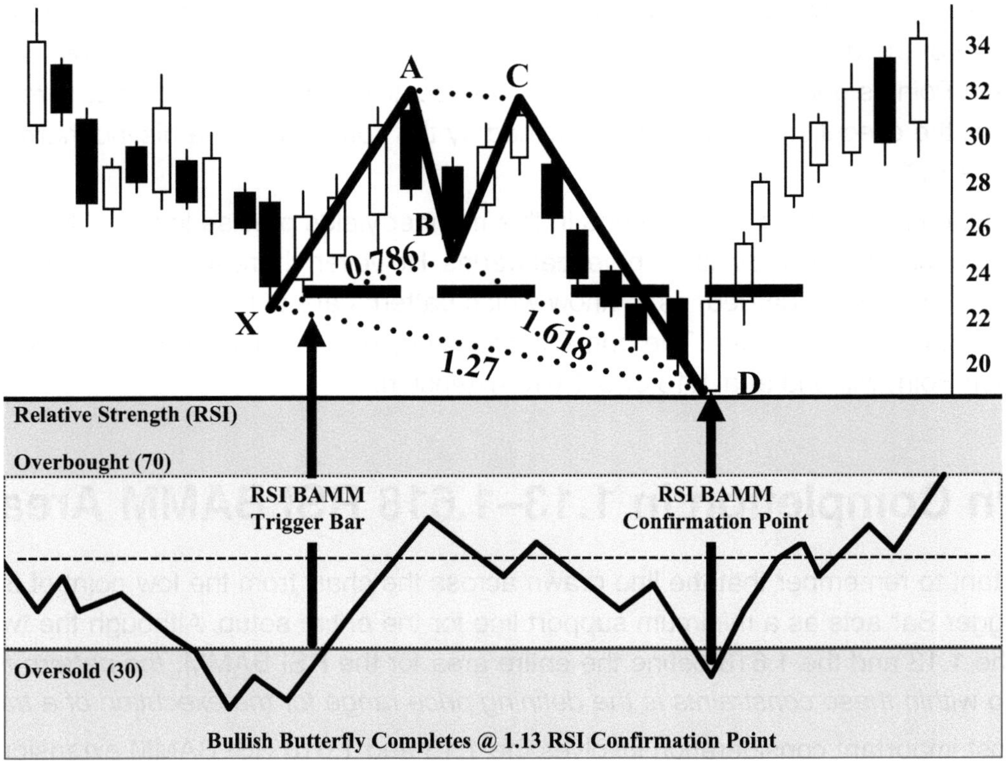

Figure 6.19

Again, the coordination of the RSI BAMM Confirmation Bar with the completion of the harmonic pattern is the special technical situation that makes this Bullish Butterfly more critical than most price structures. Essentially, the Confirmation Point represents the defining area where the overall trend bias has changed and the price is in the final stages of a complete turnaround.

Chevron-Texaco (CVX): Daily Bullish Butterfly at Bullish RSI BAMM Confirmation Point

As illustrated in the chart in Figure 6.20 of the Bullish Butterfly pattern in our Chevron-Texaco example, the stock possessed an ideal RSI BAMM setup. The completion of the pattern coincided with the RSI BAMM confirmation. As the price declined and formed the pattern structure, the secondary impulsive RSI test at the Confirmation Point reversed above the prior complex formation.

Figure 6.20

This is a fantastic example because the Bullish Butterfly pattern was such a distinct structure. The completion of the pattern marked a critical low on the daily chart, and the price action stabilized after completely testing the PRZ. The reversal turned at the completion of the pattern and the RSI BAMM, and started to rally shortly thereafter.

Chevron-Texaco (CVX): Daily Bullish Butterfly

The chart in Figure 6.21 of the Bullish Butterfly in Chevron-Texaco shows the distinct pattern that completed at the Confirmation Point (noted by the arrow). The stock reversed after completely testing the pattern's PRZ and the RSI BAMM Confirmation Point.

Figure 6.21

Although the 1.27 extension of the Butterfly pattern completed slightly below the RSI BAMM Confirmation Point, both methods identified a tight area just above $60 on the daily chart for Chevron-Texaco as a major reversal point.

Chevron-Texaco (CVX): Daily Bullish Butterfly Potential Reversal Zone (PRZ) at RSI BAMM Confirmation Point

The coordination of the pattern's completion and the RSI BAMM Confirmation Point can be seen even more clearly on this chart of the PRZ (see Figure 6.22). The price action stabilized after testing this area and reversed precisely at the completion of both the pattern and the RSI BAMM setup.

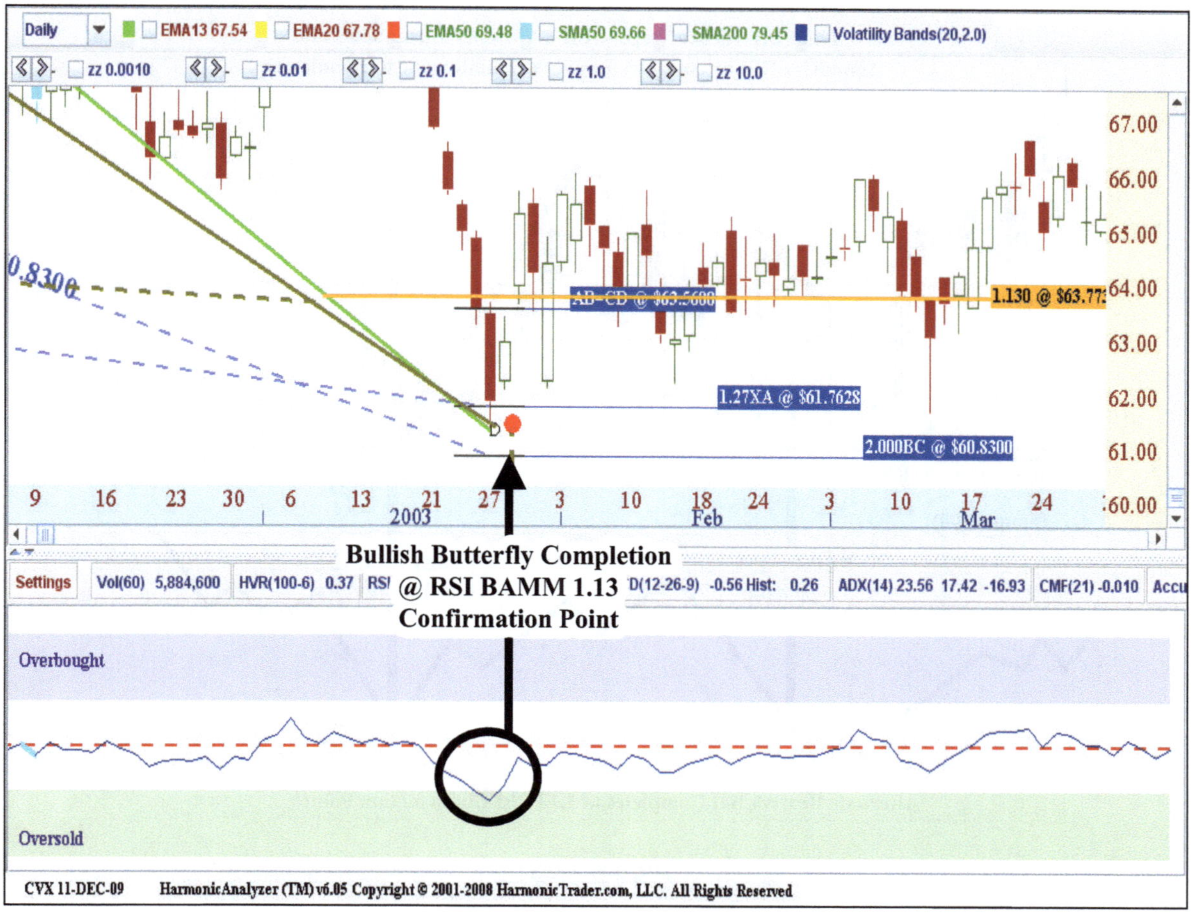

Figure 6.22

This example of Chevron-Texaco clearly shows how the technical phenomenon of the RSI and price divergence comes together at a critical point of the pattern's PRZ. The Bullish Butterfly in this example was distinct and possessed three numbers in a tight range. The ability of the stock to stabilize after testing the RSI BAMM 1.13 extension and the pattern's PRZ is the ideal type of price action in most valid reversals.

Intermediate RSI BAMM Trigger Bar Signals 1.13 Extension

The Bullish Butterfly is not the only harmonic pattern that forms at the 1.13 RSI BAMM Confirmation Point. In fact, the Alternate Bullish Bat is the most common harmonic pattern that reverses precisely at the 1.13 extension (see Figure 6.23). It's important to note that the execution of a trade from an Alternate Bat is slightly different from the standard version of the pattern. This is primarily due to the fact that the Alternate Bat's XA extension is a bit longer because of the slightly varied structure.

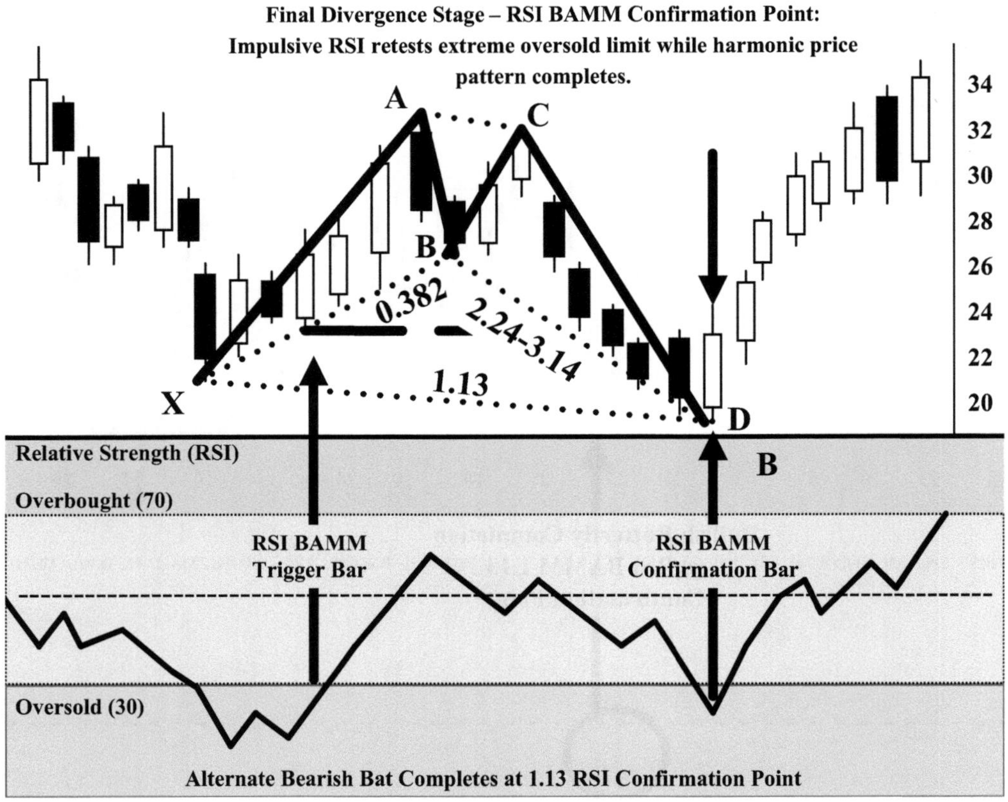

Figure 6.23

As is the case with all harmonic patterns at the RSI BAMM Confirmation Point, the coordination of the PRZ and the final impulsive indicator retest is the technical event that defines most valid reversals. In the Alternate Bat, the completion of the RSI BAMM and the ultimate execution of the trade will focus almost exclusively on the 1.13 extension at the Confirmation Point.

Standard and Poor's June 2009 Mini-Contract (ES_M9): 5-Minute Alternate Bullish Bat with Bullish RSI BAMM

The example in Figure 6.24 shows the entire Bullish RSI BAMM setup that incorporates a Alternate Bullish Bat at the Confirmation Point. Again, the trade execution at the completion of the Alternate Bullish Bat will be dictated by the price action at the 1.13 extension.

Figure 6.24

In this example, the June 2009 S&P 500 mini-contract developed a fantastic RSI BAMM that formed a distinct Alternate Bullish Bat at the RSI BAMM Confirmation Point. The price action formed all of the required elements to validate the setup.

Standard and Poor's June 2009 Mini-Contract (ES_M9): 5-Minute Alternate Bullish Bat with Bullish RSI BAMM

The pattern shown on the enlarged chart in Figure 6.25 was distinct and completed in conjunction with the RSI BAMM. In fact, the price action reversed exactly at the 1.13 extension.

Figure 6.25

This example possessed all of the ideal elements of a valid RSI BAMM. The RSI formation was nearly perfect, the pattern was distinct, and the price action reversed precisely in this projected completion area.

Pattern Completion Before 1.13 RSI BAMM Extension: Bullish Bat

Although the 1.13 RSI BAMM extension is a critical technical level in the completion of the setup, especially in the Alternate Bullish Bat, other retracement patterns such as the Bat and the Gartley frequently develop during this final phase. The dilemma arises when these retracement patterns complete simultaneously, as they successfully retest the oversold RSI 30 level triggering a valid buy signal (see Figure 6.26).

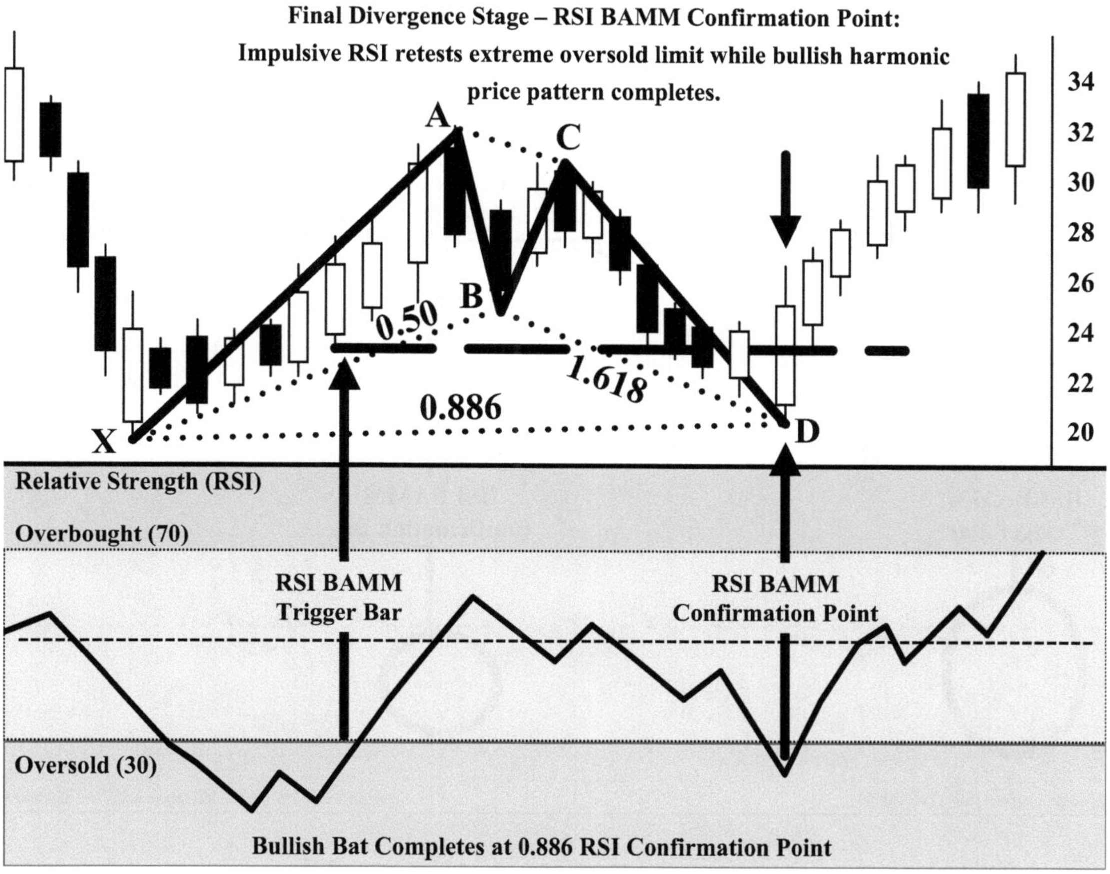

Figure 6.26

In this situation, the completion of the harmonic pattern takes precedence over the requirement of testing the 1.13 RSI BAMM extension. Although the minimum support of the low point of the RSI BAMM Trigger Bar (dotted line) offers another technical level in retracement pattern situations such as these, the price action must be distinct and reverse after testing the PRZ to validate the best trading opportunities. Furthermore, the pattern completion must coincide with a successful impulsive RSI retest. Although the 1.13 RSI BAMM extension exception makes room for retracement patterns, the coordination of the RSI and the PRZ still employs the powerful confirmation of multiple technical methods to provide greater confirmation of a valid reversal and a profitable move.

Philadelphia Semiconductor Index ($SOX): Bullish Bat

On this 5-minute chart shown in Figure 6.27, the Philadelphia Semiconductor Index ($SOX) formed a distinct the Bullish Bat that possessed ideal RSI BAMM conditions. As the $SOX entered the final phase of the RSI BAMM Confirmation Point, the price action tested the PRZ and completed the successful impulsive indicator retest.

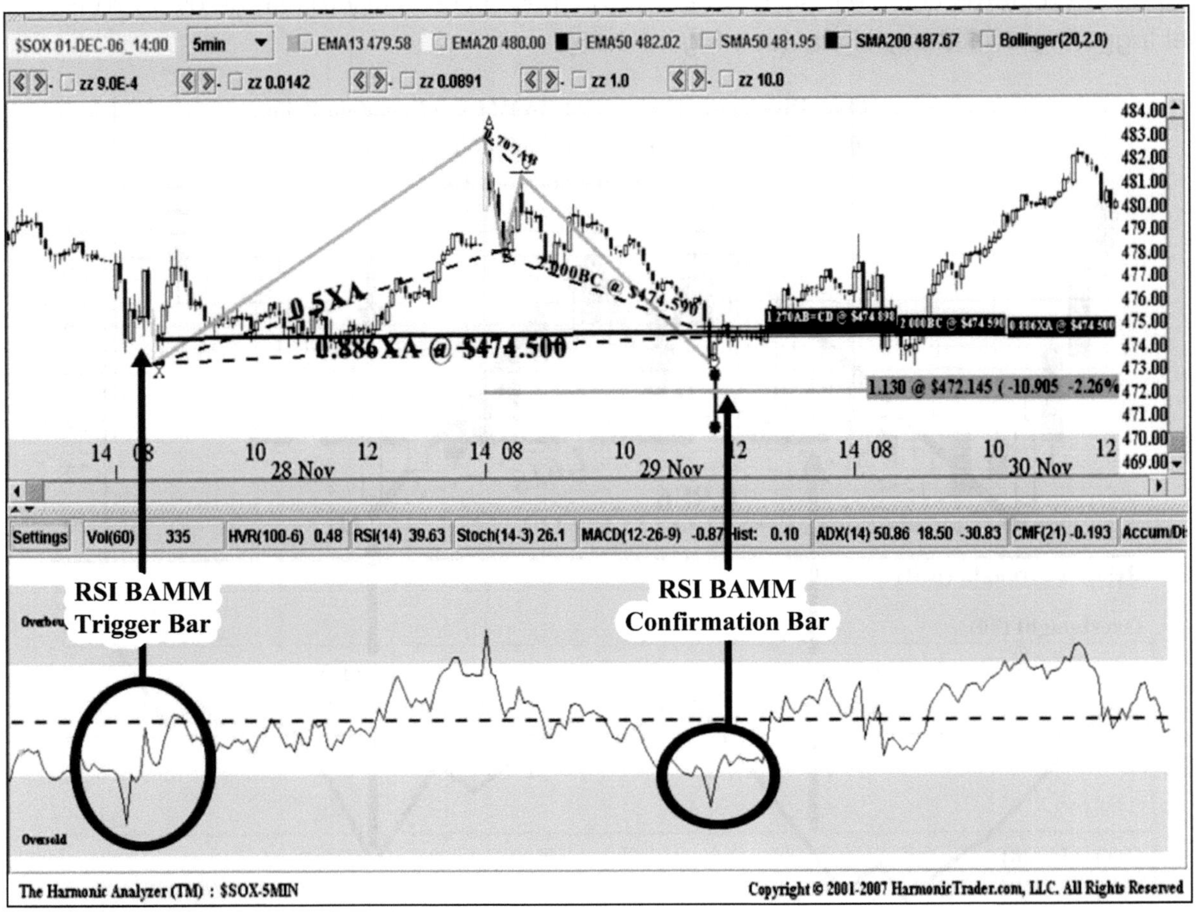

Figure 6.27

Clearly, the stock stabilized at the completion of the pattern, and the RSI was able to reverse quickly thereafter. In these cases, the impulsive RSI test will frequently be a leading signal at the completion of the pattern to indicate a valid reversal.

Philadelphia Semiconductor Index ($SOX): 5-Minute Bullish Bat Potential Reversal Zone at RSI BAMM Confirmation Point

This close-up snapshot of the PRZ and the RSI BAMM Confirmation Point in Figure 6.28 distinctly shows how the price action stabilized after completing the pattern and reversing from the impulsive indicator retest.

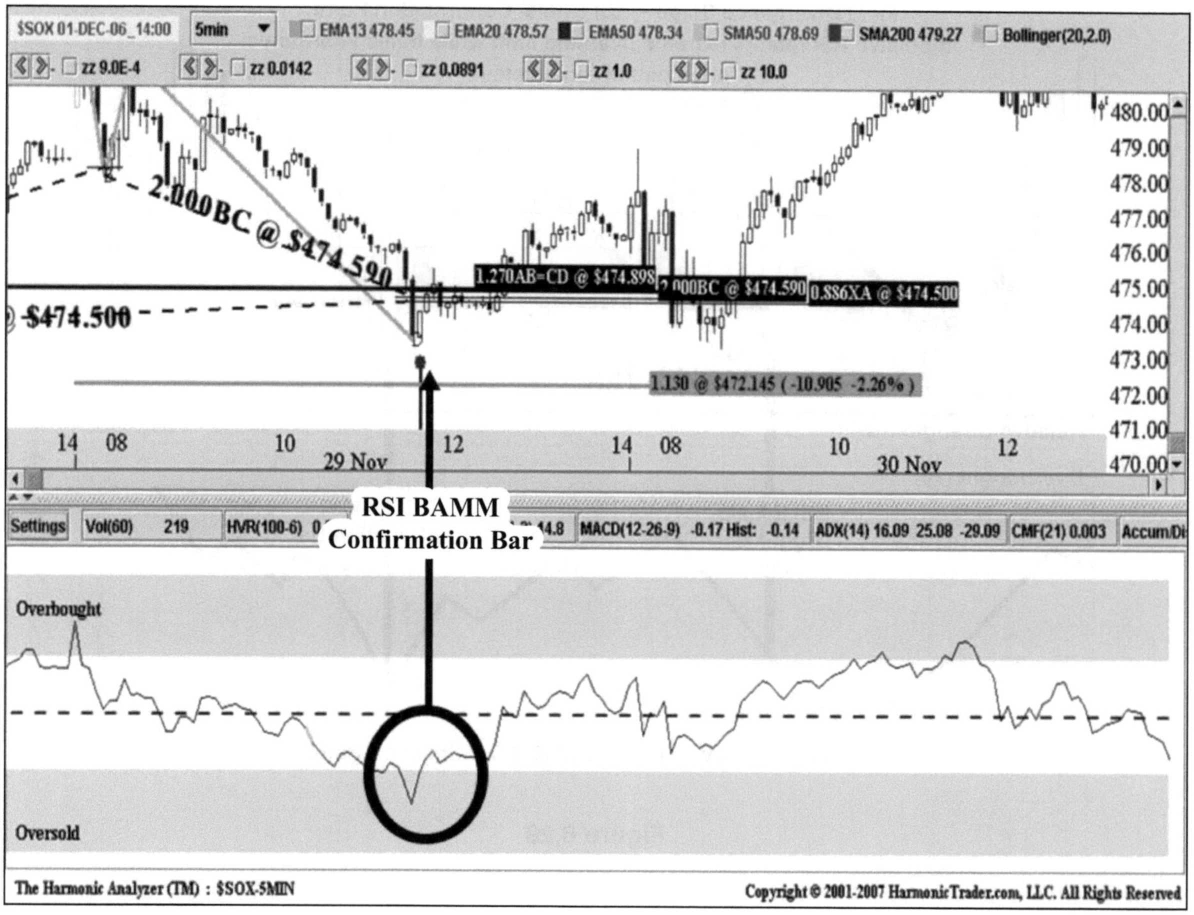

Figure 6.28

Although the 1.13 RSI BAMM extension was only a few points lower, the price action stabilized in the PRZ. This example of the $SOX clearly demonstrates the importance of focusing on the harmonic numbers after the impulsive RSI test has completed. The true advantage of this technique occurs best when the trade is executed after both conditions of the pattern completion and the RSI BAMM are satisfied.

Pattern Completion Before 1.13–1.618 RSI BAMM Area: Bullish Gartley

In the case of the Bullish Gartley, illustrated in Figure 6.29, the structure of the pattern is extremely important. Although the PRZ is typically well above the minimum 1.13 RSI BAMM extension, this situation still relies on coordinating the completion of the pattern with the final impulsive RSI retest.

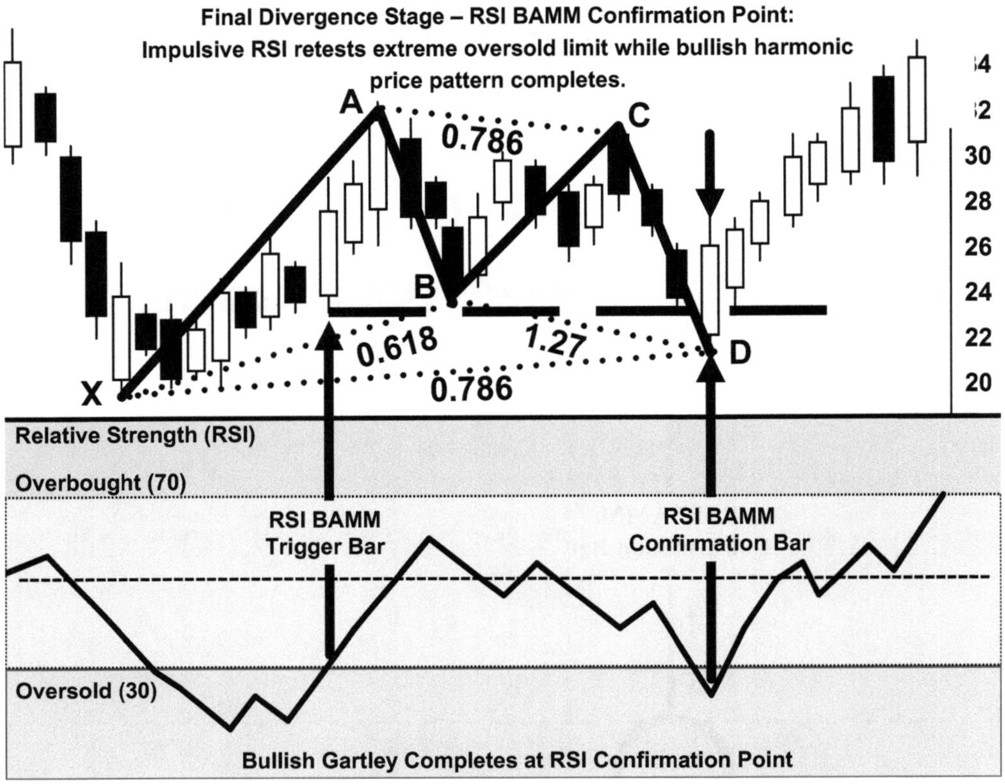

Figure 6.29

Although the Trigger Bar low point support (dotted line) complements this area, the coordination of these two technical events is critical in validating the best trade opportunities.

IBM (IBM): Weekly Bullish Gartley at RSI BAMM Confirmation Point

The fantastic Gartley pattern in IBM shown in Figure 6.30 was distinct with a precise PRZ. In addition, the RSI BAMM conditions were ideal on this weekly chart to validate the setup, as the Confirmation Point reversed in tandem with the completion of the pattern.

Figure 6.30

It is important to note that the RSI BAMM structure of both the complex and the impulsive indicator readings were exemplary. Although retracement patterns like the Bullish Gartley may be difficult to execute, the conditions of the RSI BAMM can indicate the validity of the opportunity. IBM exhibited all of the essential requirements necessary to establish the RSI BAMM setup. In combination with a distinct Bullish Gartley, this was an ideal combination of both approaches that defined a critical turning point in the price action.

IBM (IBM): Weekly
Bullish Gartley Potential Reversal Zone (PRZ) at RSI BAMM Confirmation Point

The coordination of these approaches can be seen even more clearly on the enlarged chart of the PRZ at the RSI BAMM Completion Point shown in Figure 6.31.

Figure 6.31

Retracement patterns like the Bullish Gartley can be more difficult to execute. However, the coordination of both approaches serves to filter the best opportunities and to optimize trading decisions.

Bullish 5-0 Pattern Completion at RSI BAMM Confirmation Point

The Bullish 5-0 is probably the most difficult pattern to incorporate with the RSI BAMM. This is due simply to the fact that the completion of the pattern occurs nowhere near the minimum 1.13 RSI BAMM extension (see Figure 6.32). As is the case with all harmonic patterns in the RSI BAMM setup, coordination of both approaches is still the key.

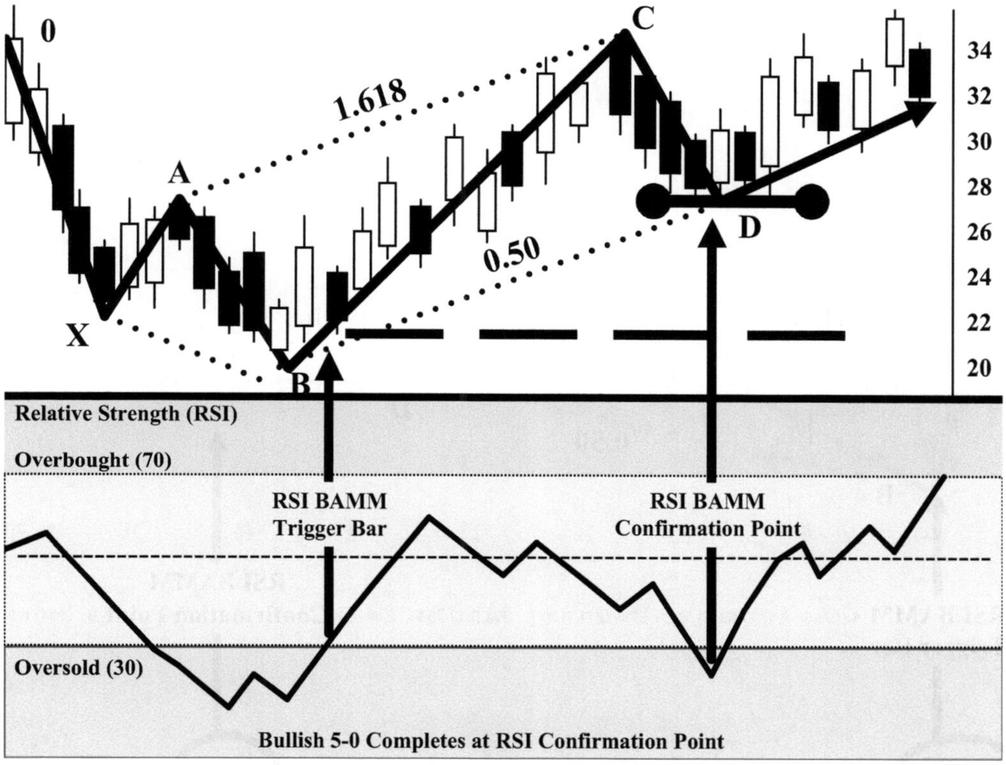

Figure 6.32

As is the case of the Bullish Gartley, the 5-0 pattern requires a distinct structure that must complete in tandem with the RSI BAMM Confirmation Point. It is important to focus on the completion of the impulsive RSI retest, as this will typically be a significant signal within the PRZ of the pattern.

British Pound (GBP_A0-FX): 5-Minute Bullish 5-0 at RSI BAMM Confirmation Point

The Pound formed a Bullish 5-0 pattern on this intra-day chart that completed at the Confirmation Point of a distinct RSI BAMM (see Figure 6.33). Although the 5-0 pattern may have seemed of little consequence after the price action declined sharply into the PRZ, the completion of the RSI BAMM Confirmation Point pinpointed the support and marked a critical short-term low.

Figure 6.33

British Pound (GBP_A0-FX): 5-Minute Bullish 5-0 Potential Reversal Zone (PRZ) at RSI BAMM Confirmation Point

The chart of the PRZ of the 5-0 pattern in Figure 6.34 shows how the price action stabilized and reversed immediately after testing the RSI BAMM Confirmation Point. The impulsive RSI retest was the ultimate trigger, as the price action rallied sharply after the indicator bounced from the 30 level.

Figure 6.34

When incorporating the 1.13 RSI BAMM extension with harmonic pattern completions, the key to successful trade executions is coordinating these two technical events to optimize trading decisions and to filter the best opportunities. In the example of the Pound, the price action provided early clues of a valid reversal as the price action held immediately after testing the entire PRZ. After covering all possible patterns that involve the 1.13 RSI BAMM Confirmation Point, it's now time to cover all possible patterns within the context of the 1.618 extension.

1.618 Extension at RSI BAMM Confirmation Point

In the Bullish RSI BAMM, the general rule for the Confirmation Point extension must focus on the location of the Trigger Bar, as it relates to the extreme prior low (see Figure 6.35). *If the Bullish RSI BAMM Trigger Bar IS the extreme low, the 1.618 extension is utilized to quantify the Confirmation Point and the execution area for the trade.*

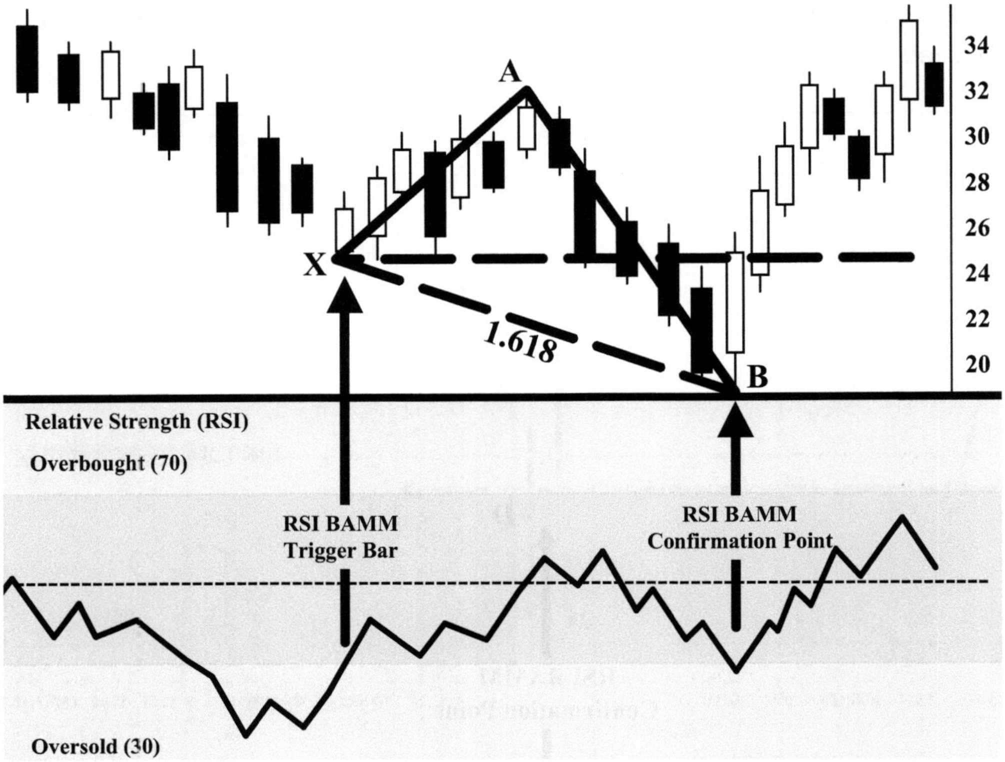

Figure 6.35

Although other factors will be considered, the importance of the extreme low to signal a 1.618 RSI BAMM extension helps to define the ultimate execution point for the trade. Two patterns—the Bullish Crab and the Deep Bullish Crab—utilize the 1.618 extension. Regardless of which Crab defines the PRZ, the crucial technical event occurs when the price action tests this area at the same time it completes the RSI BAMM Confirmation Bar.

Extreme RSI BAMM Trigger Bar Signals a 1.618 Extension: Bullish Crab

When the RSI BAMM Trigger Bar is the extreme low, the corresponding retest and the Confirmation Point will occur at the 1.618 extension (see Figure 6.36). In combination with a distinct bullish pattern such as the Crab, the 1.618 projection represents an immensely critical harmonic support point.

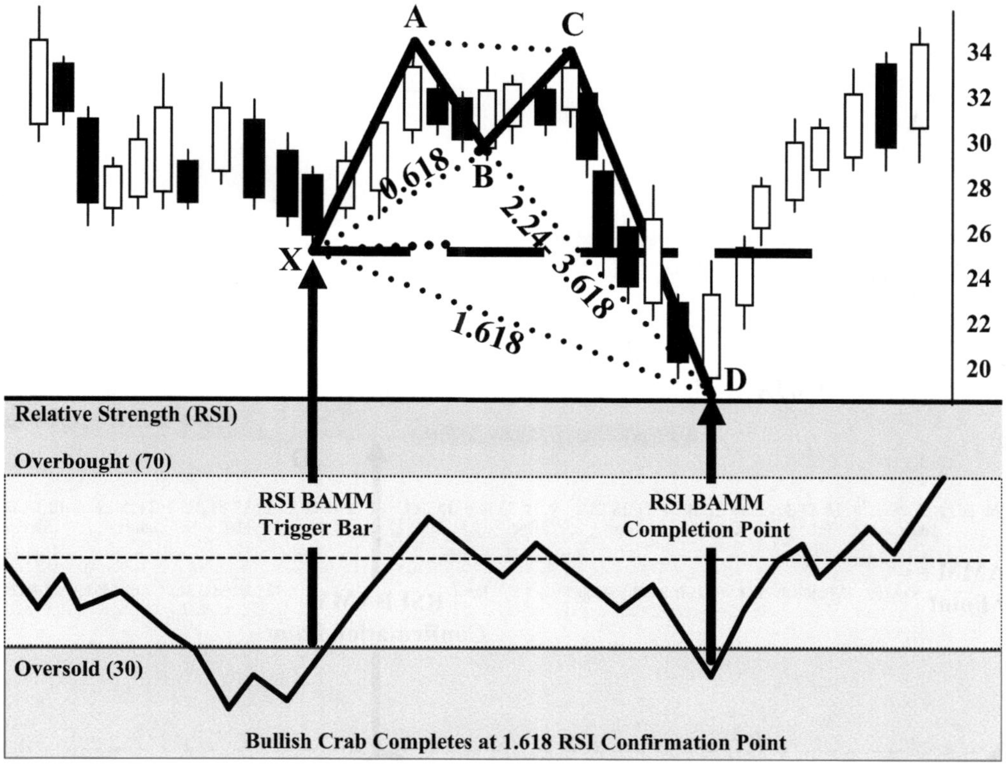

Figure 6.36

Although these situations can be difficult to distinguish, distinct pattern formations in the final phase of the RSI BAMM provide significant indication of the validity of the opportunity and act as a confirmation signal for the setup. Due to the extended nature of the 1.618 extension, the Bullish Crab will frequently possess volatile price action that can reverse sharply after testing the entire PRZ.

Coca-Cola (KO): Daily Bullish Crab at RSI BAMM Completion Point

In the example in Figure 6.37, Coca-Cola formed a distinct Bullish Crab that possessed an ideal RSI BAMM setup. The pattern started to form after the complex RSI structure was completed. After the initial bounce and retest to the RSI midpoint 50 level, the stock consolidated and eventually declined lower while forming a distinct pattern.

Figure 6.37

Although the RSI Confirmation Point experienced a deeper retest than is typical, the impulsive reading did not exceed the lowest point of the complex indicator formation. Furthermore, the PRZ accurately defined the precise area that comprised less than a 1-point range for the execution of the long position.

Coca-Cola (KO): Daily Bullish Crab Potential Reversal Zone (PRZ) at RSI BAMM Completion Point

The enlarged chart in Figure 6.38 of the PRZ at the RSI BAMM Confirmation Point shows an ideal situation where the completion of the pattern and the impulsive indicator retest combined to mark a critical turning point on this daily chart.

Figure 6.38

It is important to note that the stock did not reverse until the entire PRZ of the Bullish Crab was tested. Again, this is where the coordination of the RSI BAMM Confirmation Point at the completion of the pattern is tremendously advantageous in optimizing trade decisions and in defining the best area to execute the trade. In the case of Coke, the 1.618 extension required a few more weeks until the execution signal was triggered.

Deep Bullish Crab at RSI BAMM Completion Point

In the same manner as the Bullish Crab, the Deep Bullish Crab employs a 1.618 extension at the RSI BAMM Confirmation Point (see Figure 6.39). Again, the RSI BAMM Trigger Bar must be the extreme low of the pattern.

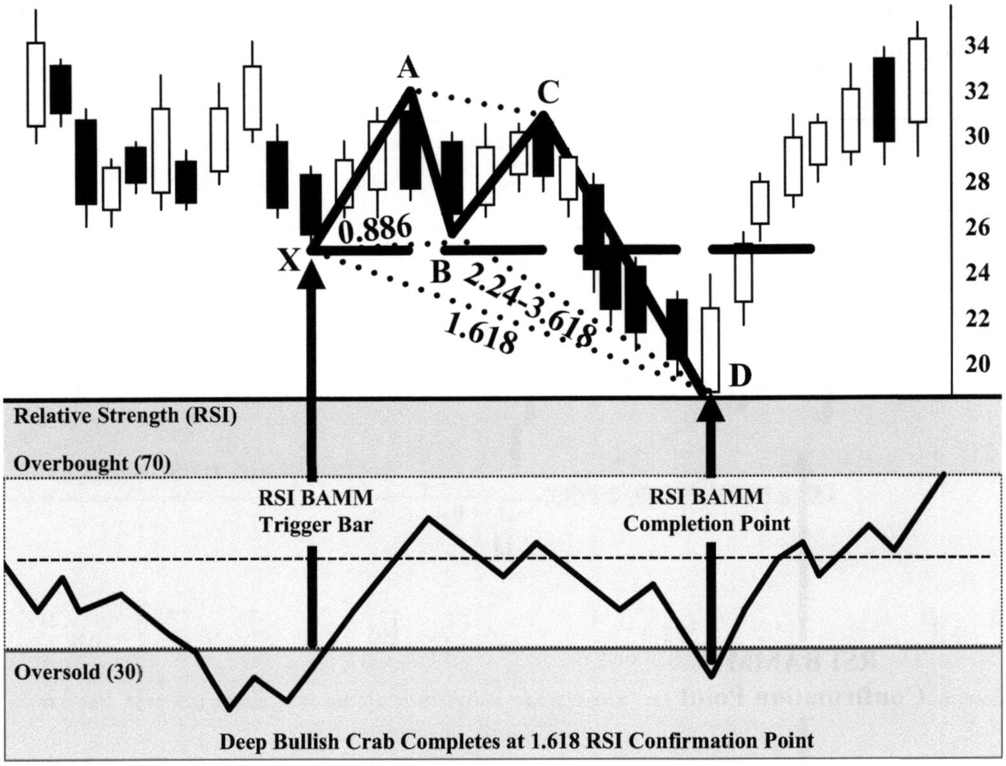

Figure 6.39

In my opinion, the Bullish Crab is the most prevalent pattern that forms with the 1.618 RSI BAMM Confirmation Point. Although many Deep Bullish Crabs present excellent opportunities, they don't seem to materialize as frequently as the regular version.

Japanese Yen (JPY_A0-FX): 60-Minute Deep Bullish Crab at RSI BAMM Confirmation Point

The 60-minute chart of the Yen in Figure 6.40 shows an excellent intra-day RSI BAMM setup. When applying the RSI BAMM to intra-day trading situations, the 15-minute or 60-minute intervals seem to produce the best results, but it is important to remember that these are still short-term day trades.

Figure 6.40

Although RSI BAMM setups that materialize on daily and weekly charts usually possess more significant reversal zones, these typically take longer to complete. But I thought it was important to show an example of a day trading situation.

Japanese Yen (JPY_A0-FX): 60-Minute Deep Bullish Crab Potential Reversal Zone (PRZ) at RSI BAMM Confirmation Point

In the Yen example shown in Figure 6.41, the stock formed a Deep Bullish Crab that reversed exactly at the 1.618 extension. The completion of the pattern occurred simultaneously with the RSI BAMM Confirmation Point.

Figure 6.41

It is important to note that the coordination between the RSI BAMM Confirmation Point and the pattern's completion should occur closer to each other in shorter-term day trading type situations. Although longer-term setups such as a 60-minute or a daily opportunity may require more time for the entire scenario to complete, 1-minute and 3-minute opportunities should exhibit more precise price action and reverse closer in proximity to each other. In essence, short-term trading situations require stricter application of the rules and allow less room for variation.

RSI BAMM Confirmation Point—Reversal Acceleration Trigger

There is an additional technical trigger that serves as secondary confirmation of a valid reversal. Although this final trigger does not develop in every situation, when this additional structural formation develops in the RSI reading at the final test of the Confirmation Point, it typically represents an area of acceleration of the reversal.

Bullish Confirmation Point—Reversal Acceleration Trigger

The most important aspect of the RSI BAMM Confirmation Point is that both the indicator structure and the price action must demonstrate a decisive continuation of the reversal trend (see Figure 6.42). In many cases following the completion of the RSI BAMM Confirmation Point, the indicator structure will form a specific W-type formation above the oversold 30 level. This structure serves as a technical acceleration point that frequently marks the beginning of a decisive new price move.

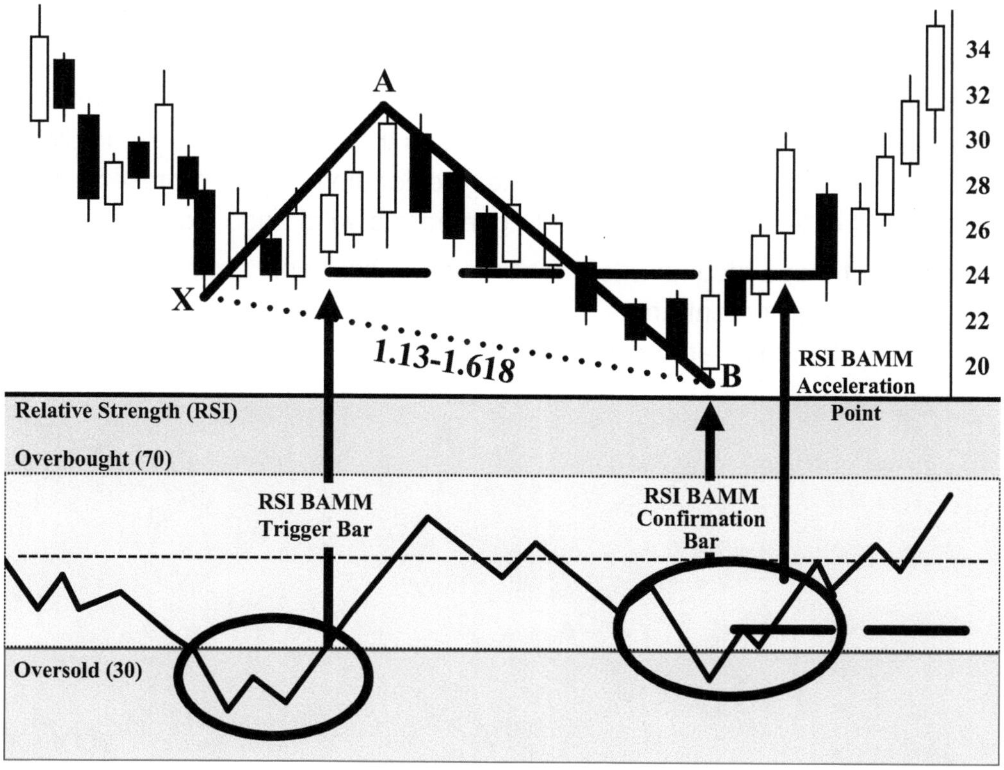

Figure 6.42

This magnified illustration of the RSI BAMM Confirmation Point clearly shows the ideal indicator structure that serves as a penultimate technical level for the entire setup. It is important to note that the Acceleration Trigger of the additional RSI structure is an immediate signal for the reversal. Sometimes, the initial pullback following a reversal from the RSI BAMM Confirmation Point may only be one or two price bars after the indicator structure rallies back above the 30 level. Despite the pause in the price action, the internal dynamics of the RSI typically gain strength at this point and signal a quick acceleration of the new trend.

Although waiting for this extra RSI signal to execute a trade may result in paying a slightly higher price, the Acceleration Trigger does provide a reliable sign of a valid reversal at hand. Furthermore, waiting for this breakout trigger prevents executions at invalid RSI BAMM Confirmation Points, where the impulsive test at the 30 level flounders and does not provide decisive reversal continuation. In these cases, it is important to act appropriately and to exit the trade at a small loss or break even due to the fact that the price action languishes after completing the RSI BAMM Acceleration Trigger. Essentially, the price action should move quickly and decidedly after the final acceleration is triggered. The price bar that completes the breakout of the W-type structure above the oversold 30 level in the RSI indicator reading will typically mark the acceleration point of the new reversal trend.

When this last trigger materializes, it definitely creates a "do-or-die" situation. After satisfying all conditions of the RSI BAMM and successfully reversing from the impulse test at the Confirmation Point, this last little caveat of the indicator reading possesses powerful price action implications. In fact, this last confirmation trigger within the final phase of the RSI BAMM represents the most precise technical setup within the entire Harmonic Trading approach. In no other technical situation of this entire methodology does the "do-or-die" scenario dictate an immediate reaction in the price action. Hence, the Acceleration Trigger represents the realization of a gamut of technical conditions to generate a valid trade signal.

The combination of these measurement techniques of harmonic patterns and the ability of the RSI BAMM to define divergent areas of price action represent the most complex system of technical conditions within the Harmonic Trading approach.

The final phase of the RSI BAMM represents a powerful technical measuring technique in its own right (see Figure 6.43). When harmonic patterns converge at the Confirmation Point of the RSI BAMM, the technical information garnered from this approach serves as an immensely accurate consensus reading to validate the setup.

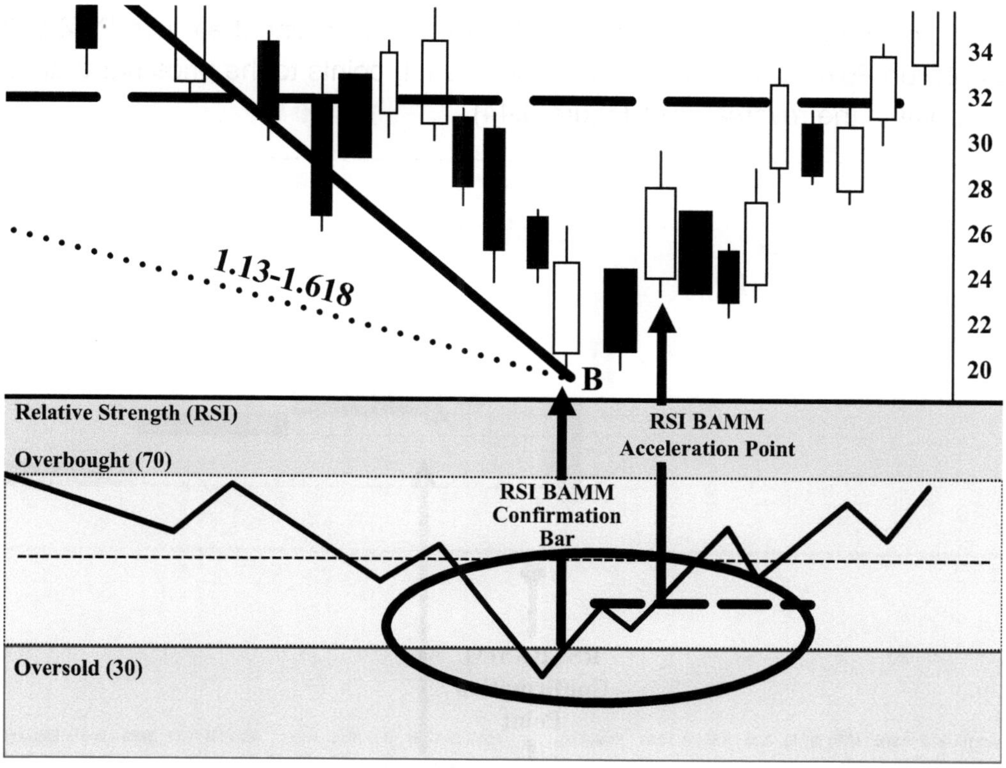

Figure 6.43

IBM (IBM): Weekly
Bullish Gartley Potential Reversal Zone (PRZ) at RSI BAMM Confirmation Point with Acceleration Trigger

Referring back to the example of IBM, the stock rallied after testing the entire PRZ at the RSI BAMM Completion Point. The second arrow from the left points to the price bar that marked the acceleration point in the reversal (see Figure 6.44).

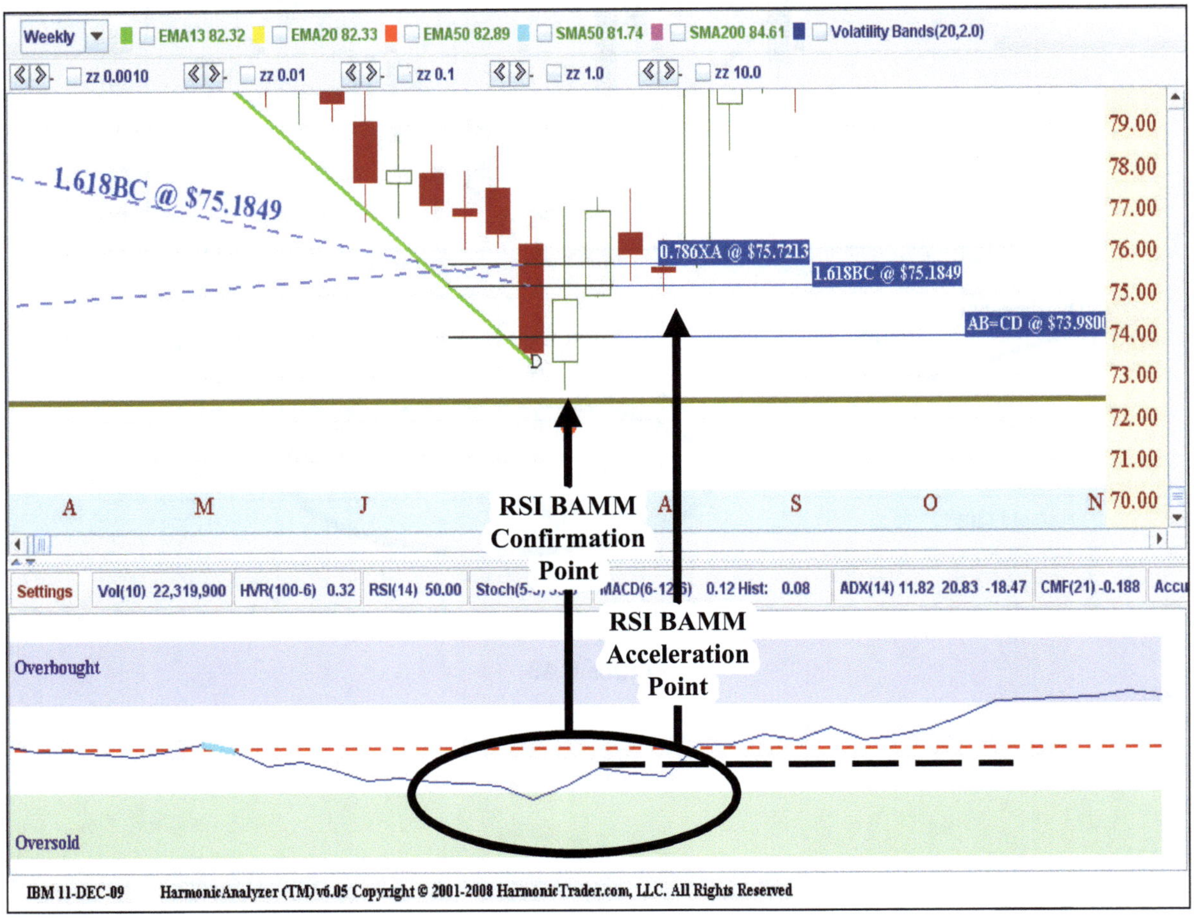

Figure 6.44

The interesting aspect of this situation is that the Acceleration Point signaled a valid long position while the stock was still trading within its PRZ. In this case, the additional confirmation of the Acceleration Point triggered the trade before the reversal began in earnest. Although waiting for the Acceleration Point to develop may result in delayed trade executions, these are very effective signals in most valid reversals.

Bullish RSI BAMM Violations and Stop Loss Considerations

After defining the entire range of the RSI BAMM Confirmation Point extension and harmonic pattern completion points, the only consideration beyond the execution is the stop loss limit. Again, the stop loss determination will also include the price levels that are defined by the larger harmonic patterns included in the trading setup. However, from a pure RSI BAMM perspective, the key validation truly occurs beyond the Completion Point extension. The stop loss is typically a combination of the price limit established by the RSI BAMM extension and the specific pattern completion that occurs in the same area as the Confirmation Point.

RSI BAMM violations involve two factors that determine the validity of the setup. First, the RSI BAMM extension—whether it is a 1.13 or a 1.618—is the primary technical level that dictates the validity of the setup. Although it is important to differentiate between whether the RSI BAMM utilizes a 1.13 or a 1.618 extension, the validation of the technical phenomenon becomes questionable beyond the 2.00 extension of the final move for either situation. But, the price action at the RSI BAMM extension at the Completion Point should be quite precise, as valid reversals usually do not exceed these areas by much. As a general rule, the 1.13 extension typically employs the area beyond the 1.618 to define its stop loss zone. In comparison, those situations that trigger a 1.618 extension will typically define the area beyond the 2.0 as a violation of the setup.

As is the case for harmonic pattern failures, price action that violates these price levels, especially on the first test, should raise a red flag that the primary trend is quite strong. Most important, the area defined by the RSI BAMM is truly a "do or die" price level that does not leave much room for discretion. I discussed pattern violations thoroughly in *Harmonic Trading: Volume One*. Although I will not review those strategies in detail in this book, the essence of pattern violations is usually witnessed after the price action has tested the entire PRZ.

The tandem violation of the relative RSI BAMM extension and the pattern's PRZ is a definite signal that the setup has failed. However, there are many instances where violations will offer warnings in the form of strong price action that provide early signs of an impending failure at hand. In many cases, the price action will violate a bullish PRZ that is in the upper range of the entire harmonic support area, signaling the violation even before the RSI BAMM extension is tested. Again, the preferred situation in most violations is price action that declines sharply through *the combined harmonic area* of both the relative RSI BAMM extension and the pattern's PRZ.

Standard & Poor's 500 March 2010 Mini-Contract (ES_H0): 15-Minute Bullish Crab and Bullish RSI BAMM Failure

The Standard & Poor's 500 March 2010 Mini-Contract formed this distinct RSI BAMM on the 15-minute chart (see Figure 6.45). The RSI BAMM Trigger Bar was the initial low, which established a projected 1.618 extension at the Confirmation Point.

Figure 6.45

Although the RSI structure was exemplary, the price action failed to stabilize at this harmonic support. The breakdown in this area was overwhelming and the distinct Bullish Crab reinforced the importance of the 1.618 extension as the defining level in this setup.

Standard & Poor's 500 March 2010 Mini-Contract (ES_H0): 15-Minute Bullish Crab and Bullish RSI BAMM Failure

The enlarged chart in Figure 6.46 clearly shows the violation of the pattern's PRZ and the RSI BAMM extension. The price action hit all the numbers on the initial test of the PRZ but quickly continued lower, sinking below the 1.618 extension.

Figure 6.46

The intra-day price action clearly violated the pattern's PRZ. This should have served as a severe warning sign well before the 1.618 RSI BAMM extension was violated. This example clearly demonstrated a failed RSI BAMM setup. The critical aspect, as is the case with most violations, is the inability of the price action to stabilize on the secondary test of the indicator at the completion point of the pattern despite a clear prior complex RSI structure.

Bearish RSI BAMM

The Bearish RSI BAMM begins with a complex reading above 70. Referring to the RSI BAMM illustration in Figure 6.47, the entire process requires several elements to validate this specific scenario. Although the entire illustration might seem a bit overwhelming upon first examination, this represents the ideal RSI BAMM model. I recommend that you thoroughly study this material before employing these strategies in your live trading. Each step will be broken down to illustrate the ideal RSI BAMM model. Obviously, the ideal situation does not occur every time. It is important to remember that the real application of the RSI BAMM principles will require a degree of flexibility.

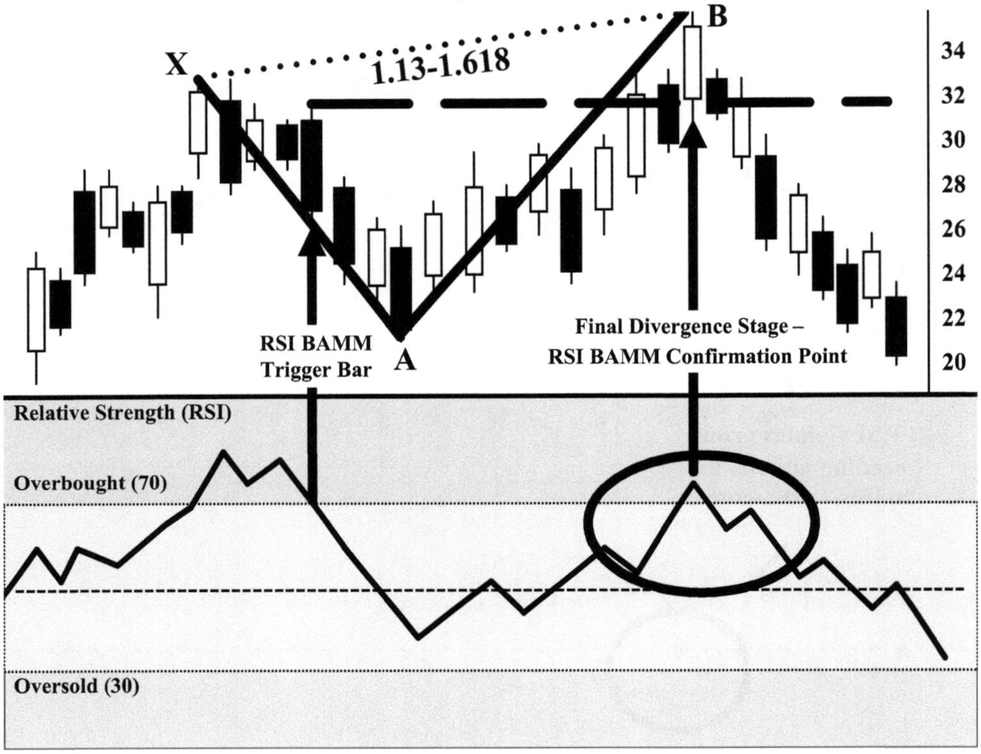

Figure 6.47

The ideal model does present all of the critical elements that clearly explain the effectiveness of this strategy. But, it will take a period of study to fully comprehend all aspects of the RSI BAMM approach. In much the same manner that the initial rules of harmonic pattern identification and differentiation may have seemed overwhelming, the RSI BAMM rules—albeit a bit complex upon first study—provide a coherent and comprehensive method for accurately measuring potential areas of divergence. Furthermore, it is essential to maintain the patience to execute only those trades that possess all required elements that validate a trade signal based upon the rules of the RSI BAMM setup. Again, it is important to remember that this illustration represents an *ideal model* and a framework to provide a set of guidelines that attempt to quantify precise technical events and to optimize overall trading decisions. However, the RSI BAMM strategy in combination with harmonic patterns effectively validates PRZs and improves the overall accuracy of the entire Harmonic Trading approach. The following example of the British Pound (versus the U.S. Dollar) clearly demonstrates these concepts.

British Pound/USD (GBP_A0-FX): Weekly Bearish RSI BAMM

The weekly chart of the British Pound in Figure 6.48 exemplifies the ideal RSI BAMM approach. It is important to study this chart as a model to distinguish and to validate RSI BAMM setups. This situation required more than a year to develop, but it possessed all of the necessary elements to establish the ultimate reversal at the RSI BAMM Confirmation Point on the weekly chart.

Figure 6.48

Step 1: Initial RSI Test of Extreme Bearish Limit

In the Bearish RSI BAMM scenario, the first step is to identify price action that possesses an RSI reading in the extreme zone above 70. As I mentioned previously, the 70 level for the overbought limit, as well as the 30 level to define the oversold area, were first outlined by Welles Wilder in his book *New Concepts and Trading Systems*. In addition, a 14-period average is calculated from his approach.

Step 2: Complete a Bearish M-Type Complex RSI Structure

The initial focus should be on the formation of the indicator readings in the entire extreme overbought range rather than looking for a specific numeric level. As I outlined earlier in this chapter for the bullish scenario, it is important to differentiate the two types of indicator structures that form at RSI extremes.

Two Types of Bearish Indicator Structures

In much the same vein as harmonic patterns, it is important to classify the general types of indicator structures that form in an overbought RSI area. Although each type could be assigned more specific classifications, indicator readings form either an impulsive or a complex structure. It has been my experience that most bearish RSI readings that are above 70 will be impulsive in nature and do not yield the required structure to be considered a valid setup. However, valid complex structures that are correctly identified offer a tremendous technical advantage because this situation is especially unique and represents a vital potential reversal area within the overall trend of the price action.

Sometimes, a complex RSI BAMM formation can be frustrating because the setup may not ideally unfold following the initial trigger. This can be particularly frustrating when a potential setup is followed for quite some time and fails to adhere to the RSI BAMM model. In the same manner that not all patterns form ideally, it is important to wait for only those situations that clearly provide all the required elements to validate the setup. Regardless, the primary focus of the initial step is to identify a complex the RSI BAMM M-type structure in the extreme area.

Bearish Impulsive Indicator Structures

A bearish impulsive indicator structure reflects price action that is experiencing a quick test of the extreme overbought resistance area, usually reversing quickly without any consolidating price action (see Figure 6.49). Since the price action commonly reverses sharply in these cases, the RSI rolls over and sinks below the 70 level typically within one or two price bars of the first overbought reading.

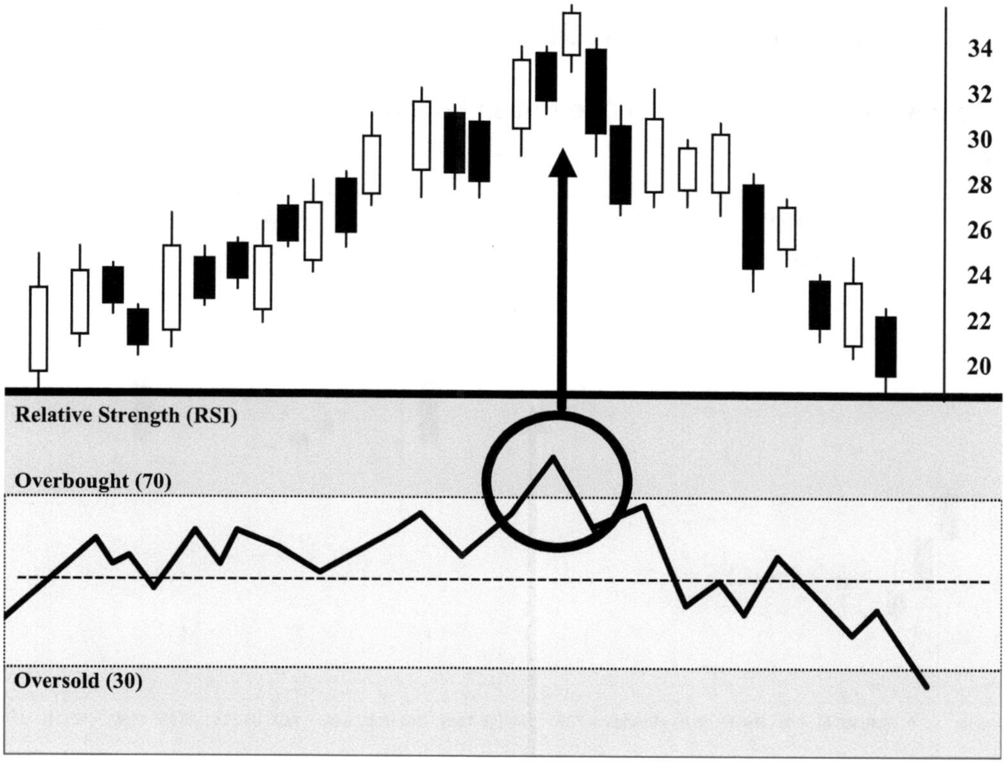

Figure 6.49

Although such impulsive formations may test the extreme bearish RSI level, it is important to focus on the nature of the indicator structure and not necessarily the exact numeric reading (as long as it is above the 70 limit). The exact indicator level is critical in quantifying the extreme state of RSI, but the general indicator formation is the critical factor, as it serves as the essential trigger to validate a potential trade opportunity.

Impulsive structures can be effective technical measures as they can serve to confirm bearish patterns and other trading signals. But it is important to note that the signals generated from extreme RSI readings do not constitute a comprehensive approach to trading the market. As mentioned previously, I believe that this is a common misconception for Relative Strength and most other technical indicators and oscillators. In my opinion, such technical measures must be utilized as a complementary methodology rather than as an exclusive approach. A Relative Strength reading above 70 does not automatically signify a trade opportunity. In fact, certain extreme impulse structures can signal significant continuations of the predominant trend. These strategies will be covered later in the book. For now, it is important to keep in mind the general types of structures. Furthermore, as is the case with all technical indicators, other methods must be employed to validate any potential trade opportunity on a multiple confirmation basis.

British Pound/USD (GBP_A0-FX): Weekly Bearish Impulse Indicator Structure

Figure 6.50 shows the impulsive RSI in the British Pound that reversed sharply after exceeding the 70 level.

Figure 6.50

It is important to note how the price action stalled after testing the extreme overbought area. In this case, the price action reversed decidedly after the impulsive RSI test was completed.

Bearish Complex Indicator Structure

A complex structure represents an indicator formation that initially exceeds the 70 level and forms an M-type structure entirely in the extreme area (see Figure 6.51). The complex structure remains above the extreme 70 limit longer than an impulsive formation, and it should be distinct from other types of indicator readings.

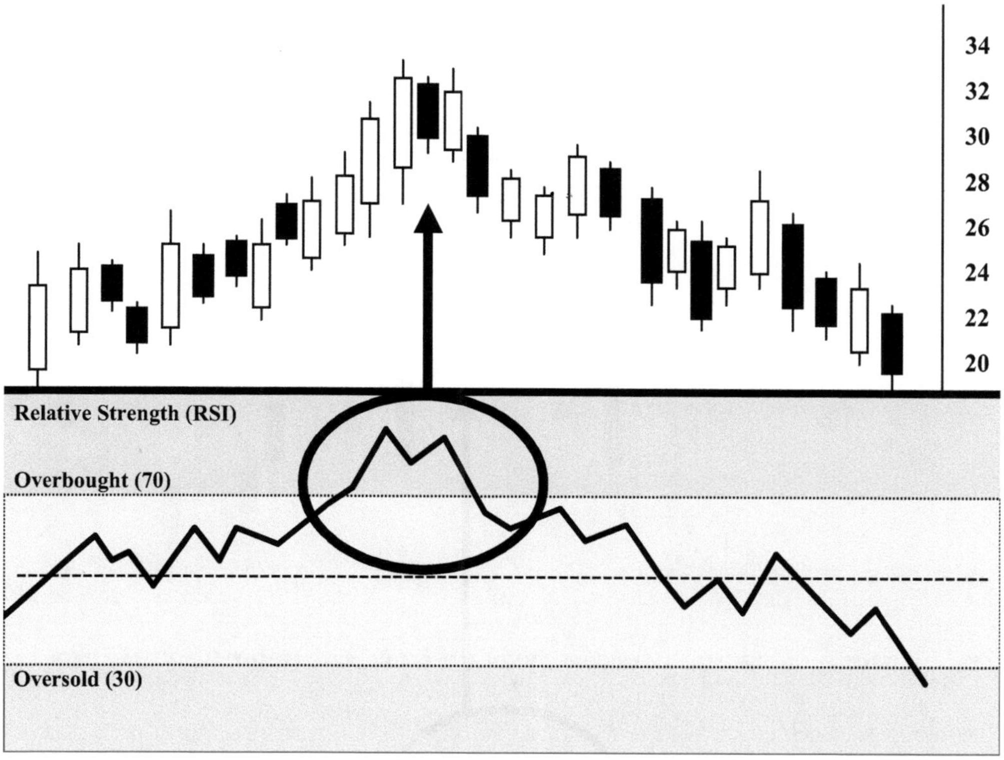

Figure 6.51

Despite representing a more significant technical condition than an impulsive formation, the bearish complex structure is typically an early trading signal. In fact, it is common for price action to accelerate to the upside while the complex formation of the RSI reading completes. Furthermore, the initial reaction to the complex RSI structure may not seem to indicate a change in trend due to such strong price action. Despite this perceived strength, *the validity of the entire RSI BAMM technique is not determined until the M-type structures has entirely formed in the overbought area above 70.* Although the advanced concepts will be clearly presented later in this chapter, it is important to keep in mind that a complex indicator reading is merely the starting point for the entire approach not the defining event of the RSI BAMM methodology.

British Pound/USD (GBP_A0-FX): Weekly Bearish Complex Indicator Structure

The example of a complex RSI structure in the British Pound shown in Figure 6.52 possessed all of the necessary elements to establish the RSI BAMM. As this chart example demonstrates, the initial test of the complex indicator formation typically experiences an acceleration of the predominant trend. Despite the perceived strength of the rally, the complex formation establishes the beginning of the most critical aspect of the entire RSI BAMM methodology—the divergence phase.

Figure 6.52

The bearish divergence occurs when the RSI reading weakens while the price action continues to rally. Although the price action may seem to be maintaining its current uptrend, valid complex RSI structures usually trigger a reversal sooner rather later and mark a critical area for a potential change in the overall direction. Although a few other elements must fall into place for the RSI BAMM to be validated, the complex RSI structure is the starting point for the entire process. Most important, this is an early signal, and it is critical to wait for the M-type structure to break under the 70 line. After the RSI formation has been completed, the other considerations of potential pattern completions and specific RSI BAMM harmonic measurements can be projected to determine the optimal reversal area. This leads us to our next step, which includes the defining and measuring of the price level that triggers this breakdown.

Step 3: Define the RSI Trigger Bar

After defining the complex RSI formation, the next step requires a measurement of the price area where the M-type indicator structure has completed. The price bar that causes the complex RSI indicator reading to complete the M-type structure and to decline below the extreme 70 limit is known as the *RSI BAMM Trigger Bar* (see Figure 6.53).

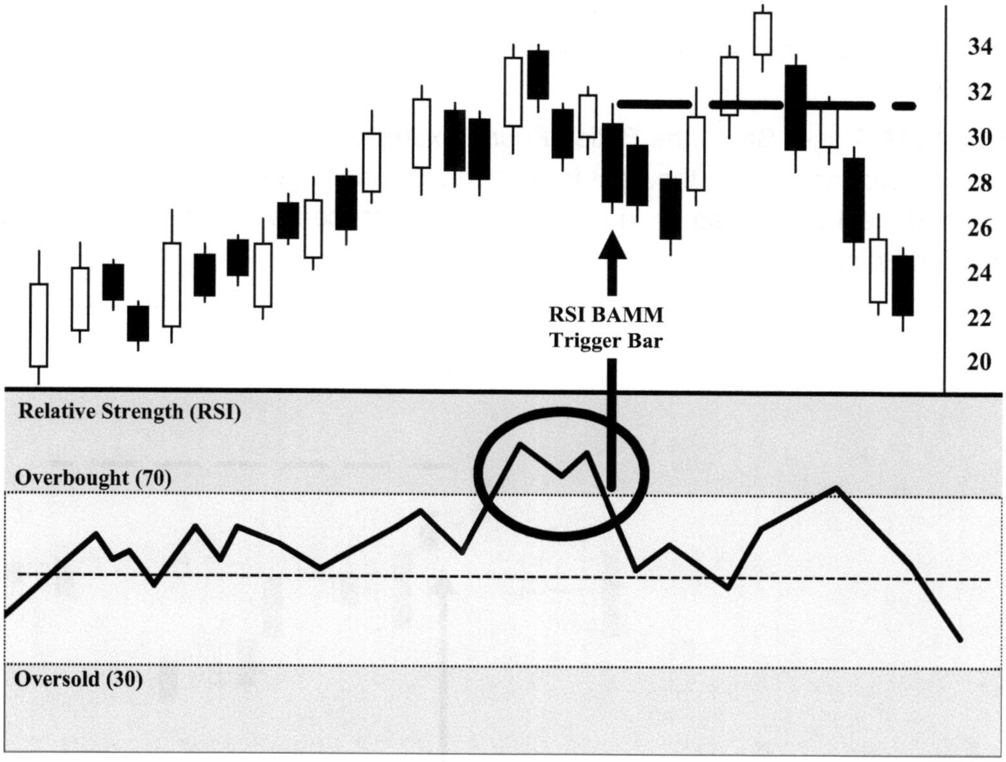

Figure 6.53

After identifying the RSI BAMM Trigger Bar, it is critical to mark the top of this price bar by drawing an extended line from the peak, projecting the resistance to the right of the chart, as illustrated in Figure 6.53. This RSI BAMM Trigger Bar resistance level serves as a minimum technical area for the corresponding retest and the anticipated execution area of the completion of the final phase of the RSI BAMM. From a general perspective, the RSI BAMM Trigger Bar denotes the starting point for the critical divergence phase that the entire methodology is attempting to define and to quantify. Again, the completion of the complex RSI structure is only a starting point of the process. Although there are strategies that I will present later in this chapter to capitalize on the initial indicator breakdown, from a broader perspective the RSI Trigger Bar can reveal a great deal about the validity of the setup and the state of the potential price action. For now, the most critical element of the RSI BAMM approach begins after the indicator has reversed from the overbought reading by completing the complex M-type structure.

British Pound/USD (GBP_A0-FX): Weekly Bearish RSI BAMM Trigger Bar

The position of the Bearish RSI BAMM Trigger Bar in relation to the prior extreme high point is critical. Although its significance will be further explained later in this section, it is important to remember that the RSI BAMM Trigger Bar typically will be the price bar that is the prior peak of the current move or within a few intervals of the extreme high. This is critical, as the Trigger Bar's position will determine the execution area for the corresponding retest and completion of the RSI BAMM.

The RSI BAMM Trigger Bar in the British Pound example in Figure 6.54 is clearly marked. After drawing a horizontal line to the right from the top of the Trigger Bar, the complex RSI structure defined the 1.8750 area as the first critical resistance level for the ultimate retest at the Confirmation Point.

Figure 6.54

Step 4: Reaction of RSI and Price

After the Trigger Bar has been established, the initial reaction from the completion of the complex RSI structure and the price must be monitored closely. After topping out in the extreme overbought area above 70, the price action typically experiences a quick and decisive pullback. This is typically evidenced by a steady short-term downtrend (see Figure 6.55).

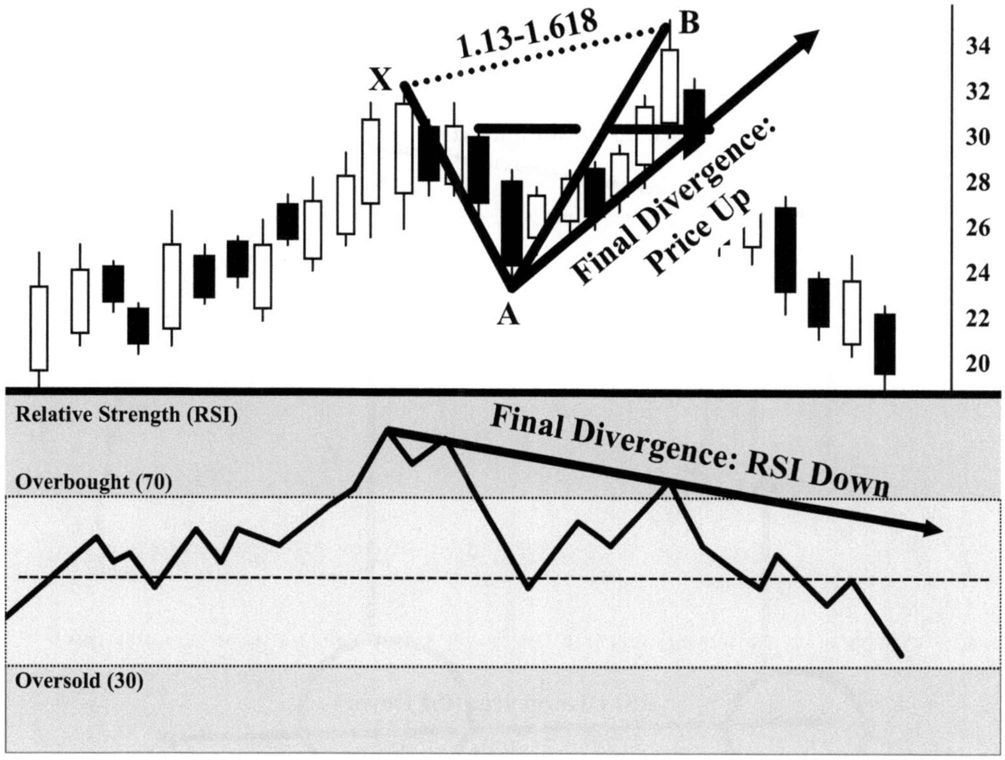

Figure 6.55

The critical divergence phase begins after this brief correction, which is normally marked by a breakout of the short-term downtrend line. This breakout is critical in defining the beginning of the divergence phase of the entire RSI BAMM methodology. Although I will review the other elements in more detail, this breakout typically will retest the RSI BAMM Trigger Bar area and rally to either a 1.13 or 1.618 extension while testing the extreme RSI overbought area above 70.

British Pound/USD (GBP_A0-FX): Weekly Reaction of RSI and Price

After breaking out of the short-term downtrend line, the British Pound started to rally for the final divergence phase. The final rally included an impulsive retest of the 70 limit (see Figure 6.56).

Figure 6.56

As the RSI and the price react during this divergence phase, a few technical aspects must unfold to validate the final test and ultimate execution of the entire setup.

Specific Type of Retest

One of the most critical aspects of this divergence phase occurs during the initial reaction following the complex RSI structure completion. After the Trigger Bar has been established, *the RSI reading MUST decline to at least the 50 level before completing the final divergence—where the price rallies while the RSI fails to exceed the readings established by the prior complex indicator formation.* Although there is room for interpretation as the RSI reading may exceed the 50 level on this initial reaction, it serves as a minimum requirement that precedes the corresponding retest of the resistance area established by the RSI BAMM (see Figure 6.57).

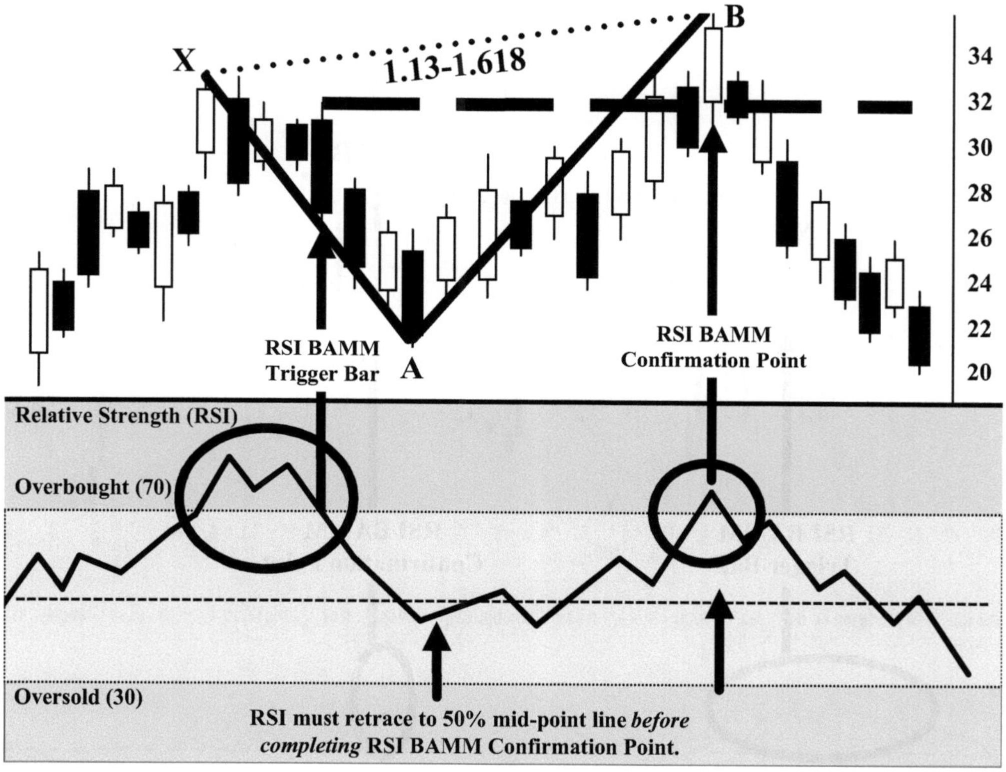

Figure 6.57

Again, this specific type of retest offers other short-term trading opportunities that I will explain a bit later in this chapter. But, the important aspect of this element of the process is a *minimum retest to the mid-point (50) level of the RSI.* At this point in the RSI BAMM methodology, the price action typically declines fractionally while the indicator experiences a sharp correction. So, it is essential to focus on the indicator reading. After the mid-point 50 limit is tested, the final divergence phase of the entire approach will begin.

British Pound/USD (GBP_A0-FX): Weekly Specific Type of Retest: RSI Mid-Point (50 Limit) Requirement

Following the initial reaction after the complex RSI formation, the British Pound declined sharply in price and, more importantly, in the RSI reading (see Figure 6.58). Although the setup consolidated at the 50 line for several months, the eventual breakout from the initial downtrend line and the rally in the RSI marked the beginning of the final phase to complete the RSI BAMM Confirmation Point.

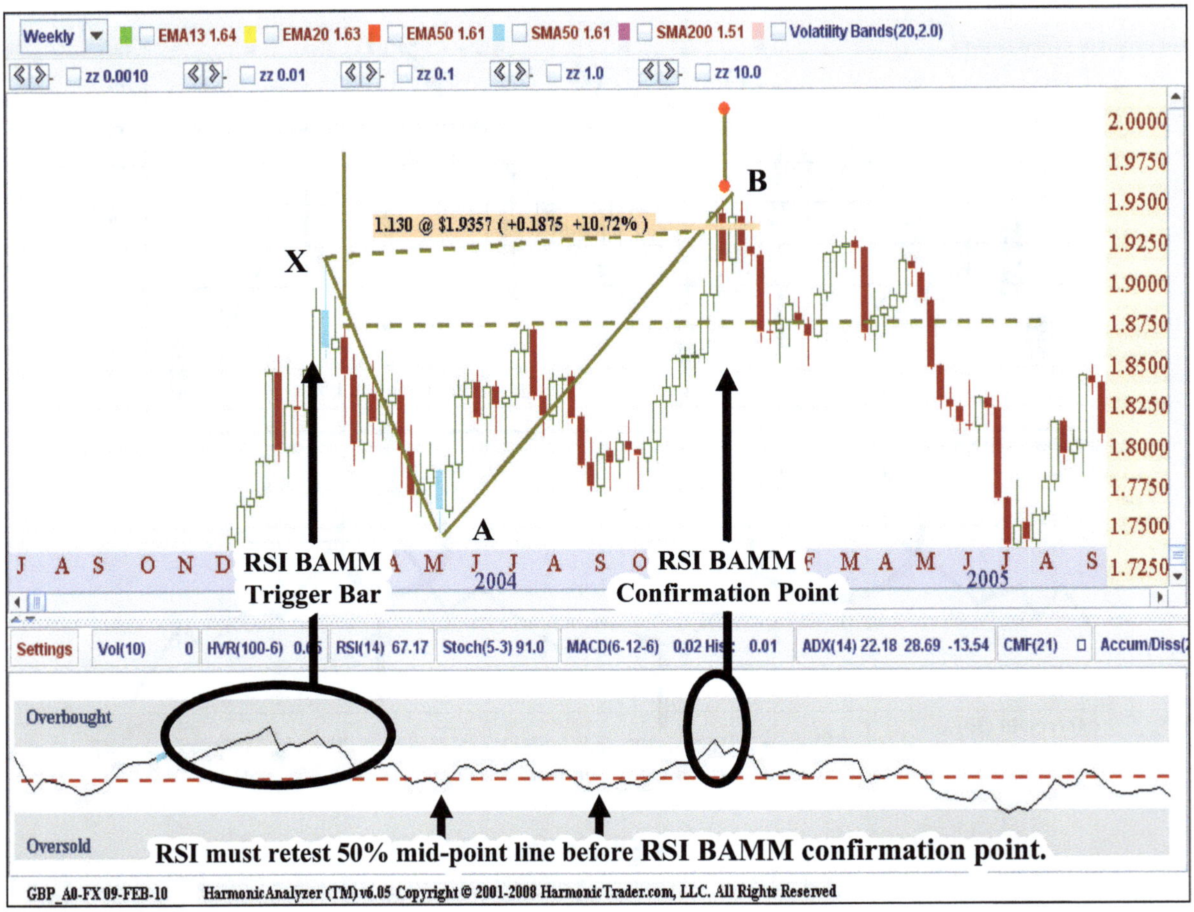

Figure 6.58

Step 5: The Final Phase—Divergence of RSI Versus Price

Figure 6.59 clearly shows the concept of this final divergence. As the RSI and the price retest their prior respective resistance points, they diverge in direction. As the RSI reading reverses after testing the 70 limit, the price action "spills over" the prior high in an attempt to continue the predominant trend. The "spillover" rally usually experiences a brief move above the prior high to either a 1.13 or 1.618 extension of the initial breakdown (X-A).

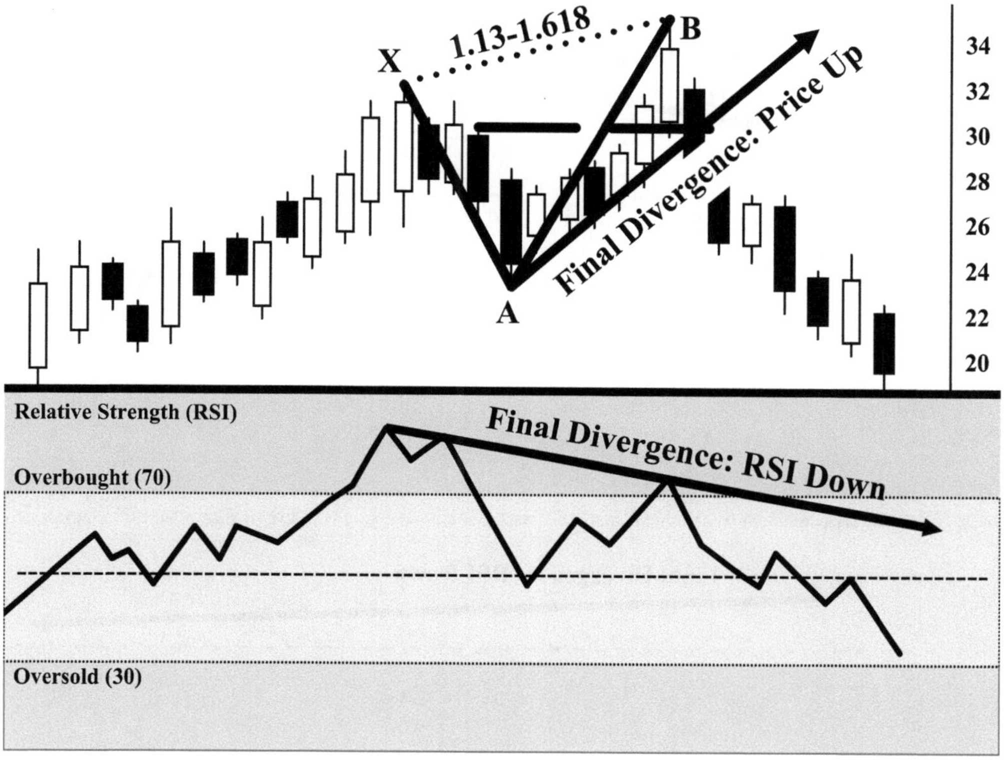

Figure 6.59

Later in this chapter, I will outline the rules that distinguish which harmonic projection works with the final divergence phase. But, the beauty of this technical phenomenon is that the breakout is inherently flawed due to the RSI failure, as the "internal strength" no longer supports the predominant trend. It is in situations like these where the general technical divergence between the RSI and the price offers tremendous trading opportunities.

British Pound/USD (GBP_A0-FX): Weekly Final Divergence Phase of RSI Versus Price

The British Pound clearly exemplifies the ideal divergent technical situation. After completing the complex RSI structure, the price action rallied to a nominal new high (see Figure 6.60).

Figure 6.60

The secondary test of the RSI failed to exceed the prior reading. Moreover, the impulsive nature of the test further underscored the weakness, as the internal strength of the last rally barely penetrated the overbought limit above 70. The price bar that triggers the completion of the impulsive indicator retest is called the *Bearish RSI BAMM Confirmation Bar.*

Bearish RSI BAMM Confirmation Bar

The critical divergence between the price and the RSI can be seen in Figure 6.61. The RSI BAMM Confirmation Bar usually completes at either a 1.13 or a 1.618 extension of the prior decline and defines the divergence point for the entire setup. As the trend of the price action continues up (notice uptrend arrow), the RSI reading fails to continue higher, completing an impulsive structure that defines the RSI BAMM Confirmation Bar.

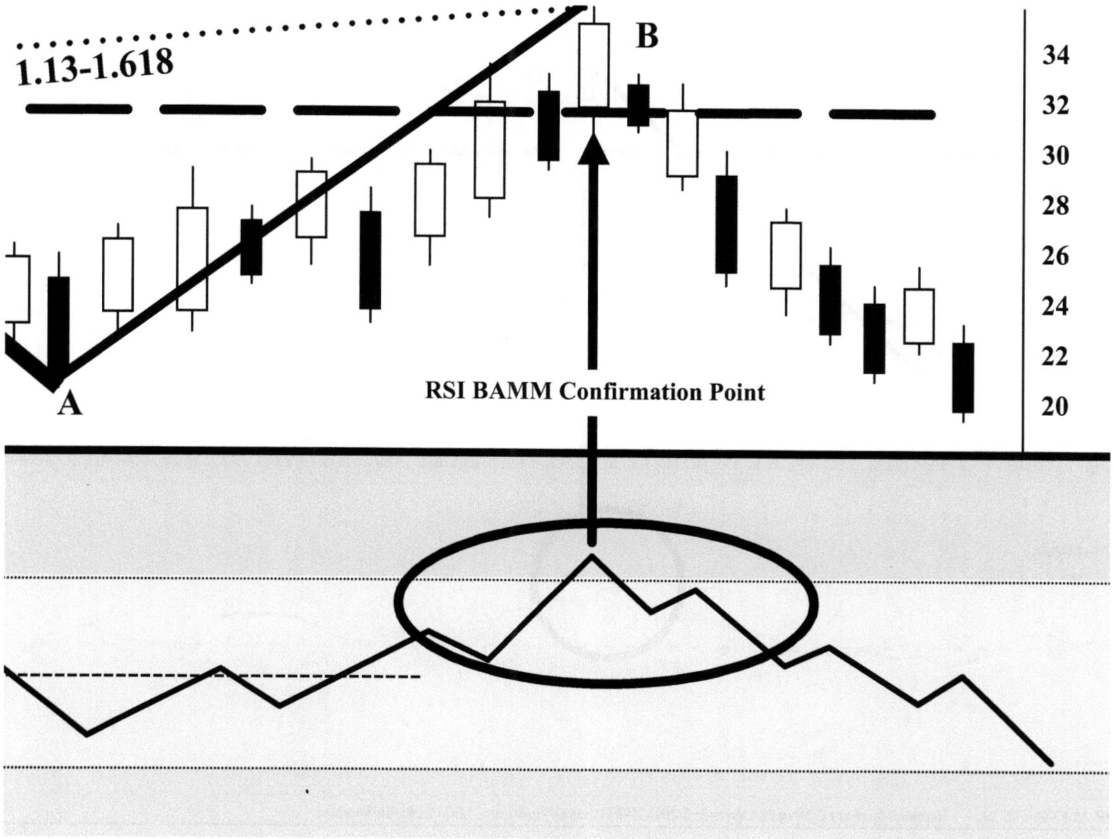

Figure 6.61

If the RSI Confirmation Bar is a valid resistance signal indicating a reversal at hand, typically the price action will decline quickly after exceeding the initial prior high level. Although I will outline the advantages of utilizing Harmonic Trading techniques of pattern recognition and Fibonacci measurement strategies with the RSI BAMM, it is important to examine this technical phenomenon on its own before trying to understand the advanced concepts. Most important, the simple divergence as marked by the Bearish RSI BAMM Confirmation Bar provides an effective technical situation that can be further refined with other trading strategies to define profitable opportunities.

British Pound/USD (GBP_A0-FX): Weekly Bearish RSI BAMM Confirmation Bar

The illustration of the British Pound in Figure 6.62 clearly shows the divergence of the RSI versus the price.

Figure 6.62

The price action at the RSI BAMM Confirmation Point reveals a great deal about the strength of the predominant trend and defines the trading opportunity at hand. In essence, the divergent price action at the Confirmation Point rallies in a "last gasp" from the indicator reading. However, the extent of this "last gasp" must be determined, and specific harmonic measurement techniques provide the tools necessary to further refine these technical levels to define excellent trading opportunities.

Review of RSI and Price

Before examining the final divergence stage, let's review the steps for the RSI BAMM up to this point. The entire process started with a complex RSI structure. Following this completion, the divergence phase begins, as the RSI reading pulls back to at least the 50 level. After mid-level RSI check back, the price action breaks out of the short-term downtrend line of the initial reaction to initiate the final divergence phase (see Figure 6.63).

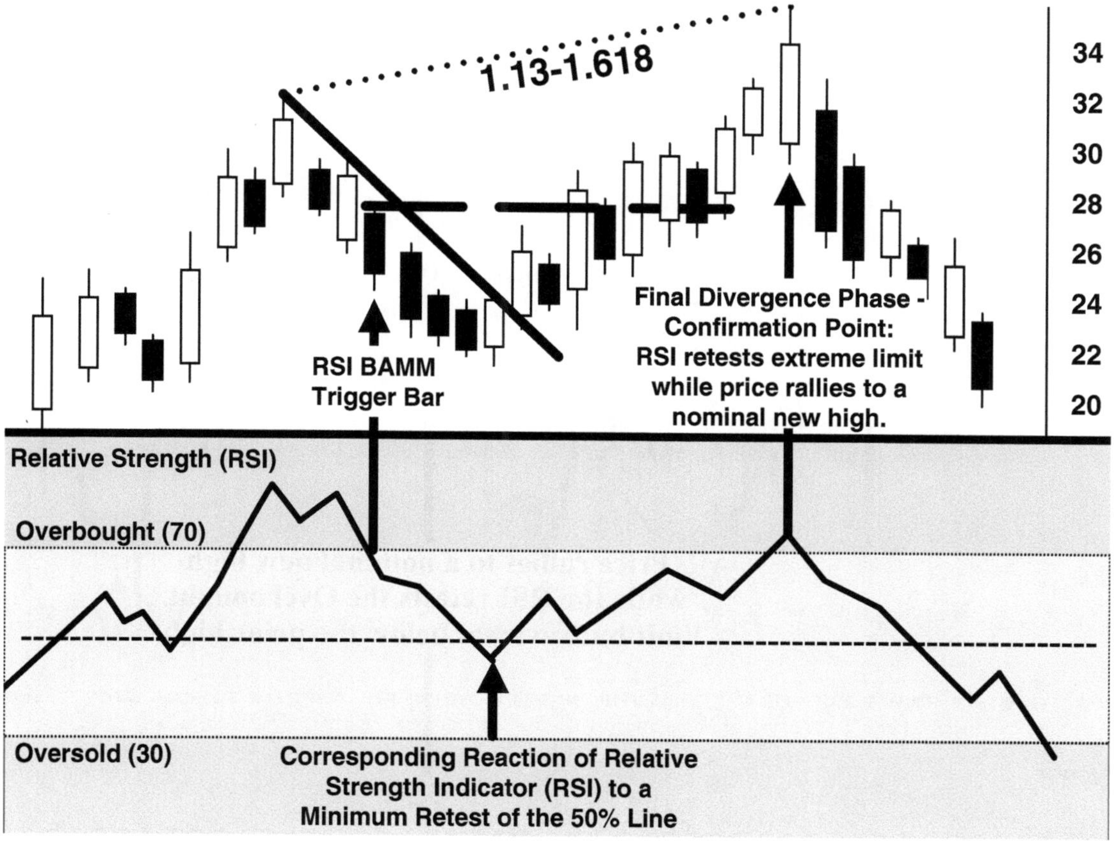

Figure 6.63

It is important to note that the entire RSI BAMM concept is encompassed within this retest of the resistance, as established by the top of the RSI BAMM Trigger Bar. Remember, this is a situation where the Relative Strength is providing an early signal to the end of the predominant trend. Although this signal may be the end of the trend technically, the price action usually experiences one last rally to retest the resistance area established by the complex RSI structure. When the price continues to rally as the RSI fails to exceed its prior resistance established by the complex reading, the final divergence phase has begun and the Confirmation Point is near completion.

British Pound/USD (GBP_A0-FX): Weekly Reaction of RSI and Price

The British Pound example possesses all of the ideal elements and price action that encompasses the RSI BAMM methodology. Figure 6.64 illustrates all of the stages of the RSI divergence. However, the last phase of this approach employs advanced harmonic measurement techniques and other trading strategies to determine the validity of the setup and to quantify the price level for the entry of the trade.

Figure 6.64

Essentially, the various technical measurements are employed to determine an advanced PRZ, where both RSI BAMM projections and harmonic patterns complete. Although this may seem a bit complex upon first study, the overwhelming advantage of the combination of harmonic patterns at the completion of the RSI BAMM pinpoints critical technical levels and defines incredibly accurate trading opportunities.

Step 6: Bearish RSI BAMM Confirmation Point: 1.13 Versus 1.618

In the development of the RSI BAMM, I was challenged for quite some time to discern the correct extension to employ for the Confirmation Point. Although the difference between 1.13 and 1.618 may appear small, in real trading situations this gap frequently can be expensive. With respect to the primary tenets of Harmonic Trading and pattern identification, exact specification of these areas is critical in pinpointing the precise completion of the setup and in determining the validity of the overall trading opportunity. Although these are general rules, I noticed a difference in the RSI BAMM extension within the final divergence phase. These rules outline two areas—depending upon the position of the Trigger Bar relative to the prior high—to examine for a completion of the setup. If the RSI BAMM Trigger Bar is a few price bars (typically 2–4) from the prior high, the execution of the trade will occur at the corresponding 1.13 extension. However, an RSI BAMM Trigger Bar that develops at the extreme high for the move will result in a 1.618 extension at the Confirmation Point.

1.13 Extension at RSI BAMM Confirmation Point

Although the general rule regarding the Confirmation Point extension differentiates the 1.13 and 1.618 ratios, the focus of the Trigger Bar should be on the extreme prior peak. Essentially, if the RSI BAMM Trigger Bar is *not* the high price bar, the 1.13 extension is utilized to quantify the execution area for the trade (see Figure 6.65).

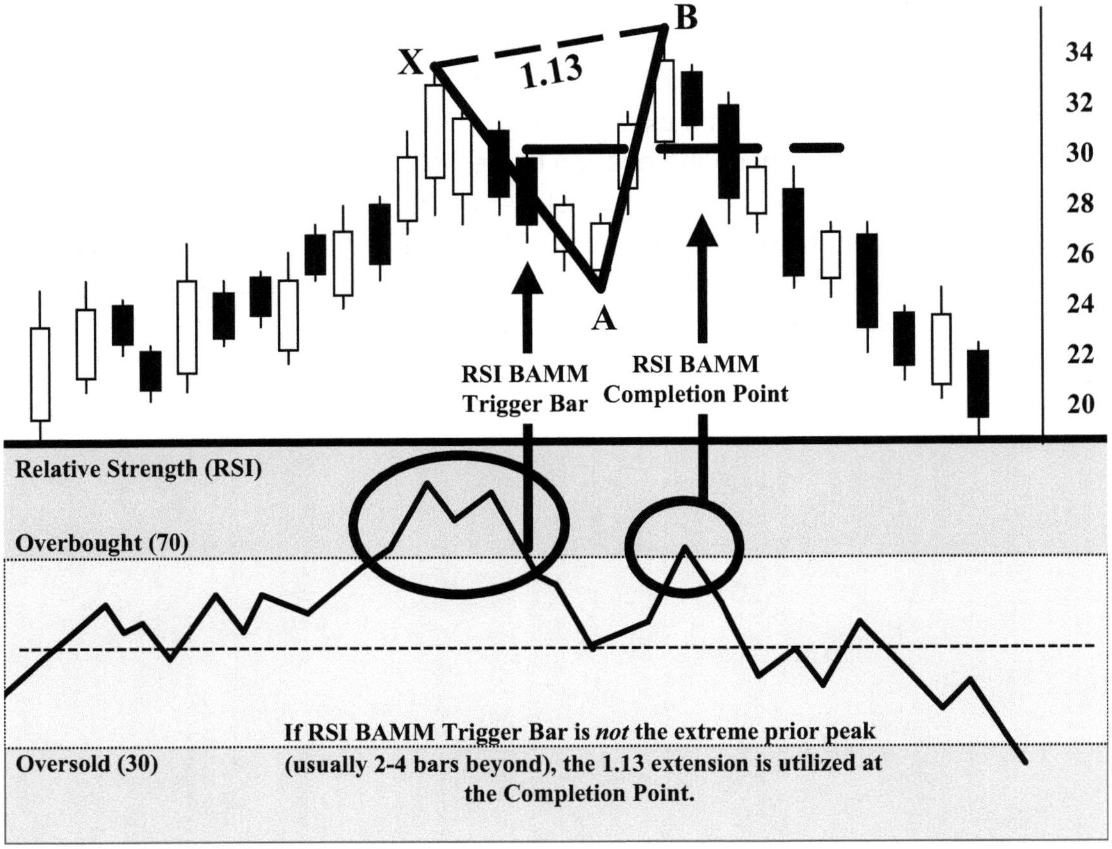

Figure 6.65

British Pound/USD (GBP_A0-FX): Weekly 1.13 Extension at RSI BAMM Confirmation Point

Referring to the British Pound example, Figure 6.66 shows an enlarged image of the RSI BAMM Trigger Bar. Again, the Trigger Bar is the price bar that results in the RSI reading falling under the extreme overbought 70 limit. In the case of the British Pound, the RSI BAMM Trigger Bar occurred three bars from the prior high. Therefore, the corresponding retest should possess a Confirmation Point that completes at or around the 1.13 extension of the prior initial reaction.

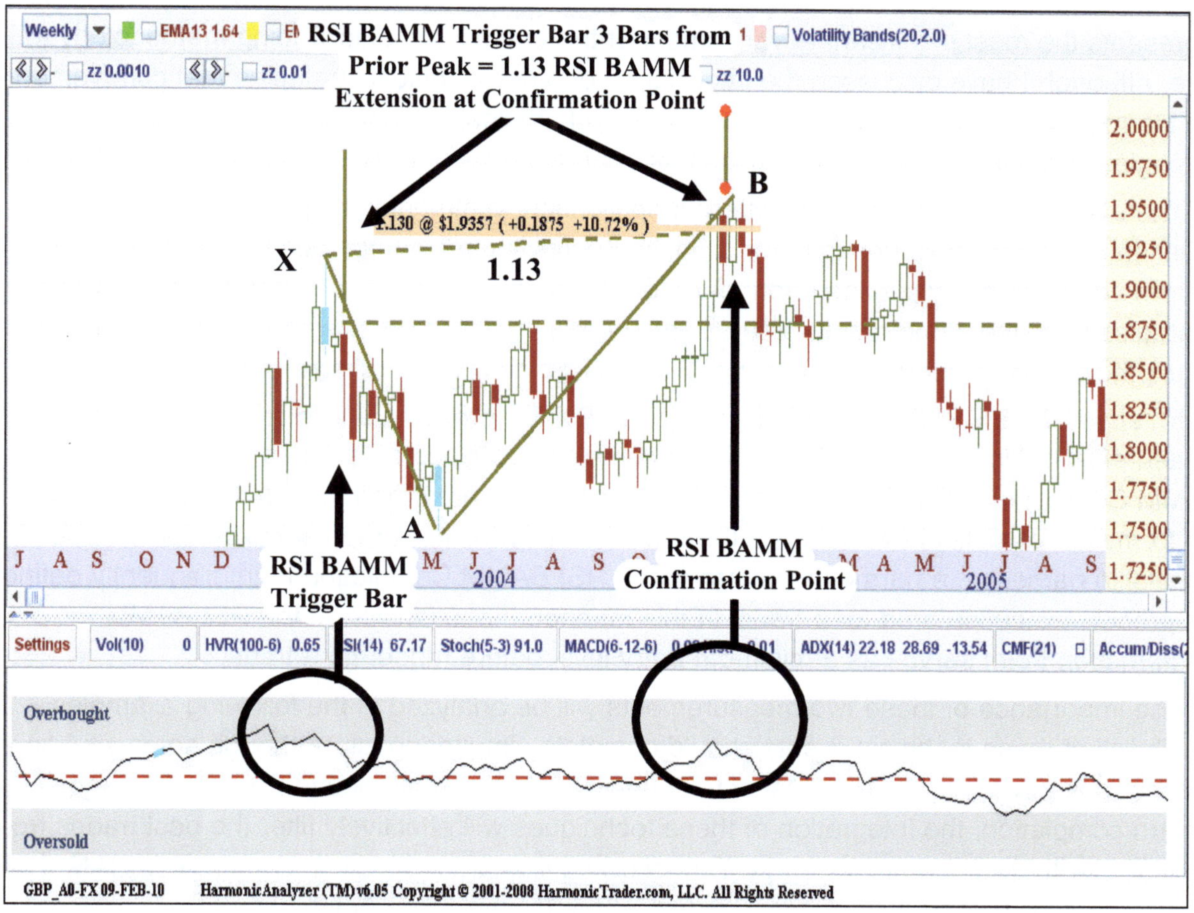

Figure 6.66

If the RSI BAMM Trigger Bar is the extreme high, the 1.618 extension would be projected to define the area where the Confirmation Point completes. I will show the 1.618 variation later in the chapter.

Step 7: Pattern Completion at the RSI BAMM Confirmation Point

After establishing the necessary steps to define the final divergence phase of the RSI BAMM, the addition of harmonic pattern recognition techniques effectively complements the target execution area for the completion of the Confirmation Point. This integration immensely improves the accuracy of the Harmonic Trading techniques to quantify critical technical levels and to define profitable trading opportunities, as well.

From a general perspective, the integration of harmonic patterns at the Confirmation Point represents the most significant advancement of the entire Harmonic Trading methodology to date. Although I have discussed the importance of other technical strategies that complement the Harmonic Trading approach in prior books and articles, the application of advanced trading strategies such as the RSI BAMM takes this approach to a new level.

The additional specification of pattern identification within uniquely prescribed technical situations yields multiple confirmation signals. Such refinement improves the determination of pattern completions by placing stronger emphasis on the PRZ, as two separate measurement strategies yield the same result. When a variety of technical measurement tools yield the same result, the technical information being provided is typically more reliable and accurate.

In terms of the RSI BAMM, the Confirmation Point represents only one primary technical measurement. Albeit as a result of a rather complex sequence of technical events, the RSI BAMM Confirmation Bar defines more of a general price area than an exact range. However, the formation of distinct harmonic patterns within this price area represents powerful trade signals. In particular, a harmonic pattern at the RSI BAMM Completion Point frequently defines the precise execution area for a trade. In this manner, the extension at the RSI BAMM Confirmation Point serves as a minimum entry level before triggering a trade.

The importance of these two measurements will be analyzed in the following examples. Ideally, all of these technical events should complete simultaneously. Although some situations may not possess all of the ideal aspects of an RSI BAMM Confirmation Point and harmonic pattern completion, the integration of these techniques will effectively filter the best trades from the losers with tremendous accuracy. The following illustrations show the entire RSI BAMM methodology with various harmonic patterns at the Confirmation Point.

Pattern Completion at the 1.13–1.618 RSI BAMM Extension Area

Although the position of the RSI BAMM Trigger Bar in relation to the prior high defines the execution area of the completion of the RSI BAMM, *the formation of distinct harmonic patterns during this final divergence stage is the defining confirmation signal for the execution of the trade.* The pattern's PRZ combined with the RSI BAMM extension provides significantly more accurate technical evidence of a probable reversal at hand. Although the execution of the trade is more dependent upon the completion of the pattern, the RSI BAMM extension is a critical minimum technical level that must be tested. Most importantly, the key to this final phase is to be patient and wait for distinct patterns to develop in these areas.

Bearish Butterfly at 1.13 RSI BAMM Confirmation Point

One of the most common patterns associated with a 1.13 RSI BAMM Confirmation Point extension is a Bearish Butterfly (see Figure 6.67). Typically, the RSI BAMM Trigger Bar will indicate a 1.13 extension, while the price action forms a distinct Bearish Butterfly, indicating that the potential reversal will occur at the 1.27 extension.

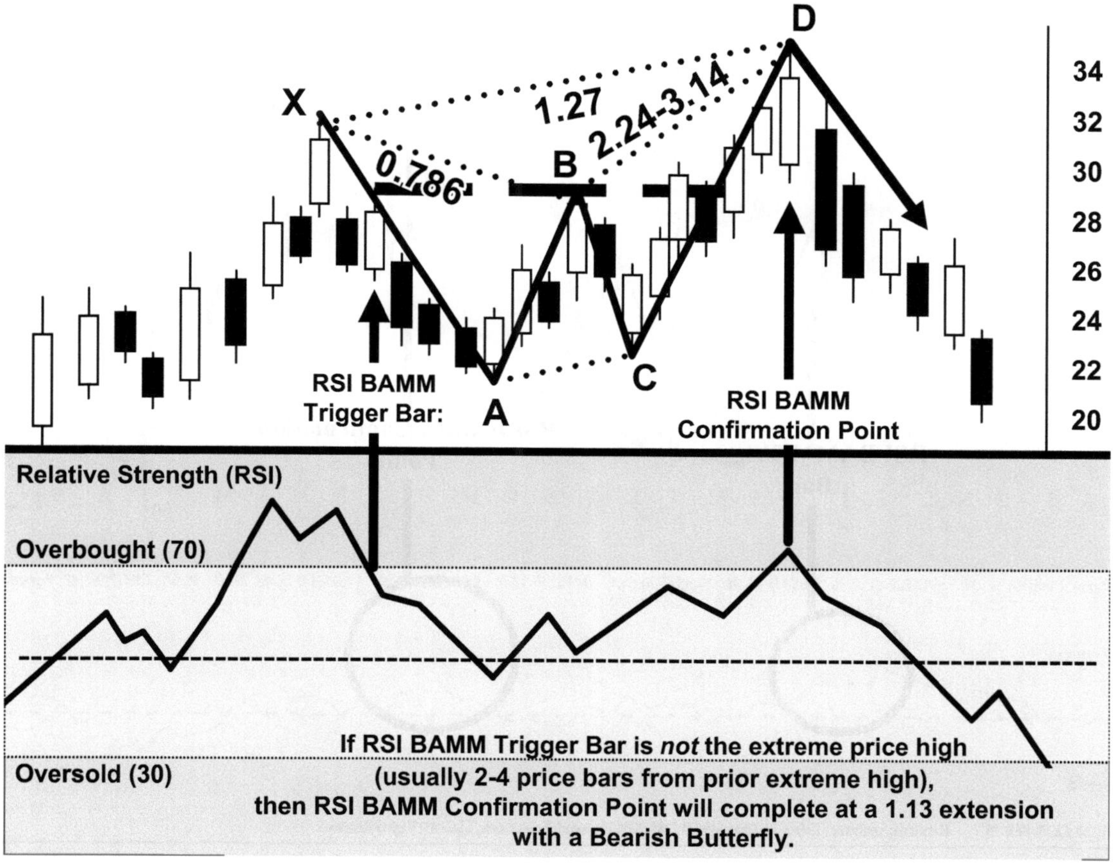

Figure 6.67

Although this may create some confusion, it is important to remember that the pattern completion point represents the most critical price level in this area. This underscores the importance of the PRZ within the RSI BAMM limits (1.13–1.618) as the most critical price area for the ultimate execution of the trade.

British Pound/USD (GBP_A0-FX): Weekly Bearish Butterfly at 1.13 RSI BAMM Confirmation Point

Referring back to our weekly example of the British Pound, the Bearish Butterfly clearly complemented the RSI BAMM Confirmation Point. Although the 1.13 extension was slightly below the pattern's PRZ, the combination of the Bearish Butterfly and the Bearish RSI BAMM defined critical long-term resistance in the 1.95–1.96 area on the weekly chart.

The chart in Figure 6.68 shows the indicator and price action that possesses a distinct bearish harmonic pattern at the RSI BAMM Confirmation Point.

Figure 6.68

British Pound/USD (GBP_A0-FX): Weekly Bearish Butterfly Potential Reversal Zone (PRZ) at 1.13 RSI BAMM Confirmation Point

The enlarged chart in Figure 6.69 of the British Pound shows the PRZ of the weekly Bearish Butterfly at the 1.13 RSI BAMM Confirmation Point.

Figure 6.69

Clearly, the PRZ of the pattern with the RSI BAMM Confirmation Bar identified critical long-term resistance, as the British Pound reversed sharply in the weeks following the completion of the setup.

Alternate Bearish Bat at 1.13 RSI BAMM Confirmation Point

Although a Bearish Butterfly possesses powerful harmonic implications at the 1.13 RSI BAMM Confirmation Point extension, there are many instances where an Alternate Bat Pattern may be the only structure forming at the completion of the setup (see Figure 6.70).

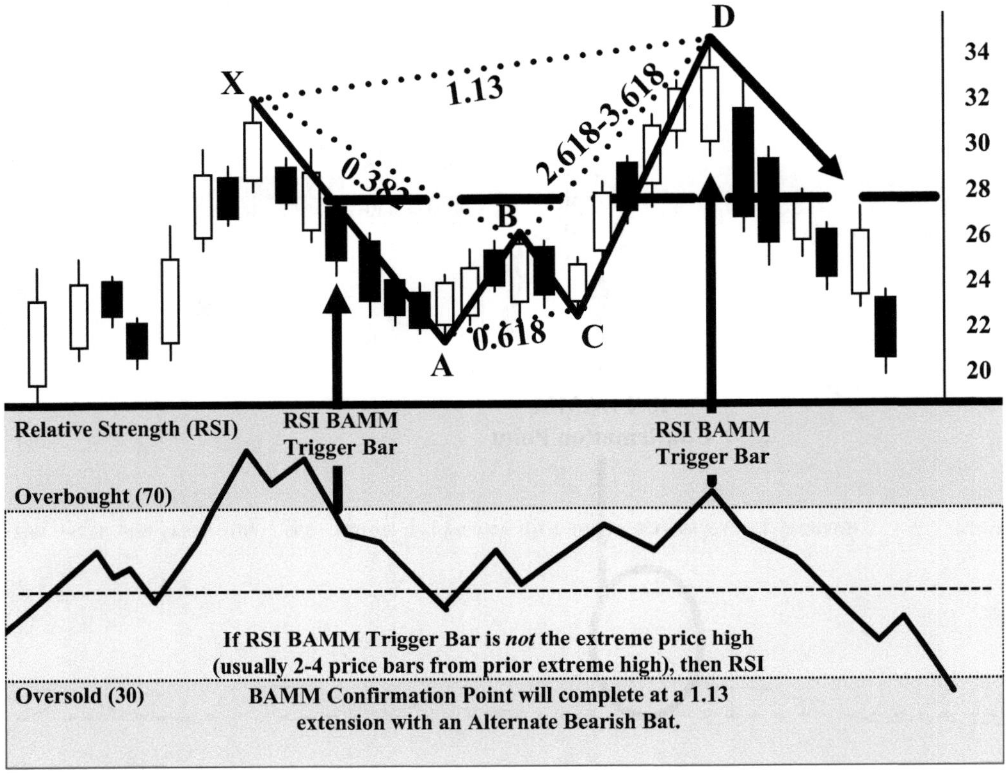

Figure 6.70

In the case of the Alternate Bat, the completion of the setup will typically reverse very close to the 1.13 extension. It is important to focus on this extension level and the RSI Confirmation Point for an indication that the reversal has completed. As long as the other elements of the RSI BAMM and the pattern alignment complete in the same area, the trade execution at the 1.13 extension is valid.

On a side note, you may be wondering about other retracement patterns like the Gartley or the Bat that may form in conjunction with a 1.13 extension. Although these patterns will typically complete before the 1.13 extension, the position of their RSI BAMM Trigger Bar will typically be 5 or more price bars from the prior high. I will show an example a bit later in this chapter. As for the Alternate Bat pattern, the Trigger Bar will typically be 3–4 price bars from the prior high.

Standard and Poor's 500 ETF (SPY): 5-Minute Alternate Bearish Bat at RSI BAMM Confirmation Point

The chart of the SPY in Figure 6.71 shows a distinct RSI BAMM setup with a Bearish Alternate Bat converging at the Completion Point. The price action reversed sharply after testing the PRZ and the overbought 70 limit. The precise reversal and decisive continuation following the completion of the setup were clear signs of a valid reversal at hand.

Figure 6.71

Although the SPY reversed just shy of the 1.13 extension, the price action tested most of the PRZ at the same time it completed the impulsive retest at the RSI Completion Point. Again, the coordination of these technical events is the defining element of all valid reversals. When the completion of the pattern occurs simultaneously with the RSI retest, the reversal is likely to yield a significant move.

Standard and Poor's 500 ETF (SPY): 5-Minute Alternate Bearish Bat Potential Reversal Zone (PRZ) at RSI BAMM Confirmation Point

The enlarged chart in Figure 6.72 of the Alternate Bearish Bat PRZ at the RSI BAMM Confirmation Point reveals the ideal elements for a valid reversal. The price action stalled immediately in the PRZ and exemplified the model technical coordination between the completion of the pattern and the RSI BAMM.

Figure 6.72

The SPY "kissed" the 70 level on the RSI retest as the pattern completed. In addition, the overwhelming downside continuation following the completion of the setup helped to quickly confirm its validity.

Pattern Completion Before 1.13–1.618 RSI BAMM Extension at Confirmation Point: Bearish Bat

The Bearish Bat structure that completes at an RSI Confirmation Point offers a unique trade opportunity. The structure of the pattern is extremely important to distinguish the optimal execution for the trade. The price action will usually test the PRZ and the overbought extreme zone before an execution signal is generated. The impulsive retest will occur at the 0.886 retracement—not the minimum 1.13 RSI BAMM extension (see Figure 6.73).

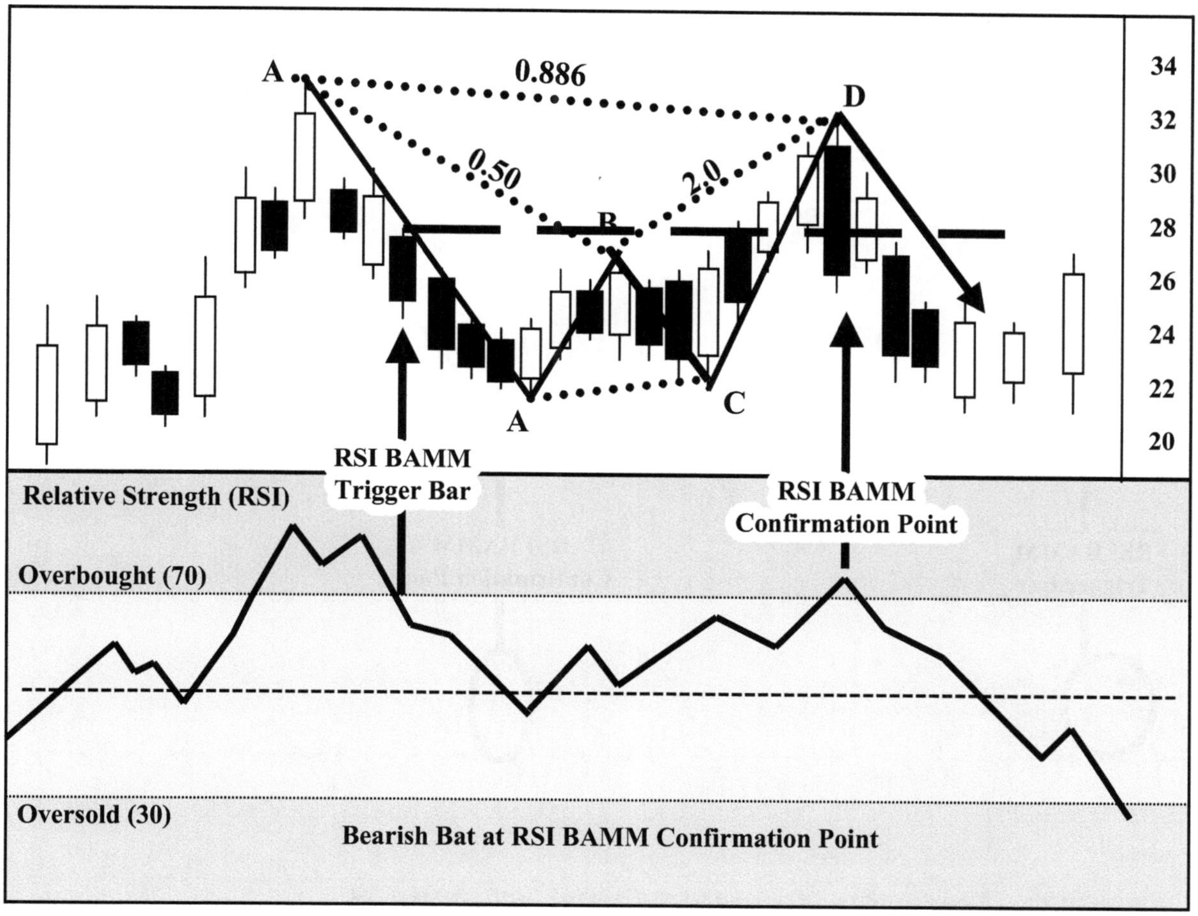

Figure 6.73

Although the Trigger Bar high point resistance (dotted line) complements this area, the coordination of these two technical events is critical in determining the minor reactive moves from the major reversals.

Standard and Poor's 500 March 2010 Mini-Contract (ES_H0): 15-Minute Bearish Bat at RSI BAMM Extension

Figure 6.74 shows a Bearish Bat that completed in conjunction with the RSI BAMM Confirmation Point (see Figure 6.74). The interesting aspect of this situation was the slightly delayed test of the PRZ, as the price action tested the RSI BAMM Completion Point well before the ultimate reversal.

Figure 6.74

Standard and Poor's 500 March 2010 Mini-Contract (ES_H0): 15-Minute Bearish Bat Potential Reversal Zone (PRZ) at RSI BAMM Confirmation Point

Figure 6.75 shows an enlarged chart of the price action the PRZ. Although the RSI rolled over much earlier, this example underscores the need to coordinate the pattern completion with the indicator divergence. Also, this situation demonstrates that the RSI BAMM completion is a minimum technical signal and relies on the completion of the pattern to dictate when and where to execute the trade.

Figure 6.75

Pattern Completion Before 1.13–1.618 RSI BAMM Extension at Confirmation Point: Bearish Gartley

In the case of the Bearish Gartley, the structure of the pattern is extremely important. Although the PRZ is typically well below the minimum 1.13 RSI BAMM extension, this situation still relies on coordinating the completion of the pattern with the final impulsive indicator retest (see Figure 6.76).

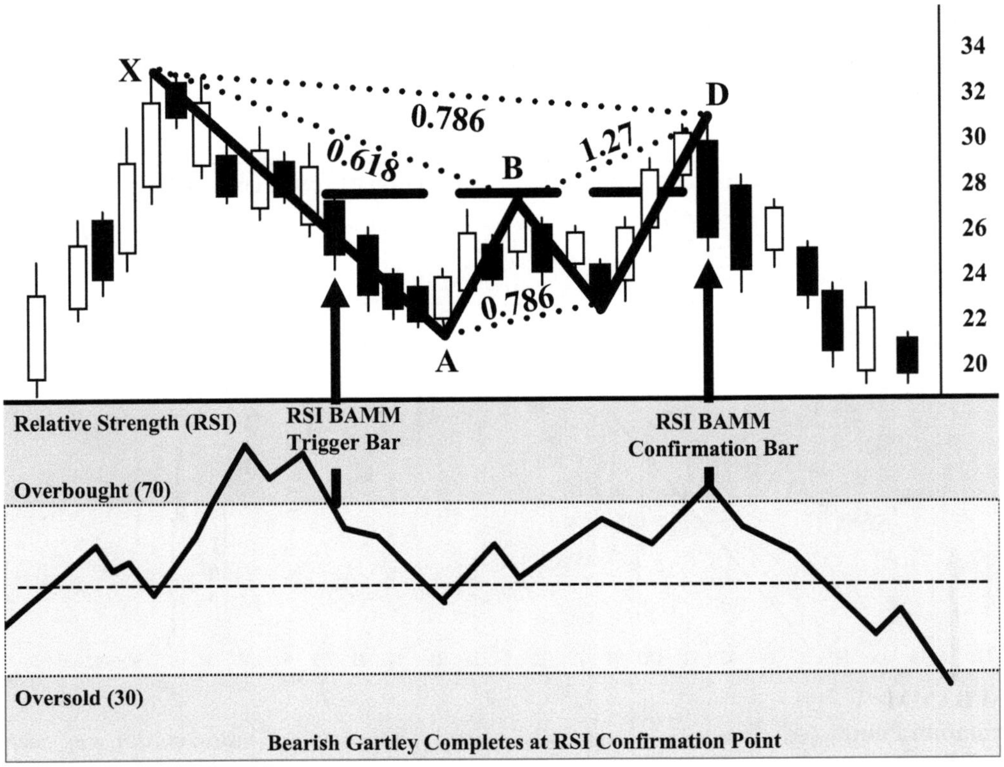

Figure 6.76

Although the Trigger Bar high point resistance (dotted line) complements this area, the coordination of these two technical events is most critical in validating the best trade opportunities.

Eurodollar (EUR_A0-FX): 5-Minute Bearish Gartley at RSI BAMM Extension

In this example, the price action possessed a distinct bearish Gartley pattern that completed in conjunction with the RSI BAMM Confirmation Point (see Figure 6.77).

Figure 6.77

Although the Euro rallied sharply as it tested the PRZ, the price action stalled immediately after hitting the overbought 70 level at the RSI BAMM Confirmation Point.

Eurodollar (EUR_A0-FX): 5-Minute Bearish Gartley Potential Reversal Zone (PRZ) at RSI BAMM Confirmation Point

The price action the PRZ is illustrated particularly well on the enlarged chart in Figure 6.78. The arrow points to where the RSI BAMM Confirmation Point completed.

Figure 6.78

Both technical events of the pattern's completion and the successful impulsive RSI retest occurred nearly on the same day. This situation exemplifies the type of coordination between the two approaches that yields the best trading opportunities.

Pattern Completion Before 1.13–1.618 RSI BAMM Extension at Confirmation Area: Bearish 5-0 Pattern

The Bearish 5-0 pattern is probably the most difficult to incorporate with the RSI BAMM. This is due simply to the fact that the completion of the pattern occurs nowhere near the minimum 1.13 RSI BAMM extension (see Figure 6.79).

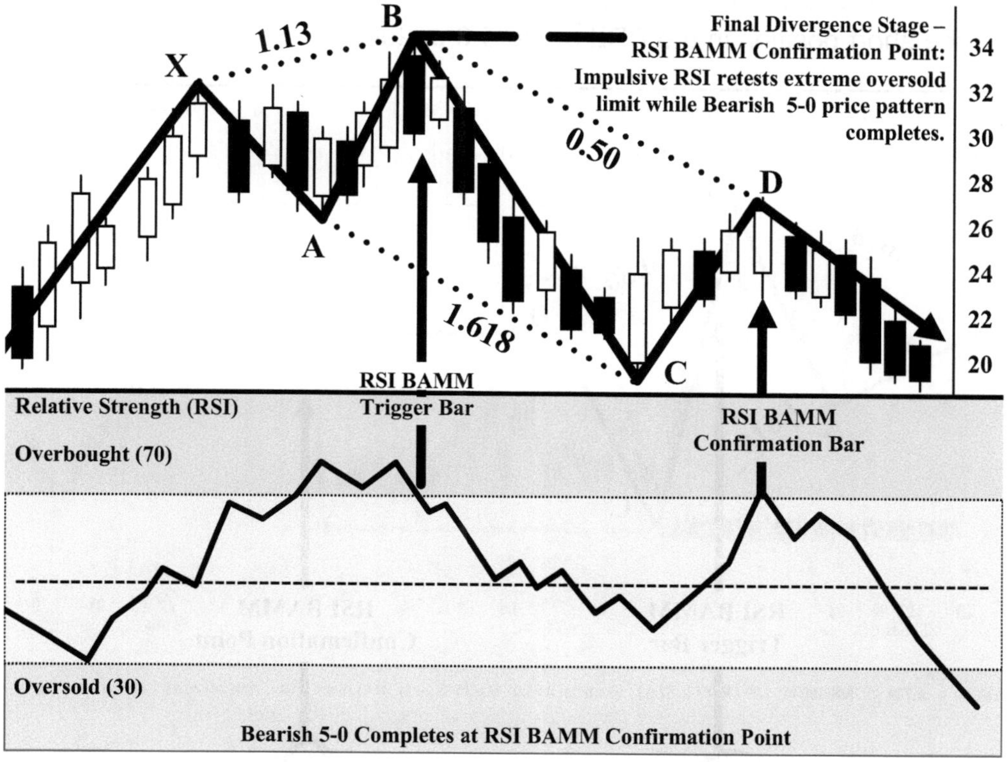

Figure 6.79

As is the case with all harmonic patterns in the RSI BAMM setup, coordination is the key. The best 5-0 patterns require a distinct price structure that must complete in tandem with the RSI BAMM Confirmation Point. It is important to focus on the completion of the impulsive RSI retest, as this will typically be the most significant signal within the PRZ of the pattern.

Google (GOOG): 15-Minute Pattern Completion Before 1.13–1.618 RSI BAMM Extension at Confirmation Area: Bearish 5-0 Pattern

The intra-day chart of Google in Figure 6.80 shows a distinct Bearish 5-0 pattern that completed simultaneously with the RSI BAMM Confirmation Point. The successful reversal following the impulsive retest at the Confirmation Point was a definitive signal to confirm the execution of the short position in the PRZ of the 5-0 pattern.

Figure 6.80

Although the typical 1.13 or 1.618 extension does not factor into these situations, the coordination of the impulsive RSI retest and the completion of the pattern continually provides accurate signals and effectively filters the best setups. Therefore, the 5-0 relies on the coordination of the indicator readings and the price action more than any other pattern applied to the RSI BAMM approach.

1.618 Extension at RSI BAMM Confirmation Point

The general rule for the Confirmation Point extension must focus on the location of the Trigger Bar, as it relates to the extreme prior peak. If the RSI BAMM Trigger Bar is the high price bar, the 1.618 extension is utilized to quantify the execution area for the trade (see Figure 6.81).

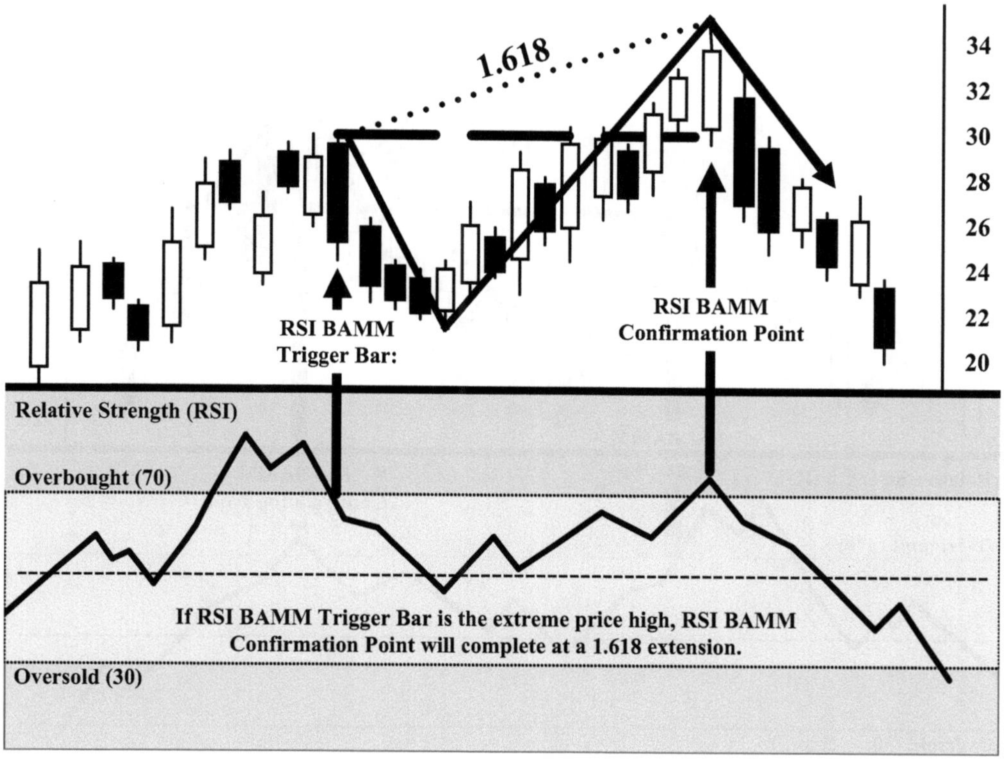

Figure 6.81

The two patterns that are utilized in these situations are the Bearish Crab and the Deep Bearish Crab. The following case studies are fantastic examples of pattern completions within the final phase of the RSI BAMM that converge with a 1.618 Confirmation Point. Although the 1.618 extension is the most critical harmonic number in this setup, the PRZ of the pattern defines the exact price range to execute the trade but still relies on the coordination of the RSI BAMM Confirmation Point to optimize trading decisions.

Bearish Crab at 1.618 RSI BAMM Confirmation Point

In the Bearish RSI BAMM, the general rule for the Confirmation Point extension must focus on the location of the Trigger Bar, as it relates to the extreme prior low. *If the Bearish RSI BAMM Trigger Bar is the extreme high, the 1.618 extension is utilized to quantify the Confirmation Point and the execution area for the trade* (see Figure 6.82).

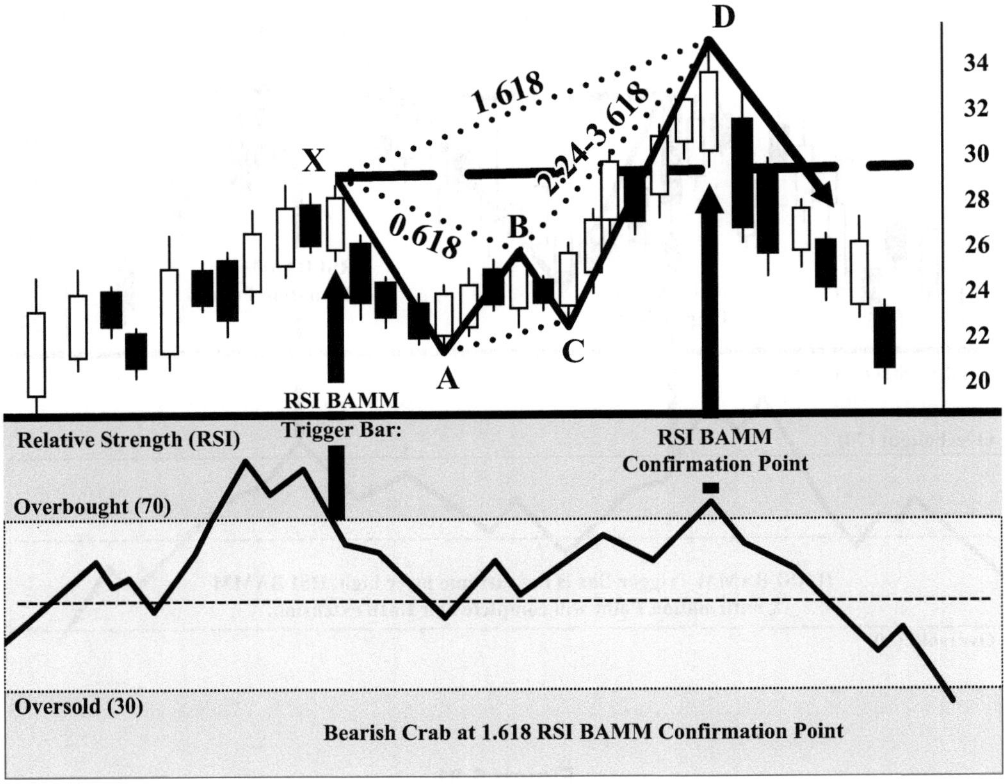

Figure 6.82

Although other factors will be considered, the importance of the extreme high to signal a 1.618 RSI BAMM extension helps to define the ultimate execution point for the trade. Two patterns—the Bearish Crab and the Deep Bearish Crab—utilize the 1.618 extension. Regardless of which Crab defines the PRZ, the crucial technical event occurs when the price action tests this area at the same time it completes the RSI BAMM Confirmation Bar.

Family Dollar (FDO): Daily Bearish Crab with Bearish RSI BAMM

The daily chart of Family Dollar in Figure 6.83 shows a Bearish Crab that completed with a distinct Bearish RSI BAMM setup. Since the extreme prior high at the X point represented the Trigger Bar, the ultimate completion occurred at the 1.618 extension.

Figure 6.83

The stock reversed immediately after testing the 1.618 RSI BAMM Completion Point. The decisive downside continuation accelerated after the RSI impulsive retest reversed from the 70 level. Again, the coordination of the reversal in both the pattern and the RSI BAMM signaled a valid setup at hand.

Deep Bearish Crab at 1.618 RSI BAMM Confirmation Point

Similar to the 1.13 RSI BAMM extension, the 1.618 extension is dictated by the position of the Trigger Bar. In this case, a Trigger Bar that is the extreme prior high will result in a corresponding pattern that utilizes a 1.618 projection. Within the Harmonic Trading arsenal of patterns, this will usually manifest as a Crab or Deep Crab pattern.

The Deep Bearish Crab presents a unique situation at the RSI BAMM Completion Point (see Figure 6.84). The 1.618 extension is the defining level for both the completion of the pattern and the RSI BAMM. In these situations, the 1.618 extension becomes even more significant, and the price action should not exceed this resistance level. Furthermore, most valid reversals will occur quickly after this area has been tested.

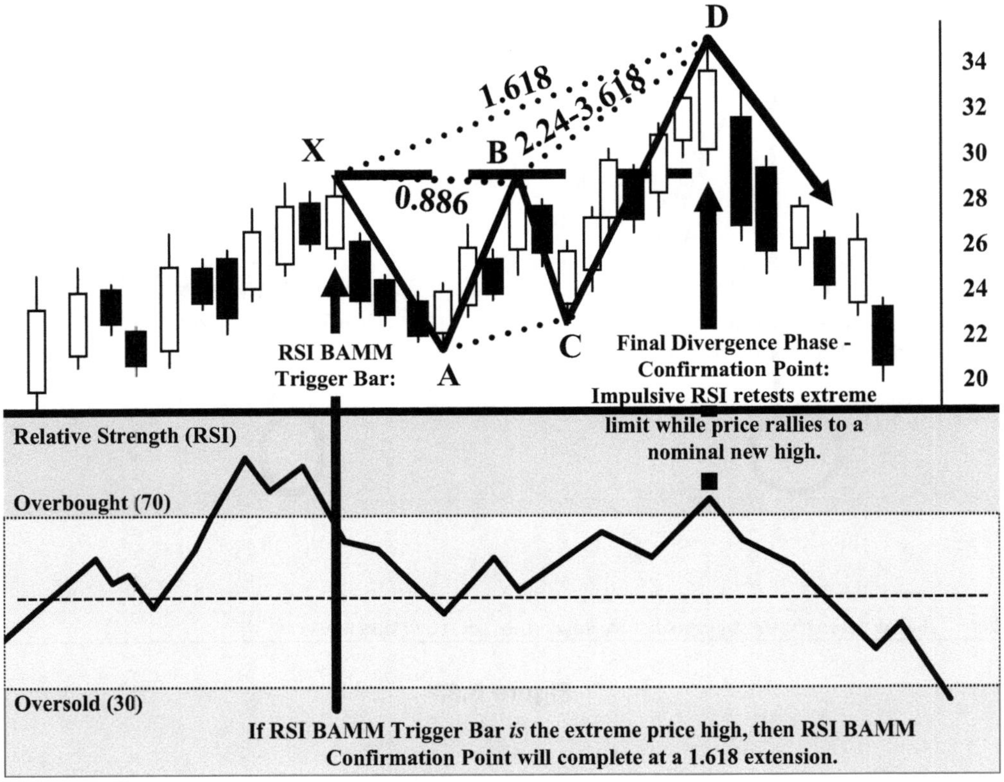

Figure 6.84

Boeing (BA): Daily
Deep Bearish Crab with Bearish RSI BAMM

The Boeing chart in Figure 6.85 shows the entire RSI BAMM and the distinct Bearish Crab that formed during the divergence phase of the RSI BAMM. Although there were other numbers in the PRZ to complement this harmonic resistance, the 1.618 extension was the defining technical level in the setup. The convergence of the completion of the pattern with the impulsive RSI retest marked a critical reversal for the stock on the daily chart.

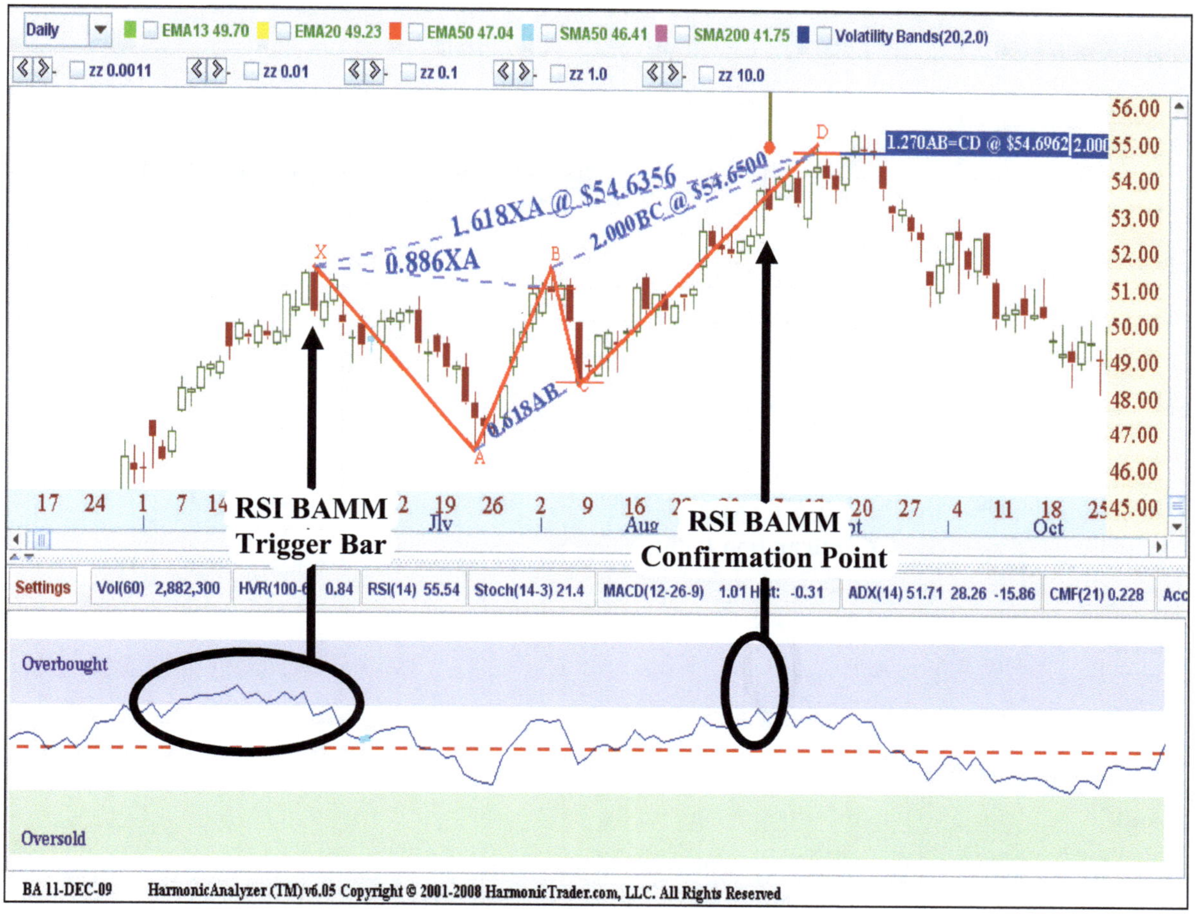

Figure 6.85

Although the RSI BAMM Confirmation Point completed before the entire test of the PRZ, both methods indicated the distinct area where this trend would change. In addition, this example of Boeing truly shows how distinct harmonic patterns that form in the final phase of the RSI BAMM can pinpoint precise reversal zones.

Boeing (BA): Daily
Deep Bearish Crab Potential Reversal Zone (PRZ) at 1.618 RSI BAMM Confirmation Point

The enlarged chart in Figure 6.86 of the price action in the PRZ at the RSI BAMM Confirmation Point clearly shows how the uptrend stalled as it tested this area and rolled over shortly after completing the pattern.

Figure 6.86

On a side note, the impulsive RSI retest reading literally kissed the 70 limit and reversed. These situations may be difficult to assess because the RSI BAMM Confirmation Point typically involves a sharp and brief indicator test. Although these situations may be tricky, the PRZ of the pattern serves to indicate the optimal price level for the trade execution. Remember, both conditions of a pattern completion and a successful test of the Confirmation Point are required to validate the entire RSI BAMM setup.

RSI BAMM Confirmation Point—Reversal Acceleration Trigger

An additional technical trigger serves as a secondary confirmation. Although this final trigger does not develop in every situation, when present after the final test of the Confirmation Point, it typically represents an area of acceleration of the reversal.

Bearish Confirmation Point—Reversal Acceleration Trigger

The important focus of this Acceleration Trigger is the impulsive test of the RSI in conjunction with the price action. The structure of the RSI reading is critical after it sinks *below the 70 level*, as it can offer an important technical trigger that marks the area where the reversal should begin to accelerate (see Figure 6.87).

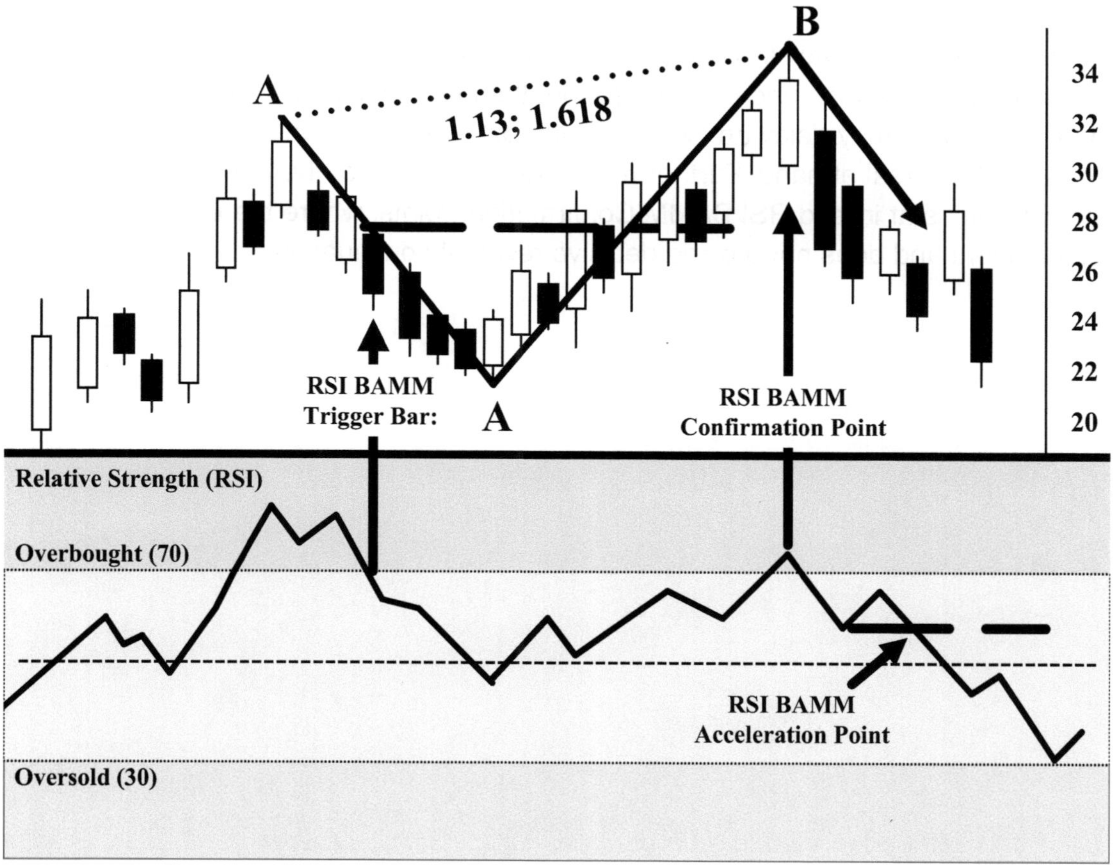

Figure 6.87

Typically, the RSI reading forms a brief “corrective pause” before accelerating to the downside. This “corrective pause” usually occurs within a few price bars of the breakdown. The trigger is determined by the price bar that results in the (accelerated) breakdown of the indicator reading following the completion of the RSI BAMM Confirmation Point.

It is important to expect that the RSI trigger signal will develop *before* the price begins to move. Although the RSI trigger is a bit early, the RSI BAMM Acceleration Trigger marks the most critical area within the entire strategy. This price level marks where an acceleration of the reversal price action *must occur* at this point or shortly thereafter. After the reaction from the overbought area, the indicator reading of the final RSI BAMM Confirmation Point should accelerate decidedly following the impulsive test of this last phase. In particular, the structure of the RSI reading is critical after it sinks *below the 70 level*, as it must demonstrate a decisive continuation of the reversal trend. Specifically, an M-type formation following the impulsive RSI test at the Confirmation Point should serve as an acceleration level that marks the beginning of the new trend.

The magnified illustration of the Bearish RSI BAMM Confirmation Point in Figure 6.88 clearly shows the ideal indicator structure that serves as a definitive confirmation trigger. It is important to note that the ideal structure is more visibly seen in the RSI than the price. Sometimes, the initial pullback following a reversal from the RSI BAMM Confirmation Point may only be a one or two bearish price bar pause, but the internal action is weakening. Although waiting for this trigger may delay an execution, the extra confirmation does provide a reliable signal of a valid reversal at hand. Furthermore, this breakdown of the Acceleration Trigger prevents executions at invalid RSI BAMM Confirmation Points, where the impulsive test at the 70 level flounders and does not provide decisive reversal continuation.

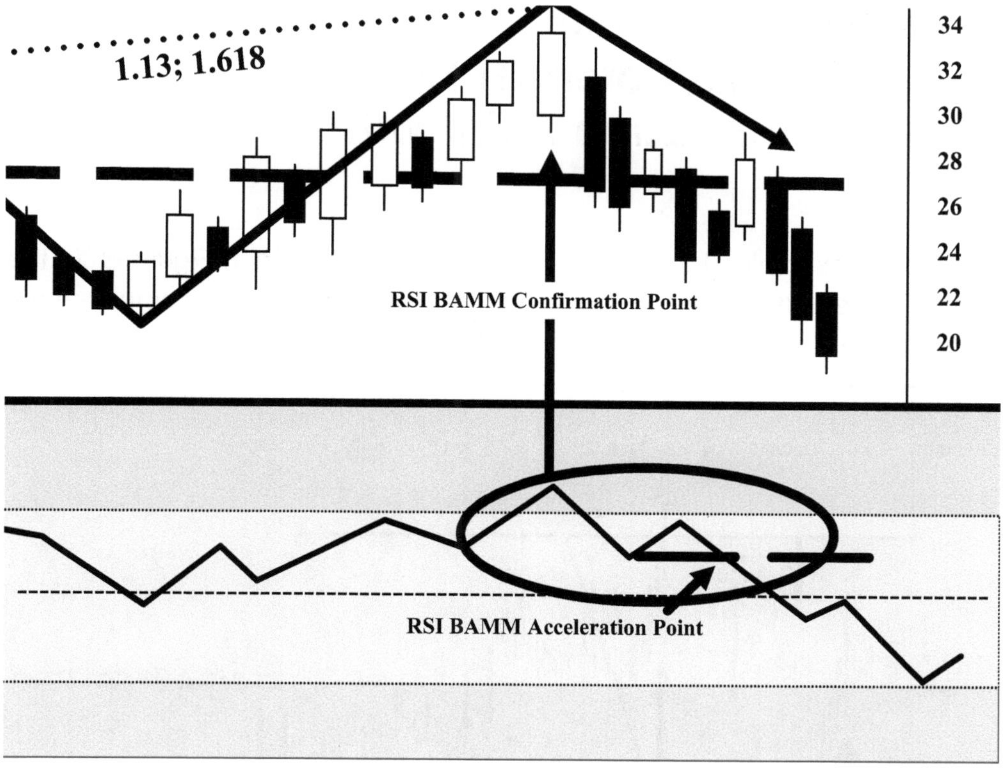

Figure 6.88

In these situations, it is important to respond appropriately and exit the trade at a small loss or break even due to the fact that the price action languishes after completing the RSI BAMM Confirmation Point.

The price action should move quickly and decidedly after the Acceleration Trigger is confirmed. The price bar that completes the breakdown of the M-type structure in the RSI reading will typically mark the acceleration point of the new reversal trend. When this trigger materializes, it creates a "do-or-die" situation while possessing powerful price action signals. In fact, the Acceleration Trigger represents the most sophisticated technical setup within the entire Harmonic Trading approach.

Google (GOOG): 5-Minute Bearish 5-0 Pattern Potential Reversal Zone (PRZ) at RSI BAMM Confirmation Point with Acceleration Trigger

Referring back to the example of the Bearish 5-0 pattern in Google in Figure 6.80, the stock reversed precisely after hitting the entire PRZ at the same time the RSI completed a successful impulsive retest of the overbought extreme limit above the 70 level (see Figure 6.89).

Figure 6.89

The Acceleration Bar completed an M-type structure after the indicator reading broke down under the 70 level. This extra signal effectively indicated the area where the reversal would accelerate. It is important to note that the combination of the measuring techniques of harmonic price patterns and the ability of the RSI BAMM to define divergent areas of price action present an advanced methodology of technical strategies that effectively optimizes trading decisions in an unprecedented fashion. In particular, the final phase of the RSI BAMM represents a powerful technical measuring technique in its own right. When harmonic patterns converge at the Confirmation Point of the RSI BAMM, the multitude of technical readings serves to generate a consensus reading of whether to execute the trade.

Bearish RSI BAMM Failure—Stop Loss Considerations

After defining the entire range of the RSI BAMM and the harmonic pattern completion points, the only consideration beyond the execution is the stop loss limit. The stop loss is a combination of the RSI BAMM extension—typically beyond the 1.618—and the price limit of the pattern that corresponds with the setup. Again, this will also include the price levels that are defined by the larger relevant harmonic levels. From a purely RSI BAMM perspective, the key invalidation point truly occurs beyond the 1.618 extension of the final divergent move. The validation of the technical phenomenon becomes questionable beyond the 2.0 extension of the final move for either situation.

In the case of the 1.13 RSI BAMM extension, it should not experience price action beyond the 1.618 level. For the 1.618 RSI BAMM extension, the price action should not exceed the 2.0 projection. Again, these are more guidelines than strict rules, as the stop loss for each situation is dependent upon the pattern completion at the RSI BAMM Confirmation Point.

As is the case for harmonic pattern failures, price action that violates these price levels, especially on the first test, should raise a red flag that the primary trend is quite strong. Most important, the area defined by the pattern's PRZ and the RSI BAMM Confirmation Point defines a "do or die" price level that does not leave much room for discretion.

From a purely RSI BAMM perspective, the stop loss point represents the area where the entire scenario fails. Although these general rules attempt to define reliable technical levels to discern potential RSI BAMM violations, each situation still requires an ability to assess price action relative to the conditions of the setup to optimize trading decisions. Sometimes, these can be tricky situations. However, these rules provide defined limits where the reversal must occur.

As a side note, I dedicate an entire chapter to pattern failures in *Harmonic Trading: Volume One*. I will not cover the specifics of these strategies in this material. However, these violations are important technical events within the Harmonic Trading approach. It is important to recognize the violation of these precise harmonic zones and how they typically exhibit decisive price action in the continuation of the predominant trend.

Intercontinental Exchange (ICE): 5-Minute Bearish Alternate Bat and RSI BAMM Failure

The Intercontinental Exchange (ICE) example in Figure 6.90 shows a distinct Bearish RSI BAMM setup on the 5-minute chart. Despite the ideal conditions, the stock rallied sharply above the RSI BAMM Confirmation Point. In fact, the impulsive RSI retest exceeded the prior reading at the Confirmation Point as it continued above the PRZ.

Figure 6.90

This example shows the typical price action involved with a violation of the RSI BAMM setup. Specifically, ICE formed the RSI BAMM with a 1.13 extension that was projected to complete at $72 a share. However, the price action exceeded this area and continued through the 1.618 stop loss projection.

Intercontinental Exchange (ICE): 5-Minute Bearish Alternate Bat and Bearish RSI BAMM Failure

The chart in Figure 6.91 shows the Bearish Alternate Bat that completed at the RSI BAMM Confirmation Point. The combination of the bearish pattern and the RSI BAMM setup clearly defined the $72 level as critical short-term resistance. Despite the ideal conditions, the price action rallied sharply through the PRZ and the RSI BAMM Confirmation Point after a brief consolidation.

Figure 6.91

The inclusion of the pattern with the RSI BAMM Confirmation Point helped to define a more precise area and to determine the violation of the setup. Although the violation of the 1.618 RSI BAMM extension was a substantial signal, the strong price action through the pattern's PRZ was the definitive technical evidence that indicated a failure at hand.

Intercontinental Exchange (ICE): 60-Minute Bearish Alternate Bat Potential Reversal Zone (PRZ) and Bearish RSI BAMM Failure

The enlarged chart in Figure 6.92 clearly shows the decisive upside continuation through the PRZ. Although the general rule of thumb in the case of the 1.13 RSI BAMM incorporates a 1.618 extension as the stop loss limit, the pattern's PRZ in this example of ICE signaled a violation much earlier.

Figure 6.92

It is important to note that the same rules apply with the 1.618 RSI BAMM extension. The essence of determining the validity of an opportunity is to analyze the price action as it completes the pattern *and* retests the overbought RSI 70 level. If the action in both the price and the RSI decisively violates its respective technical levels, a significant continuation of the primary trend typically follows. Although it will require some time to effectively decipher these situations, the ability of these techniques to distinguish such opportunities is immensely accurate.

Final RSI BAMM Review

The RSI BAMM represents a significant evolution in the Harmonic Trading approach. The integrative strategies embodied within the RSI BAMM clearly demonstrate effectiveness of multiple confirmation techniques to define trade opportunities. Although others—including Welles Wilder himself—have presented research that discusses the basic concepts of divergence as it relates to Relative Strength, I believe that this technique that incorporates harmonic measurement strategies is the most precise means of quantifying this technical phenomenon. In fact, the inclusion of harmonic patterns to act as structural signals to further refine these divergent situations presents an immensely accurate system that quantifies precise technical levels of potential harmonic support and resistance in an unprecedented fashion.

Since discovering the RSI BAMM, the price zones of support and resistance that incorporate both the RSI and PRZ measurements have immensely improved the basic pattern identification techniques. These unprecedented strategies advance the basic tenets of the Harmonic Trading approach to define unique situations where harmonic pattern completions are especially significant.

The RSI BAMM includes the following steps:

- Step 1: Initial Test of the Extreme RSI Limit
- Step 2: Complete M- or W-Type Complex RSI Structure
- Step 3: Define the RSI Trigger Bar
- Step 4: Assess Reaction of RSI and Price
- Step 5: The Final Phase—Divergence of RSI Versus Price
- Step 6: RSI BAMM Confirmation Point: 1.13 Versus 1.618
- Step 7: Pattern Completion at the RSI BAMM Confirmation Point

Although each step must be assessed carefully, this approach clearly defines the required elements to validate the RSI BAMM conditions. Although the pattern completion is the last step in the process, the integration of the PRZ and the RSI BAMM Completion Point is dependent upon each of the prior steps to be satisfied to trigger this technical phenomenon. These requirements must be met before any pattern can be considered to define a trade opportunity. It is important to review some of the most critical elements of the RSI BAMM.

RSI BAMM Tips

- Look for the Extreme RSI Complex indicator reading to initiate the setup.
- Look for the initial reaction of the complex RSI reading to retest the 50 limit reading at a minimum before completing the Confirmation Point.
- Wait for the divergence of RSI and price, as long as the impulsive RSI retest of the extreme limit does not exceed the reading of the prior complex structure.

- The execution of the trade is triggered at the completion of the relative harmonic pattern that completes at the appropriate RSI BAMM extension level.
- The Acceleration Trigger provides an extremely effective final confirmation signal when it develops following the RSI BAMM Confirmation Point.

The concept of divergence is quantified effectively by the RSI BAMM approach. As a trader, I am constantly analyzing charts, looking for the best opportunities that signal a significant change in the primary trend. The combination of the RSI BAMM approach with the completion of harmonic patterns creates a unique divergent situation that defines immensely accurate trading opportunities. Although these strategies may take some time to integrate into your current trading plan, the advanced techniques represent a substantial advancement of the entire Harmonic Trading approach and serve to filter the best pattern completions. In the years to come, I firmly believe that the RSI BAMM and the other advanced strategies presented in this book will go a long way in helping you to turn patterns into profits—because that's what this game is all about!

Conclusion

Harmonic Trading: Volume Two represents my most comprehensive research to date. The new patterns and trading strategies, especially the RSI BAMM, take the Harmonic Trading approach to a new level. These strategies refine the existing approach presented in my first two books. *Volume Two* incorporates new measurement techniques, providing more accurate technical information and optimizing trade decisions. Although these concepts include new elements to define harmonic price behavior, this analysis still adheres to the primary tenets of the Harmonic Trading approach of pattern recognition as quantified by Fibonacci ratios. Although this material encompasses new technical measures, the same analytical process is applied to identify harmonic price behavior.

Is This Really Harmonic Trading?

Despite the effectiveness of the RSI BAMM, you might be asking: "Is this really Harmonic Trading?" To answer this, we need to ask the proverbial question: "What is Harmonic Trading?" The answer is

> ***"Harmonic Trading is a methodology that utilizes the recognition of specific structures that possess distinct and consecutive Fibonacci ratio alignments that quantify and validate harmonic patterns. These patterns calculate the Fibonacci aspects of these price structures to identify highly probable reversal points in the financial markets.... The identification of historically repetitive price patterns is the primary means that these techniques utilize to interpret the market's signals. It is in this effective price pattern identification ability that Harmonic Trading possesses its greatest advantages. The precision and accuracy of the specific pattern alignments define a consistent and effective approach that can be easily applied. Furthermore, each distinct pattern acts as a model for the basis of all trading decisions. Once a potential pattern is identified, the trading opportunity can be managed according to a defined set of rules that are particular for each situation. Although each pattern possesses different elements, Harmonic Trading does identify specific repetitive situations within the chaos of the financial markets."***
>
> (Scott M. Carney, *Harmonic Trading: Volume One* [FT Press 2010], 7-8).

In essence, the techniques in *Volume Two* utilize pattern recognition and Fibonacci ratios to define unique technical support and resistance levels. Although the analysis in this material addressed indicator structures and employed new patterns to define harmonic price behavior, the measurement tools are consistent with the Harmonic Trading methodology.

What's More Important: RSI BAMM or Harmonic Patterns?

Without a doubt, the strategies presented in this material—in particular, BAMM Theory and the RSI BAMM—are practically a trading system unto themselves. This could be a costly fact for me to mention. Why trade harmonic patterns when the RSI BAMM works so well on its own? There's no doubt that both harmonic price pattern recognition strategies and the RSI BAMM approach can be effective in their own right. But their true effectiveness can be seen when they work in concert with each other. When techniques of multiple approaches come together and yield the same result, the probability for a successful trading opportunity is extremely high.

Harmonic patterns represent the starting point for the entire methodology. The effective measurement techniques presented in my first two books offered a comprehensive system that effectively deciphered price action and determined trade opportunities. However, the material within *Volume Two* identifies an unprecedented technical situation where both the RSI and the pattern completion converge to identify an extremely precise trading opportunity. Again, this is where the confirmation of multiple technical methods gives a much greater probability of a valid reversal and possibly a more significant move. Despite this "dual approach," I must emphasize that patterns are still more critical within the Harmonic Trading approach than the RSI BAMM. In fact, I would not recommend executing an RSI BAMM setup without a pattern.

As my research has continued through the years, the advantage of defining specific "technical entities" such as the RSI BAMM within the context of harmonic price behavior has yielded consistently reliable information regarding the potential state of future price action. When harmonic patterns develop in specific technical situations, their completion typically represents a critical point within the predominant trend. This specification improves the overall comprehension of the price action and creates a defined system to identify valid trade opportunities. Therefore, it is always important to be as precise as possible.

In closing, I want to thank you for taking the time to study this material. I truly believe that these unprecedented strategies are extremely effective in discovering the most profitable trading opportunities. In my opinion, the material in this book represents the most significant advancement of the entire Harmonic Trading approach since its inception, as well. Finally, I hope that these new ideas are embraced within the field of Technical Analysis as widely as the initial concepts of this approach have been accepted.

Bibliography

Carney, Scott M. *Harmonic Trading: Volume One*. Upper Saddle River, NJ: FT Press, 2010.

——. *The Harmonic Trader*. Nevada: HarmonicTrader.com, L.L.C, 1999.

Cohen, Guy. *Options Made Easy*. London: Prentice-Hall, 2005.

Edwards, Robert and John Magee. *Technical Analysis of Stock Trends*, 8th ed. Boca Raton, FL: CRC Press, LLC, 2001.

Frost, Alfred John and Robert Prechter. *Elliott Wave Principle*. Gainesville, GA: New Classics Library, 1978.

Hurst, J. M. *J. M. Hurst Cycles Course*. Greenville, SC: Traders Press, 1973.

——. *The Profit Magic of Stock Transaction Timing*. Greenville, SC: Traders Press, 1970.

Kane, Jim. *Trade Management*. Tucson, AZ: KaneTrading.com, 2005.

——. *Median Line and Fibonacci Synergy*. Tucson, AZ: KaneTrading.com, 2006.

Warren, Ted. *How to Make the Stock Market Make Money for You*. Grants Pass, OR: The Ted Warren Company, 1966.

Wilder, J. Welles. *New Concepts in Technical Trading Systems*. Greensboro, NC: Trend Research, 1978.

Wyckoff, Richard. *Stock Market Technique*. Fraser Publishing, 1934.

Index

Numerics

0.886 retracement
extreme bearish harmonic impulse waves at, 69-70
extreme bullish harmonic impulse waves at, 67-68
1.13 extension (failed wave), 58
bearish 1.13 extension, 61-62
bullish 1.13 extension, 59-60
1.13 RSI BAMM Confirmation Point
Alternate Bearish Bat pattern, 244-246
Alternate Bullish Bat pattern, 192-194
Bearish 5-0 pattern, 253-254
Bearish Bat pattern, 247-249
Bearish Butterfly pattern, 241-243
Bearish Gartley pattern, 250-252
Bullish 5-0 pattern, 201-203
Bullish Bat pattern, 195-197
Bullish Butterfly pattern, 188-191
Bullish Gartley pattern, 198-200
1.618 RSI BAMM Confirmation Point, 204, 255
Bearish Crab pattern, 256-257
Bullish Crab pattern, 205-207
Deep Bearish Crab pattern, 258-260
Deep Bullish Crab pattern, 208-210
5-0 pattern, 73-74
Bearish 5-0 pattern, 88, 253-254
AMEX Oil Index 5-minute chart example, 89
Dow Jones Industrial Average 1-minute chart example, 93
S&P 500 September 2009 mini-contract 5-minute chart example, 91
Bearish 5-0 pattern PRZ
AMEX Oil Index 5-minute chart example, 90
Natural Gas March 2010 contract 15-minute chart example, 96
S&P 500 September 2009 mini-contract 5-minute chart example, 92
Bearish 5-0 pattern with Bearish AB=CD, 94-95
Bullish 5-0 pattern, 79, 201-203
Adobe Software daily chart example, 87
Eurodollar 5-minute chart example, 80
NASDAQ 100 March 2010 mini-contract 60-minute chart example, 82
S&P 500 June 2009 mini-contract 15-minute chart example, 83
S&P 500 Trust daily chart example, 81
Bullish 5-0 pattern PRZ, 84
Bullish 5-0 pattern with Bullish AB=CD, 85-86
failed Bearish 5-0 pattern, 100-101
failed Bullish 5-0 pattern, 97-98
failed Bullish 5-0 pattern PRZ, 99
requirements, 78
9/11 terrorist attacks, effect on Dow Jones Industrial Average, 36-37
2025 (year), long-term harmonic projections for, 50
Dow Jones Industrial Average weekly chart example, 53
NASDAQ Composite weekly chart example, 52
S&P 500 weekly chart example, 50-51

A

AB=CD BAMM, 152
Bearish AB=CD BAMM, 156-158
Bullish AB=CD BAMM, 153-155
AB=CD patterns
Bearish AB=CD pattern, 152
Bearish reciprocal AB=CD patterns within trends, 121-122
Bullish AB=CD pattern, 37, 39-40
Bullish reciprocal AB=CD patterns within trends, 119-120
as continuation signals, 111
bearish AB=CD patterns, 117-118
bullish AB=CD patterns, 112-116
Adobe Software daily chart example, 87
advanced Harmonic Trading, benefits of, 8
Alternate Bat pattern, 102-109
Alternate Bearish Bat pattern, 106-109, 244-246
Alternate Bullish Bat pattern, 103-105, 192-194
AMEX gas and oil exchange daily chart example, 68
AMEX Oil Index 5-minute chart example, 89-90
Apple 5-minute chart example, 132-133
Australian dollar 15-minute chart example, 130

B

Baker-Hughes weekly chart example, 77
BAMM (Bat Action Magnet Move), 141. *See also* RSI BAMM
- AB=CD BAMM, 152
  - *Bearish AB=CD BAMM, 156-158*
  - *Bullish AB=CD BAMM, 153-155*
- Bearish BAMM breakdown, 148-149
- Bearish BAMM breakdown in CD leg, 150-151
- Bullish BAMM breakout, 144-145
- Bullish BAMM breakout in CD leg, 146-147
- RSI BAMM, harmonic patterns versus, 272

Bat pattern. *See also* Alternate Bat pattern
- Alternate Bearish Bat pattern, 244-246
- Alternate Bullish Bat pattern, 192-194
- Bearish Bat pattern, 144, 247-249
- Bullish Bat pattern, 41-43, 148, 195-197

bear market of 2000
- Dow Jones Industrial Average in, 33
  - *9/11 crash, 36-37*
  - *bearish retracements in daily chart example, 35*
  - *Bullish AB=CD pattern, 37, 39-40*
  - *Bullish Bat pattern, 41-43*
  - *bullish retracements in weekly chart example, 34*
  - *lessons learned, 47*
- harmonic patterns in, 12-13
- Harmonic Trading success/failure, 48
- lessons learned, 47
- market positions during, 15-16
- NASDAQ Composite in, 23, 32
  - *Bearish Bat pattern, 26-28*
  - *decline from 5000, 25*
  - *failed Bullish Gartley pattern, 29-31*
  - *harmonic scenario failures, 31-32*
  - *rally to 5000, 23, 25*
- pattern violations, 13-14
- S&P 500 in, 16, 23
  - *Bearish Gartley pattern, 16, 18*
  - *Bullish AB=CD pattern pattern, 18-21*
  - *Bullish Bat pattern pattern, 21-22*
- testing of Harmonic Trading techniques in, 14-15

bear market of 2008
- Dow Jones Industrial Average in, 44-46
- Harmonic Trading success/failure, 48
- lessons learned, 47

bearish 1.13 extension (failed wave), 61-62
Bearish 5-0 pattern, 88, 253-254
- AMEX Oil Index 5-minute chart example, 89
- Dow Jones Industrial Average 1-minute chart example, 93
- failed Bearish 5-0 pattern, 100-101
- S&P 500 September 2009 mini-contract 5-minute chart example, 91

Bearish 5-0 pattern PRZ
- AMEX Oil Index 5-minute chart example, 90
- Natural Gas March 2010 contract 15-minute chart example, 96
- S&P 500 September 2009 mini-contract 5-minute chart example, 92

Bearish 5-0 pattern with Bearish AB=CD, 94-95
Bearish AB=CD BAMM, 156-158
Bearish AB=CD pattern, 117-118, 152
Bearish BAMM breakdown, 148-149
Bearish BAMM breakdown in CD leg, 150-151
Bearish Bat pattern, 26-28, 144, 247-249
Bearish Butterfly pattern, 241-243
Bearish Crab pattern, 256-257
bearish extension patterns within bearish trends, 131-133
bearish failed patterns against bullish trends, 137-139
Bearish Gartley pattern, 16-18, 250-252
bearish harmonic impulse waves
- extreme bearish harmonic impulse waves, 65
- extreme bearish harmonic impulse waves at 0.886 retracement, 69-70

bearish harmonic ratio progression, 57
bearish indicator structures, 220
- complex structures, 223, 225
- impulsive structures, 221-222

bearish patterns within bearish trends, 129-130
Bearish Reciprocal AB=CD pattern, 76-77, 121-122
bearish retracements, 35
Bearish RSI BAMM, 218-219
- 1.13 versus 1.618 Confirmation Point extensions, 237
- Alternate Bearish Bat pattern, 244-246
- Bearish 5-0 pattern, 253-254
- Bearish Bat pattern, 247-249
- Bearish Butterfly pattern, 241-243
- Bearish Crab pattern, 256-257
- Bearish Gartley pattern, 250-252
- British Pound/USD weekly chart example, 219
- Confirmation Point extensions, 238-239
- Deep Bearish Crab pattern, 258-260
- divergence of RSI versus price, 231-232, 235
- indicator structures, 220
  - *complex structures, 223, 225*
  - *impulsive structures, 221-222*
- inital RSI test, 220
- M-type complex RSI structure completion, 220
- pattern completion, 240-241
- reaction of RSI and price, 227-228, 236
- Reversal Acceleration Trigger, 261-263, 265
- RSI BAMM Confirmation Bar, 183, 233-234
- RSI BAMM Trigger Bar, 225-226
- RSI retest type, 229-230
- stop loss limits, 265-268

bearish trends, bullish failed patterns against, 134-136
Boeing daily chart example, 259-260
breakdowns, 142-143
- Bearish BAMM breakdown, 148-149
- Bearish BAMM breakdown in CD leg, 150-151

breakouts, 142-143
- Bullish BAMM breakout, 144-145
- Bullish BAMM breakout in CD leg, 146-147

British Pound 5-minute chart example, 202-203
British Pound 15-minute chart example, 128
British Pound/USD weekly chart example
- 1.13 extension at RSI BAMM Confirmation Point, 239

Bearish Butterfly PRZ at RSI BAMM Confirmation Point, 243
Bearish Butterfly at 1.13 RSI BAMM Confirmation Point, 242
bearish complex indicator structure, 224
bearish impulse indicator structure, 222
Bearish RSI BAMM, 219
Bearish RSI BAMM Confirmation Bar, 234
Bearish RSI BAMM Trigger Bar, 226
divergence phase of RSI versus price, 232
reaction of RSI and price, 228, 236
bullish 1.13 extension (failed wave), 59-60
Bullish 5-0 pattern, 79, 201-203
Adobe Software daily chart example, 87
Eurodollar 5-minute chart example, 80
failed Bullish 5-0 pattern, 97-98
failed Bullish 5-0 pattern PRZ, 99
NASDAQ 100 March 2010 mini-contract 60-minute chart example, 82
S&P 500 June 2009 mini-contract 15-minute chart example, 83
S&P 500 Trust daily chart example, 81
Bullish 5-0 pattern PRZ, 84
Bullish 5-0 pattern with Bullish AB=CD, 85-86
Bullish AB=CD BAMM, 153-155
Bullish AB=CD pattern
bear market of 2000
Dow Jones Industrial Average in, 37-40
S&P 500 in, 18-21
as continuation signals, 112-116
Bullish BAMM breakout, 144-145
Bullish BAMM breakout in CD leg, 146-147
Bullish Bat pattern, 148, 195-197
bear market of 2000
Dow Jones Industrial Average in, 41-43
S&P 500 in, 21-22
Bullish Butterfly pattern, 188-191
bullish complex indicator stuctures, 172, 174
Bullish Crab pattern, 205-207
bullish extension patterns within bullish trends, 127-128
bullish failed patterns against bearish trends, 134-136
Bullish Gartley pattern, 29-31, 198-200
bullish harmonic impulse waves
extreme bullish harmonic impulse waves, 63-64
extreme bullish harmonic impulse waves at 0.886 retracement, 67-68
bullish harmonic ratio progression, 56
bullish impulsive indicator stuctures, 170, 172
bullish indicator structures, 169
complex indicator structures, 172, 174
impulsive indicator structures, 170, 172
Bullish Reciprocal AB=CD pattern, 74-76, 119-120
bullish retracement patterns
within bullish trends, 124-126
Dow Jones Industrial Average weekly chart example, 34
Bullish RSI BAMM, 167
1.13 versus 1.618 Confirmation Point extensions, 184
Alternate Bullish Bat pattern, 192-194
Bearish RSI BAMM Confirmation Bar, 183
Bullish 5-0 pattern, 201-203
Bullish Bat pattern, 195-197
Bullish Butterfly pattern, 188-191
Bullish Crab pattern, 205-207
Bullish Gartley pattern, 198-200
bullish indicator structures, 169-174
Bullish RSI BAMM Trigger Bar, 186
bullish W-type complex RSI structure completion, 169
Chevron-Texaco daily chart example, 168
Confirmation Point extensions, 185
Deep Bullish Crab pattern, 208-210
divergence of RSI versus price, 180-182
inital RSI test, 169
pattern completion, 187
reaction of RSI and price, 176-177
Reversal Acceleration Trigger, 211-214
RSI BAMM Trigger Bar, 174-175
RSI retest type, 178-179
trade execution at, 187
violations and stop loss factors, 215-217
Bullish RSI BAMM Trigger Bar, 186
bullish trends, bearish failed patterns against, 137-139
Butterfly patterns
Bearish Butterfly pattern, 241-243
Bullish Butterfly pattern, 188-191

C

Chevron-Texaco daily chart example
Bearish RSI BAMM Confirmation Bar, 183
Bullish Butterfly at Bullish RSI BAMM Confirmation Point, 189
Bullish Butterfly pattern, 190
Bullish Butterfly PRZ at RSI BAMM Confirmation Point, 191
bullish complex indicator structure, 173-174
bullish impulse indicator structure, 171-172
Bullish RSI BAMM, 168
Bullish RSI BAMM Trigger Bar, 186
divergence of RSI versus price, 181-182
reaction of RSI and price, 177
RSI BAMM Trigger Bar, 175
RSI retest type, 179
Chicago Mercantile Exchange daily chart example, 125-126
Coca-Cola daily chart example, 206-207
complex indicator structures
bearish structures, 223, 225
bullish complex indicator structures, 172, 174
Confirmation Point
1.13 RSI BAMM Confirmation Point
Alternate Bearish Bat pattern, 244-246
Alternate Bullish Bat pattern, 192-194
Bearish 5-0 pattern, 253-254
Bearish Bat pattern, 247-249
Bearish Butterfly pattern, 241-243
Bearish Gartley pattern, 250-252
Bullish 5-0 pattern, 201-203
Bullish Bat pattern, 195-197
Bullish Butterfly pattern, 188-191
Bullish Gartley pattern, 198-200

1.13 versus 1.618 extensions, 184, 237
1.618 RSI BAMM Confirmation Point, 204, 255
Bearish Crab pattern, 256-257
Bullish Crab pattern, 205-207
Deep Bearish Crab pattern, 258-260
Deep Bullish Crab pattern, 208-210
Bearish RSI BAMM Confirmation Bar, 183
Bearish RSI BAMM extensions, 238-239
Bullish RSI BAMM extensions, 185, 187
Reversal Acceleration Trigger, 211-214, 261-265
confirmation signals, 8
continuation signals, AB=CD patterns as, 111
bearish AB=CD patterns, 117-118
bullish AB=CD patterns, 112-113, 115-116
Crab patterns
Bearish Crab pattern, 256-257
bearish patterns within bearish trends, 131-133
Bullish Crab pattern, 205-207
bullish patterns within bullish trends, 127-128
Deep Bearish Crab pattern, 258-260
Deep Bullish Crab pattern, 208-210

D

decline in NASDAQ Composite (bear market of 2000), 25-28
Deep Bearish Crab pattern, 258-260
Deep Bullish Crab pattern, 208-210
Directional Movement Index (DMI), 163
Disney daily chart example
Bullish AB=CD BAMM, 157
Bullish AB=CD BAMM in CD leg, 158
bullish reciprocal AB=CD patterns within trends, 120
divergence
importance of, 165
in RSI, 164
DMI (Directional Movement Index), 163
Dow Jones Industrial Average
in bear market of 2000, 33
9/11 crash, 36-37
bearish retracements in daily chart example, 35
Bullish AB=CD pattern, 37, 39-40
Bullish Bat pattern, 41-43
bullish retracements in weekly chart example, 34
lessons learned, 47
in bear market of 2008, 44-46
in crash of 1929, 32
Dow Jones Industrial Average 1-minute chart example, 93
Dow Jones Industrial Average weekly chart example, 53
Dow Jones Industrials ETF weekly chart example, 104
Dow Jones Transportation Average daily chart example, 138-139
Dow Theory, 55
downward patterns, 129-130

E

Elliott Wave Principle (Frost and Prechter), 49
Eurodollar 5-minute chart example
Alternate Bearish Bat pattern, 107
Alternate Bullish Bat pattern, 105
Bearish Gartley pattern, 251-252
Bullish 5-0 pattern, 80
Eurodollar daily chart example, bearish 1.13 extension (failed wave), 62
Eurodollar weekly chart example
Bearish BAMM breakdown, 149
Bearish BAMM breakdown in CD leg, 151
extension patterns
bearish extension patterns within bearish trends, 131-133
bearish retracement patterns within bearish trends, 129-130
bullish extension patterns within bullish trends, 127-128
extensions
1.13 versus 1.618 Confirmation Point extensions, 184, 237
Bearish RSI BAMM Confirmation Point extensions, 238-239
Bullish RSI BAMM Confirmation Point extensions, 185-187
extreme bearish harmonic impulse waves, 65-66
extreme bearish harmonic impulse waves at 0.886 retracement, 69-70
extreme bullish harmonic impulse waves, 63-64
extreme bullish harmonic impulse waves at 0.886 retracement, 67-68

F

failed Bearish 5-0 pattern, 100-101
failed Bullish 5-0 pattern, 97-98
failed Bullish 5-0 pattern PRZ, 99
failed harmonic patterns against trends, 133
bearish failed patterns, 137-139
bullish failed patterns, 134-136
failed wave (1.13 extension), 58
bearish 1.13 extension, 61-62
bullish 1.13 extension, 59-60
Family Dollar daily chart example, 257
Fedex Corp. weekly chart example, 75-76
feel for the markets in Harmonic Trading, 48-49
Frost, Alfred, 49
future price action, signals of (bear market of 2000), 13-14

G

Gartley patterns
Bearish Gartley pattern, 250-252
bearish patterns within bearish trends, 129-130
bullish Gartley in bearish trend, 135
Bullish Gartley pattern, 198-200
bullish Gartley PRZ in bearish trend, 136
bullish patterns within bullish trends, 124-126
failed bearish Gartley in bullish trend, 138
failed bearish Gartley PRZ in bullish trend, 139

Gartley, H. M., 162
General Motors daily chart example, 98
General Motors weekly chart example, 99
Google 5-minute chart example
Bearish 5-0 pattern PRZ at RSI BAMM Confirmation Point with Acceleration Trigger, 264
Bullish 1.13 extension (failed wave), 60
Google 15-minute chart example, bearish 5-0 pattern at RSI BAMM extension, 254

H

harmonic impulse waves, 57, 71
1.13 extension (failed wave), 58-62
bearish harmonic impulse waves, 65, 69-70
bullish harmonic impulse waves, 63-64, 67-68
harmonic patterns. *See also names of specific patterns*
against trends, 133
bearish failed patterns, 137-139
bullish failed patterns, 134-136
in bear market of 2000, 12-13
breakouts/breakdowns, 142-143
magnet effect in, 142
RSI BAMM versus, 272
within trends, 111, 123
AB=CD patterns as continuation signals, 111-118
bearish extension patterns, 131-133
bearish reciprocal AB=CD patterns, 121-122
bearish retracement patterns, 129-130
bullish extension patterns, 127-128
bullish reciprocal AB=CD patterns, 119-120
bullish retracement patterns, 124-126
harmonic ratio progression, 55-56
bearish harmonic ratio progression, 57
bullish harmonic ratio progression, 56
harmonic scenario failures, NASDAQ Composite in bear market of 2000, 31-32
Harmonic Trading
benefits of, 8
defined, 271
feel for the markets in, 48-49
lessons learned from bear markets of 2000/2008, 47
long-term projections, 49-53
misinformation about, 4-5
role of trader in, 7
success/failure in bear markets of 2000/2008, 48
technical indicators and, 161-163
testing in bear market of 2000, 14-15
Home Depot daily chart example, 154
Home Depot weekly chart example, 155
How to Make the Stock Market Make Money for You (Warren), 48
Hurst, J. M., 55

I–J

IBM weekly chart example
Bullish Gartley at RSI BAMM Confirmation Point, 199
Bullish Gartley PRZ at RSI BAMM Confirmation Point, 200
Bullish Gartley PRZ at RSI BAMM Confirmation Point with Acceleration Trigger, 214
impulsive indicator structures
bearish structures, 221-222
bullish impulsive indicator structures, 170, 172
Intercontinental Exchange 5-minute chart example, 266-267
Intercontinental Exchange 60-minute chart example, 268
Intercontinental Exchange daily chart example, 101

Japanese Yen 60-minute chart example, 86, 209-210

L–M

light sweet crude March 2006 contract 15-minute chart example, 66
long-term harmonic projections, 49-53

M-type complex RSI structure completion (Bearish RSI BAMM), 220
magnet effect in harmonic patterns, 142. *See also* BAMM (Bat Action Magnet Move)
market gurus, 5-6
market positions during bear market of 2000, 15-16

N–O

NASDAQ 100 March 2010 mini-contract 60-minute chart example (Bullish 5-0 pattern), 82
NASDAQ Composite daily chart example
Bearish Bat pattern
August 2000, 27
January 2001, 28
March 2000, 26
bullish AB=CD patterns as continuation signals, 113-116
rally to 5000, 24
NASDAQ Composite in bear market of 2000, 23, 32
Bearish Bat pattern, 26-28
decline from 5000, 25
failed Bullish Gartley pattern, 29-31
harmonic scenario failures, 31-32
rally to 5000, 23, 25
NASDAQ Composite weekly chart example
failed Bullish Gartley pattern, 30
failed Bullish Gartley PRZ pattern, 31
long-term harmonic projections for 2025, 52
Natural Gas March 2010 contract 15-minute chart example
Bearish 5-0 pattern PRZ, 96
Bearish 5-0 pattern with Bearish AB=CD, 95
New Concepts and Trading Systems (Wilder), 169, 220
New Concepts in Technical Trading Systems (Wilder), 163-165, 182
Nike daily chart example (Alternate Bearish Bat pattern), 108-109

P

pattern completion
Bearish RSI BAMM, 240-241
Bullish RSI BAMM, 187

pattern violations. *See also* failed harmonic patterns against trends
in bear market of 2000, 13-14
of Bullish RSI BAMM, 215-217
Philadelphia gold and silver index daily chart example (extreme bearish harmonic impulse wave at 0.886 retracement), 70
Philadelphia Semiconductor Index 5-minute chart example (Bullish Bat PRA at RSI BAMM Confirmation Point), 197
Philadelphia Semiconductor Index chart example (Bullish Bat pattern), 196
Prechter, Robert, 49
predictions, 49-53
price action, future signals (bear market of 2000), 13-14
Principle of Harmonicity, 55
Profits in the Stock Market (Gartley), 162

Q–R

rally in NASDAQ Composite (bear market of 2000), 23, 25
Reciprocal AB=CD pattern, 74
Bearish Reciprocal AB=CD pattern, 76-77, 121-122
Bullish Reciprocal AB=CD pattern, 74-76, 119-120
Relative Strength Index, 162-164
retracements
bearish retracements, 35
bullish retracements
Dow Jones Industrial Average weekly chart example, 34
within bullish trends, 124-126
Reversal Acceleration Trigger, 211-214, 261-263, 265
RSI (Relative Strength Index), 162-164
RSI BAMM, 3. *See also* Bearish RSI BAMM; Bullish RSI BAMM
explained, 164-165
harmonic patterns versus, 272
steps in, 269
tips for, 269-270
uniqueness of, 166
RSI BAMM Confirmation Bar, 233-234
RSI BAMM Trigger Bar, 174-175, 225-226

S

S&P 500 Continuous Contract daily chart example
Bullish BAMM breakout, 145
Bullish BAMM breakout in CD leg, 147
S&P 500 December 2009 mini-contract 60-minute chart example, 64
S&P 500 ETF 5-minute chart example, 245-246
S&P 500 in bear market of 2000, 16, 23
Bearish Gartley pattern, 16, 18
Bullish AB=CD pattern, 18-21
Bullish Bat pattern, 21-22
S&P 500 June 2009 mini-contract 5-minute chart example
Alternate Bullish Bat with Bullish RSI BAMM, 193-194
bullish Gartley pattern in bearish trend, 135
bullish Gartley PRZ pattern in bearish trend, 136
S&P 500 June 2009 mini-contract 15-minute chart example, 83-84
S&P 500 March 2010 Mini-contract 15-minute chart example
Bearish Bat at RSI BAMM extension, 248
Bearish Bat PRZ at RSI BAMM extension, 249
Bullish Crab and Bullish RSI BAMM failure, 216
Bullish Crab PRZ and Bullish RSI BAMM failure, 217
S&P 500 September 2009 mini-contract 5-minute chart example, 91-92
S&P 500 Trust daily chart example, 81
S&P 500 weekly chart example
Bearish Gartley pattern, 16, 18
bearish reciprocal AB=CD patterns within trends, 122
Bullish AB=CD pattern, 18-21
Bullish Bat pattern, 21-22
long-term harmonic projections for 2025, 50-51
September 11, 2001 terrorist attacks, effect on Dow Jones Industrial Average, 36-37
stop loss limits
for Bearish RSI BAMM, 265-268
for Bullish RSI BAMM, 215-217

T–Z

technical indicators, Harmonic Trading and, 161-163
testing Harmonic Trading techniques in bear market of 2000, 14-15
Toll Brothers weekly chart example, 118
trade execution at Bullish RSI BAMM Confirmation Point, 187
traders, role in Harmonic Trading, 7
trends
harmonic patterns against, 133
bearish failed patterns, 137-139
bullish failed patterns, 134-136
harmonic patterns within, 111, 123
AB=CD patterns as continuation signals, 111-118
bearish extension patterns, 131-133
bearish reciprocal AB=CD patterns, 121-122
bearish retracement patterns, 129-130
bullish extension patterns, 127-128
bullish reciprocal AB=CD patterns, 119-120
bullish retracement patterns, 124-126
trigger bar, 174-175, 225-226

violations. *See* pattern violations

W-type complex RSI structure completion (Bullish RSI BAMM), 169
Warren, Ted, 48
Wilder, Welles, 163-165, 169, 182, 220